The Hutchinson

Diction

Phrases

The Hutchinson

Dictionary of

Battles

Ian V. Hogg

Helicon

Copyright © Helicon Publishing Ltd 1995

Helicon Publishing Ltd
42 Hythe Bridge Street
Oxford OX1 2EP

Printed and bound in Great Britain by
Cox & Wyman Ltd, Reading, Berkshire

ISBN 1 85986 057 5

British Library Cataloguing in Publication Data

A catalogue record of this book is available
from the British Library

Cover illustration: a detail of a contemporary
painting of the battle of Isandhlwana (1879),
during the Zulu War. *Topham Picture Library*

Acquisitions Director
Anne-Lucie Norton

Project Editor
Simon Hall

Editor
Paul Davis

Cartography
Simon Hall/European Map Graphics
Ltd

Page make-up
TechType

Production
Tony Ballsdon

Contents

About the author

Ian Vernon Hogg was born in 1926. He enlisted in the Regular Army (Royal Artillery) during World War II and served in Europe and the Far East during the Korean War with various field and Horse Artillery regiments. Qualifying as a gunnery instructor in 1953, Mr Hogg served on the staff of the Royal School of Artillery teaching artillery equipment, ammunition, and explosives. A further qualification in electronic warfare and counter–bombardment followed in 1959–60 and he became Warrant Officer in charge of trials 1961–66. Promoted to Master Gunner in 1965, he was posted to the instructional staff at the Royal Military College of Science. Upon reaching retirement age in 1972, Mr Hogg became a full-time writer specializing in defence journalism. He has written, contributed to, or edited over 100 books on military subjects and is a contributor to over 25 specialist magazines internationally.

Married with two sons and one daughter, Mr Hogg lives in Worcestershire.

Introduction

The past three thousand or so years are, by now, fairly well documented and recorded; and looking through those documents and records one is drawn to the conclusion that there was never a year in all that time when somebody, somewhere, was not fighting somebody else. War, like death and taxes, is always with us and always will be. Look around you; count the praiseworthy bodies striving for peace, and count the people waging war.

Some people tell us that we can improve our future by studying history; perhaps so, but not in the matter of war (except to perfect methods of waging it.) War is terrible, degrading, everything disgusting that can be imagined; these well-attested facts are recorded in countless books and works of art, and yet the human race will still go to war almost at the drop of a hat. Because, on the other hand, as many a head of state can testify, war is exhilarating, a national tonic, a reviver of national spirit, an opportunity to display the heroism and self-sacrifice for which the nation (any nation) is justly famous.

There is something to be said for both points of view, which is why one likes to have a dictionary of battles about the place, so that examples of either case can be readily provided. No dictionary can have every battle in it; the result would be an unwieldy volume. Nor can one say 'List the important battles' – every battle was important to those who fought it, otherwise they would not have exerted themselves. One can, with hindsight, say of a few battles that they were a waste of time and effort, but this was not apparent at the time.

What we have done, therefore, is to make a selection; from ancient times a handful of battles which changed the political structure of the world as it then was and thus had a determinant effect upon the course of history. From a later period, battles which began to separate and organize the European tribes into distinct geographical groups as each settled their chosen piece of countryside. After this, battles which helped to bring the world into the shape and divisions which have persisted ever since as nations strove to extend their borders, acquire colonies, and enrich themselves. Finally, we have selected the battles, principally of the last century or so, where ideology has replaced simple territorial greed as a motivating power. As we move forward in time, so the battles become more numerous; it would be pointless to enumerate every skirmish between the Greeks and Spartans or of the Hundred Years' War, but when we come down to the two Great Wars of the 20th century, much more is included since we are here within living memory and, moreover, due to modern military technology a relatively small skirmish can, in many cases, have a significant effect upon the course of a war.

Another marked feature of military development as we move through history is the concentration in time which has taken place in wars. The so-called 'Hundred Years' War' (it actually lasted 130 years) was not a continuous day-by-day combat; years went by without any fighting at all until the whole thing lumbered to its end. Contrast that with, say, the Austro-Prussian War of 1866 when everything was over in six weeks, or the Arab-Israel conflict of 1967 which lasted a mere six days of intense hour-by-hour fighting. As the time taken has contracted, so have the numbers involved expanded. During the Hundred Years' War the armies were small; they met, fought, separated, went into winter quarters, met again ... there was one battle at a time. Today when armies are numbered by the million, half-a-dozen battles can be raging in different areas on the same day. It was always a sore point with the Allied troops in Italy that their capture of Rome was obscured by events in France, since it took place on 6 June 1944 just as the Allied invasion began.

We hope that all these trends in the development of military and political history, and several other important lessons, can be discerned by considering the battles collected together here.

By way of an added bonus, the main A–Z listing which follows is supplemented by a short section of battle plans, a weapons development chronology, brief biographies of notable military commanders, and a chronology of wars and battles. The first two of these attempt to provide an insight into the changing nature of battle over the course of history, and the third assesses the strengths and weaknesses of some of history's greatest battlefield leaders. The last serves as an index to the main A–Z listing, enabling the reader to identify at a glance, for example, all the listed battles of the Seven Years' War.

I. V. H.

January 1995

A

Aboukir Bay see Battle of the ⟡Nile.

Abu Klea engagement between British forces and Dervishes in the Sudan 17 Jan 1885. A camel corps with about 1,800 troops under General Sir Herbert Stewart, part of the British expedition to relieve General Charles Gordon in Khartoum, took a short cut to avoid a large loop of the Nile. At Abu Klea, a group of wells on the track from Korti to Metemmeh, it was attacked by 10,000 Dervishes. The British force formed a square which was broken for a short time; it closed up again and beat off the attack, but Col Frederick Burnaby, noted soldier and explorer, was killed in the battle.

Abu Kru (also known as Gubat) engagement between British forces and Dervishes in the Sudan 19 Jan 1885. The column which had been attacked at ⟡Abu Klea was attacked again some 11 km/7 mi further on its route. General Sir Herbert Stewart halted the column and took up a defensive position. He was killed during the attack, but it was eventually beaten off and the column managed to reach the Nile. The new commander, General Sir Charles Wilson, decided to rest there for three days and so arrived at Khartoum too late to save General Charles Gordon.

Abu Tellul engagement between British and Turkish forces in World War I, 14 July 1918. The Turkish army advanced north and east of Jericho, capturing the village of Abu Tellul but were then halted by British advanced posts. A counterattack by the Australian Light Horse trapped the Turkish force between cavalry and advanced posts, capturing some 350 prisoners and regaining the village.

Acre unsuccessful French siege March–May 1799 of a seaport and town in Palestine, 130 km/80 mi northwest of Jerusalem, during Napoleon Bonaparte's abortive attempt to carve out a French empire. The city was defended by the Turks, aided by a small British naval force, and Napoleon began the siege 17 March. A French assault was beaten off, and the approach of a Syrian relief army forced Napoleon to withdraw most of his force to deal with this threat. The siege was then resumed, with seven more assaults being made without success, while the defenders made a number of sorties, and Napoleon finally raised the siege and departed 21 May. Acre has been the focus of many military operations throughout history, notably during the various Crusades

Actium naval battle in the Roman Civil War in which Octavian defeated the combined fleets of Mark Antony and Cleopatra 2 Sept 31 BC to become the undisputed ruler of the Roman world (as the emperor Augustus). Antony had encamped in Greece with a powerful force of infantry and cavalry, and was waiting for Octavian's smaller force to attack. However, engagements on land were indecisive and Octavian's fleet of 400 ships, commanded by Agrippa, cut off Antony's supply route, despite his larger fleet of 500. Antony and Cleopatra could have escaped overland to continue the fight but Cleopatra demanded to return to Egypt by sea. In the ensuing engagement Antony was defeated, leaving Octavian supreme in the Roman world.

Admin Box first major victory of British and Indian troops over the Japanese during World War II, Feb 1944. The 'Admin[istration] Box' was the administrative and base area of 7th Indian Division of the British Army at Sinzewa, Burma; it was besieged by the Japanese 55th Division 5–23 Feb 1944. The siege was lifted when the Japanese were taken in the rear by the 5th Indian Division advancing over the Ngakyedauk Pass.

Adrianople Gothic victory over the Roman Empire in the East 9 Aug 378. Valens, the Eastern Emperor, was lost in the battle and never seen again. This victory led to the foundation of a Gothic settlement within the frontier of the Roman Empire and was the beginning of the empire's downfall. Moreover, the success of the Gothic horsemen against the Roman foot soldiers established the superiority of mounted troops in European war for the next thousand years.

Aegospotami Spartan naval victory over the Athenians at the end of the Peloponnesian War 405 BC. An Athenian fleet of some 180 triremes lay at Aegospotami (now Gelibolu on the northern shore of the Dardanelles) and 170 Peloponnesian ships, under Lysander, lay at Lampsacus (now Lapseki) on the southern shore. On four successive days the Athenian fleet rowed across the strait, hoping to draw Lysander's force out to give battle, but without success. On the fifth day Lysander waited until the Athenians made their usual sortie and returned to their base; once they had anchored, Lysander's fleet made a sudden dash across the water, pounced on the anchored Athenians, captured 160 ships, and killed the crews. This decisive defeat broke the hitherto unchallenged Athenian naval superiority and ended the Peloponnesian War.

Agincourt English victory over the French during the Hundred Years' War 25 Oct 1415. The English army, about 5,700 troops under Henry V, had marched from Harfleur and crossed the River Somme to come into contact with the French Army, about 25,000 strong, and the two marched parallel toward Agincourt, a village in the Pas-de-Calais about 23 km/14 mi from St Pol. Henry, short of provisions, offered various concessions in return for permission to leave France peacefully but these were refused and after a rainy night the two armies deployed for battle.

The English formed up in four ranks, with archers in front. They then advanced, halted, and drove stakes into the ground to protect against cavalry. The combined effect of archery, heavy mud, and the row of stakes foiled the French cavalry, but their foot soldiers attacked and engaged in hand-to-hand fighting. This first line of the French was defeated, and the English then advanced upon the second and third lines which offered little resistance. The French Army was driven from the field with a loss of some 9,000 troops and 2,000 prisoners, while the English retired to Calais in good order with losses of about 400.

Agordat British victory over Italian forces in World War II 31 Jan 1941. Agordat, a town in Eritrea about 95 km/60 mi northwest of Asmara, had been occupied by the Italians since the Abyssinian war until it was captured by the 4th Indian Division 31 Jan. The Italian garrison, partly surrounded, was able to escape but had to abandon most of its artillery and equipment.

Agra Indian city on the Jumna river about 210 km/130 mi southeast of Delhi; the size of three major battles in its history.

1713 Jahandar Shah, with 70,000 troops, fought against a rebel force commanded by his nephew Faroukhsiyar. After a bitter struggle the rebels won and Jahandar Shah was captured and executed by his nephew, who succeeded to the throne.

4 Oct 1803 a British force under General Lake besieged the town, which fell into their hands Oct 18.

2 Aug 1857 the British garrison holding the city went out to meet a force of about 10,000 rebels stirred into action by the Indian Mutiny. Native troops in the British force deserted to the rebels and the British troops were forced to retire into the city and take refuge in the fort. They were then besieged until Oct, when a relief column was able to break through the rebel lines.

Aisne three battles between Allied and German forces in northern France during World War I.

12–20 Sept 1914 inconclusive battle on a 160-km/100-mi front between Compiègne and Tahure, near Reims. The German forces (1st, 2nd, 3rd and 4th Armies) had fallen back from the Marne and entrenched north of the river Aisne with a considerable strength of artillery. The Allies launched a frontal attack, crossing the river with great difficulty, and eventually gained the crest of the ridge and the Chemin des Dames which ran along it. The Allies were unable to make further gains as they had no heavy artillery and both sides dug into trenches and remained on this line for most of the war.

16 April–20 May 1917 disastrous French attempt on German positions. General Robert Nivelle planned to throw 27 French divisions against the main German position and force a decision within 48 hours but this plan was compromised when the Germans captured a copy of his orders for the attack. They were able to reinforce both their infantry and artillery and prepare a defence in depth and the French sustained heavy casualties.

Advancing in snow and rain, overwhelmed by machine guns, and unsupported due to the late arrival of their tanks, the French nevertheless managed to penetrate some 6.5 km/4 mi into the German positions before being stopped. Both sides ultimately sustained heavy casualties: the French lost about 187,000, the Germans 163,000. The severe casualty rate was one of the causes of the mutinies in the French Army in the following month.

27 May–18 June 1918 partly successful German breakthrough toward Paris. The attack was launched by the German 1st and 7th Armies against the British 9th Army Corps and 5th French Army. The Germans broke through and advanced about 16 km/10 mi to Château-Thierry, placing Paris under threat, before their lack of reserves and stretched lines of supply brought them to a halt.

Alam Halfa abortive German attack in World War II on the southern sector of the British defensive line at El Alamein 30 Aug 1942. However, this move had been foreseen by General Sir Claude Auchinleck, plans had been prepared, and they were put into action by General Bernard Montgomery, who now had 700 tanks to meet Rommel's force of 446 tanks. A coordinated defence with artillery, tanks, and tactical air forces stopped Rommel and on 2 Sept he called off the attack and retreated, having lost 3,000 troops, 49 tanks, 60 guns, and 400 trucks.

Alamein, El in World War II, two decisive battles in the western desert, north Egypt, 1942 resulting in British victory over Axis forces under Field Marshal Erwin Rommel.

1–27 July 1942 the British 8th Army under General Sir Claude Auchinleck held off the German and Italian forces. Neither side can be said to have won, but the British had the strategic advantage of short supply lines and so could reinforce faster than the Germans.

23 Oct–4 Nov 1942 General Bernard Montgomery launched a diversionary British attack in the south, aiming to draw Axis forces into the area so that the main attack in the north could cut two corridors through the extensive minefields, enabling British armoured divisions to pass through and exploit the gaps. Progress was slow however and Montgomery decided to change tactics to fight what he called a 'crumbling' battle, constantly switching the main emphasis of his attack to chip away at Rommel's front line and keep him guessing. On 26 Oct the 9th Australian Division attacked along the coastal road, drawing the Axis forces toward them. Montgomery promptly launched a fresh attack further south, forcing the German armour to react in what became a major tank battle. By 3 Nov Rommel had only 30 serviceable tanks in action and on the following day began organizing his withdrawal. He was able to disengage and escape as the British were hampered by heavy rain and a shortage of fuel.

Before Alamein we never had a victory. After Alamein we never had a defeat.

On the *Battles of El Alamein* Winston Churchill *The Hinge of Fate* 1951

Albert inconclusive engagement during the 'Race to the Sea' in World War I between French and German forces 20–30 Sept 1914. Elements of the French 2nd Army attempted to outflank General Alexander von Kluck's German forces which were also attempting a flanking movement. A stalemate developed which was resolved by the arrival of the German 6th Army under Prince Rupprecht. The French were forced back but in turn augmented their force by adding the French 10th Army under General Maud'huy and the outflanking movements began once more, ending in entrenched lines from Albert to Noyon. There was no subsequent major change in these positions until the German retreat of 1917.

Albuera in the Peninsular War, British victory over the French 16 May 1811 at Albuera, a village some 21 km/13 mi southeast of ◊Badajoz, Spain. A French army of about 23,000 troops under Marshal Nicolas Soult was marching to Badajoz, which was under siege by the British, intending to break through the British lines and raise the siege. The Duke of Wellington ordered General William Beresford to abandon the siege and turn to meet the approaching enemy. Beresford selected Albuera as a suitable place for the battle and disposed his troops – 6,000 British and 24,000 Spanish and Portuguese – on a ridge overlooking the village.

On the morning of the 16th, Soult launched a feint attack against the Allied left flank while directing his main force against the Allied right. Beresford had expected a frontal attack and was unable to wheel his troops before the French struck. The Spanish troops on the left were shattered by French musketry and a cavalry charge, and the British 2nd Division was brought from the other side of the field to stop the attack. The 57th Foot (Middlesex Regiment) lost 423 of their 575-strong contingent and earned themselves the nickname 'The Die-Hards'. There was little room to manoeuvre on the ridge, so the battle became a fierce hand-to-hand affair. Beresford narrowly escaped capture and was preparing to retreat when the British and Portuguese reserves were brought up and, charging up the hill into the face of the French, routed them. The French were able to retire in good order, taking about 500 prisoners with them, but the siege of Badajoz had not been raised. Of the 6,000 British troops, only 1,500 were not wounded.

The rain flowed after in streams discoloured with blood; and fifteen hundred unwounded men, the remnant of six thousand unconquerable British soldiers, stood triumphant on that fatal hill.

Sir William Napier on the *Battle of Albuera*, *History of the Peninsular War*

Alesia, Siege of during the Gallic Wars, final defeat of the Gauls 52 BC by Roman forces under Julius Caesar which completed the Roman conquest of Gaul. The town was the Gauls' last stronghold, held by about 80,000 foot and 15,000 horse troops under Vercingetorix, while the Romans besieging them consisted of about 50,000 troops, mainly legionaries. The Belgii, another Gallic tribe, sent a relief force which attempted to break through the Roman lines but was so decisively defeated that the town immediately surrendered. Napoleon III erected a statue of Vercingetorix on the site of the battle 1864.

Alma during the Crimean War, Allied attempt on Sevastopol 20 Sept 1854 held off by 40,000 Russians under General Alexander Menshikov. The Allied (British, French, and Turkish) armies, some 63,000 strong, under General Lord Raglan and Marshal Jacques St Arnaud, had landed at Eupatoria, intent upon marching to attack Sevastopol; in response, Menshikov placed his force on high ground close to the river Alma. The British and part of the French made a frontal advance on the Russian lines, while the remainder of the French and the Turks made a flanking movement through difficult and hilly country and surprised the Russians. The French forces in the centre were moved to the flank to exploit this success, leaving the British to complete the frontal attack. Due to confused orders part of the British line retired while the remainder advanced, but this was corrected and the Russians were driven from their position to fall back into Sevastopol. The Allies could have then attacked the city, but failed to press the advantage so that the Russians had sufficient time to complete their defences.

Amba Alagi during World War II, last stand of Italian forces in Ethiopia under the Duke of Aosta against British invasion 1941. Amba Alagi was a mountain held by 7,000 Italian troops with 40 guns, whose positions were attacked 3–19 May by a mixed force of British, Indian, South African, and Ethiopian troops. The battle took place at altitudes of 10,000 feet and more and the Italians put up a spirited defence until they were forced to surrender 19 May.

Ambon Island in World War II, Japanese attack on a small island in the Dutch East Indies, held by a mixed force of Dutch and Australian troops 31 Jan–3 Feb 1942. Some 809 Australian troops were taken prisoner; over half were later killed or died from starvation after torture.

Amiens in World War I, intermittent fighting between Allied and German forces around the capital of the Somme *département*, ancient city of northeast France at the confluence of the rivers Somme and Avre. An important rail junction, it became the hub of military communications in northern France during World War I and was awarded the *Croix de Guerre*. It was occupied by the German Army for several days before the battle of the ◊Marne Sept 1914 but thereafter remained in French hands. The ◊German Spring Offensive 1918 brought it within the sound of gunfire and it was in some danger for several weeks, during which the main railway line to Paris was cut. The danger was finally lifted by the Allied counter-offensive Aug 1918.

Ancre in World War I, closing episode of the series of battles between German and Allied forces in the Somme area 1916–17. The British advance on the Somme Oct 1916 had left a heavily fortified German salient, containing the village of Beaumont-Hamel, thrusting into the British line on both banks of the river Ancre.

The battle began 11 Nov 1916 with a one-day artillery bombardment, the infantry attack starting at 0512 hrs the following day. Fighting was heavy, but Beaumont-Hamel was finally captured by the 51st Highland Division 13 Nov. The British had advanced about a mile by 15 Nov, when the severe winter weather made the ground impassable, supplying the forward troops became difficult, and fighting impossible. The battle died out in the appalling weather and the line stabilized.

Antietam battle between Confederate forces under General Robert E Lee and Union forces under Maj-Gen George McClellan in the American Civil War, 17–18 Sept 1862. Tactically Antietam was inconclusive, but strategically it was a significant Confederate loss, marking the end of Lee's dreams of converting Maryland to the Confederate cause. It was also the bloodiest battle of the Civil War: the Confederates lost 2,700 dead, 9,000 wounded, and 2,000 missing out of 51,844 troops; the Union forces lost 2,100 dead, 9,500 wounded, and 750 missing out of 75,316 troops.

The Confederates were aiming north toward Harrisburg, intending to destroy a rail bridge and then see what further opportunity offered. Lee halted at Frederick, sending a detachment off to deal with the Union garrison at Harper's Ferry while he pushed on to Hagerstown. Unfortunately McClellan obtained a discarded copy of Lee's orders and he dispatched the Union Army toward the gap between Lee's two forces. After a skirmish with McClellan's leading troops, Lee fell back to Sharpsburg to await his detachment's return from Harper's Ferry, taking up a defensive line along the Antietam Creek east of Sharpsburg, about 16 km/10 mi north of Harpers Ferry. The Union Army closed in but did not attack until the following day. By noon on 17 Sept both sides had fought themselves to a standstill, but then the Confederate detachment from Harper's Ferry came up just as the Union forces brought up fresh troops. More bitter fighting ensued but the Union commander, General Charles Sumner, believing that further Confederate reinforcements were arriving, decided that further attacks were useless. McClellan ordered a flanking attack by General Ambrose Burnside's corps, but more Confederates arrived from Harper's Ferry just in time to take this attack in its flank. This proved to be the final engagement: both armies spent the night gathering their wounded, and on the following day each waited for the other to attack. Neither did, and Lee was able to withdraw his force and make his way back to Virginia.

Antwerp British operation in World War II to liberate the port from the Germans who had occupied it since 1940. When it was liberated by the British 11th Armoured Division 4 Sept 1944, the Allies hoped to secure the port in working order to provide Allied forces with a supply port close to the front line. Unfortunately the banks of the river Scheldt were still held by German troops, denying the Allies use of the river, and special operations had to be mounted to remove them. It was not until 28 Nov that the first supply ships reached the port.

Anzio in World War II, the beachhead invasion of Italy 22 Jan–23 May 1944 by Allied troops; failure to exploit the initial surprise of the landing led to Allied troops being held on the beachhead for five months before the breakthrough after Monte Cassino allowed the US 5th Army to dislodge the Germans from the Alban Hills and allow the Anzio force to begin its advance on Rome.

We sought to throw a raging lion ashore; what we got was a stranded whale.

Winston Churchill on the *Anzio* landings

Arakan series of British offensives in World War II to dislodge the Japanese from Burma (now Myanmar). Arakan is a coastal region offering an invasion route from India with access to central Burma.

The British mounted three offensives in this area; the first Dec 1942 had limited objectives and was largely in order to give British forces confidence in operating against the Japanese. It was halted by the Japanese at Donbailk and withdrew. The second Dec 1943 advanced as far as Maungdaw before being halted. The third offensive was more a renewal of the second offensive which eventually captured Rangoon 3 May 1945.

Archangel, Expedition to Allied operation to secure Western interests in Bolshevik-held territory in northern Russia in the spring of 1918. The expedition had three main objectives: to safeguard the large concentration of military stores which had been sent to the Russians and which lay in Archangel; to safeguard the flank of the Murmansk Expedition; and to try to stabilize the Eastern Front and make contact with the Czech Legion and the White Russian forces of Admiral Alexander Kolchak.

A mixed force of British, French, and US troops occupied Murmansk July 1918. Using this as a base, the Allied naval squadron, with air support, attacked and captured Modiuga Island, some 48 km/30 mi north of Archangel, which allowed them to bypass Bolshevik defences and enter Archangel. A land force then cleared the valleys of the rivers Dvina and Vaga and defeated the Bolshevik forces which had been occupying Archangel. A local government was formed and formally recognized and several thousand Russians enlisted with the Allies.

After the Armistice, the Bolsheviks were able to concentrate troops in the area and by early 1919 there seemed little point in holding on to this enclave in a country which had almost entirely become Bolshevik. Archangel was successfully defended until Aug, when withdrawal began, and the British naval base was finally closed and the last troops evacuated 27 Sept, having handed their equipment over to White Russian forces.

Argenta Gap World War II operation by British troops to breach German defences in Italy April 1945. The Gap was a heavily defended strip of dry land between Lake Comacchio and the Lombardy marshes in northern Italy blocking the route to the Lombardy plain and northeast Italy. The British 5th Corps used amphibious armoured vehicles to outflank the German positions and breach the Axis lines, allowing the British 6th Armoured Division to pass through the gap in the final Allied advance in Italy.

Argesul unsuccessful Romanian operation in World War I to hold off Austrian and German armies on the line of the Argesul river in the defence of Bucharest 30 Nov–3 Dec 1916. The Austrians under the German general August von Mackensen attacked from the south and southwest, while the Germans under General Erich von Falkenhayn attacked from the north and west in a pincer movement. Although the Romanians initially put up fierce resistance, they eventually collapsed after German reinforcements arrived and their own reserves failed to arrive due to treason by General Sosescu. Bucharest was occupied by the Germans 6 Dec 1916 and Sosescu was later court-martialled and imprisoned.

Argonne, Campaigns in the series of battles in World War I between French and German forces; the Argonne was of considerable strategic importance as a German advance through this area could threaten Verdun, outflank Châlons, and render the French front on the river ◊Meuse untenable.

In 1914 the right flank of the German Army passed through the Argonne, but fell back to the area of Varennes after the Battle of the ◊Marne. Trenches were dug and apart from local movements the lines remained stable until a German attack June 1915. Savage fighting ensued but what small gains the Germans made were lost to French counterattacks and the battle was a stalemate. There was a series of minor battles and raids throughout 1916–17 but neither side made any significant impact.

In the autumn of 1918 the French general Ferdinand Foch determined to clear the area and strike at the Mézières-Montmédy railway line, the main German line of communication. By this time the area was well defended by the Kriemhilde Line, part of the larger Hindenburg Line system of fortifications. Foch was beset with difficulties: the major component of his force was 22 divisions of US troops of which only three had taken part in previous operations; there was a grave shortage of transport; and many of the US troops were untrained in the latest methods of attack. The US troops were to advance through the Argonne and up the west bank of the Meuse, while General Henri Gouraud's French 4th Army simultaneously advanced west of the Argonne.

The US troops attacked and overran the German lines 26 Sept, but communication and transport breakdowns caused severe problems: many troops received no food or ammunition for four days and the initial momentum could not be maintained. After resolving these problems the Allied advance resumed 4 Oct and gained 11 km/7 mi, and on 14 Oct the US force broke the Kriemhilde Line at several points. Hard fighting continued until 29 Oct when the Germans finally fell back to the west bank of the Meuse. The attack was resumed 1 Nov and by 6 Nov Sedan was taken. A further advance began but was ended by the Armistice.

US casualties were 115,519 with only 15,599 killed, an unusually low proportion; French casualties were about 7,000; and 17,659 German prisoners and 468 guns were captured.

Arnhem in World War II, airborne operation by the Allies, 17–26 Sept 1944, to secure a bridgehead over the Rhine, thereby opening the way for a thrust toward the Ruhr and a possible early end to the war. Arnhem itself was to be taken by the British while US troops were assigned bridges to the south of the city. Unfortunately, two divisions of the SS Panzer Corps were refitting in Arnhem when the British landed and penned the British troops in, while the US force captured the bridge at Nijmegen but were unable to secure the bridge at Elst. Despite the arrival of Polish reinforcements 21 Sept, General Bernard Montgomery ordered a withdrawal four days later. British losses came to 1,130 killed and 6,000 taken prisoner, compared with 3,300 German casualties.

Arras in World War I, effective but costly British attack on German forces April–May 1917. The attack was launched in support of a French offensive on the Siegfried Line which was only partially successful. British casualties totalled 84,000 as compared to 75,000 German casualties.

Arras in World War II, Allied victory over German forces 21 May 1940. Although the Allies were eventually beaten off, the German general Erwin Rommel's report of being attacked by 'hundreds of tanks' led to a 24-hour delay in the German advance which gave the British vital time to organize their retreat through Dunkirk.

To stem the German advance through northern France, a hastily assembled force of the British 1st Tank Brigade, 6th Durham Light Infantry, and the French 3rd Light Armoured Division, under the overall command of Maj-Gen Franklyn, launched a counterattack against Rommel's 7th Panzer Division. The attack cut the Panzers in two, shattered two German rifle regiments, and caused part of the 3rd SS Division to panic and run. Rommel eventually got his troops under control and was able to beat off the British tanks using 88 mm anti-aircraft guns, the first time they were used in an anti-tank role.

Artois in World War I, French offensive north of Arras May–July 1915 intended to hold German forces in France and prevent their movement to the Eastern Front. The 8th and 10th French Armies (under generals Victor d'Urbal and Maud'huy respectively), supported by British troops under General Sir John French, were employed in the attack. The main axis of attack was against Lens, a heavily fortified German position and was initially successful, having been prepared by a 1,200-gun artillery bombardment and a diversionary attack by the British against Aubers Ridge. Although the French advance captured two major German positions and gave them a line from which Vimy Ridge could subsequently be attacked, the German line held and the battle died away into sporadic trench fighting.

Ascalon victory for the Crusaders under Godfrey de Bouillon over the Saracens 1099. Following their defeat, Muslim resistance to Christian occupation of the Holy Land ended for some time, although the city itself was recaptured by Saladin 1187.

Asiago Plateau series of battles in World War I between Austrian and Italian forces in the mountainous country north of the Venetian plain and between the Adige and Piave rivers Nov 1917–Oct 1918.

An Austrian attack 10 Nov 1917 captured the town of Asiago, forcing the Italians to fall back on a defensive line. The Austrians battered this line for several days before capturing part of it and some 15,000 prisoners 7 Dec. Although they made further small gains in the area, the main attack was directed away from this line until 23 Dec when Austrian troops captured more ground and prisoners.

The Italians launched a minor attack which gained some ground Jan 1918, after which there was a quiet period until a major Austrian attack in June which included an artillery gas bombardment. By this time, however, the Italian line had been strengthened by French and British troops, and the Austrians made little impression. An Allied counterattack June 15–16 1918 drove the Austrians back with severe losses in prisoners and equipment. This victory had important consequences on a broader scale: it not only led to riots in Austria and a serious attempt at a general strike in Hungary, but it also allowed the Allied commander Marshal Ferdinand Foch to use his reserves on the Western Front. The line was thereafter stable until a final Allied attack Oct 1918 which broke the Austrian line and led to a general retreat, ending with a local armistice 4 Nov.

Aspern Austrian victory over French troops 21–22 May 1809; Napoleon Bonaparte's first ever defeat. Following the French occupation of Vienna, Archduke Charles gathered the Austrian Army across the river Danube. Napoleon sent an opposing force of 40,000 troops to the Marchfeld plain, between the villages of Aspern and Essling. A confused battle ensued, after which the Austrians held Essling and the French Aspern. On the following day Napoleon attacked again and broke the Austrian centre, but the

Austrians held firm and sent a force to destroy the bridges behind the French. Napoleon ordered the attack to cease and the French then fell back, fighting a rearguard action, to the village of Lobau.

Atlantic continuous battle fought in the Atlantic Ocean during World War II by the sea and air forces of the Allies and Germany, to control the supply routes to the UK. The Allies destroyed nearly 800 U-boats during the campaign and at least 2,200 convoys of 75,000 merchant ships crossed the Atlantic, protected by US naval forces. Prior to the US entry into the war 1941, destroyers were supplied to the British under the Lend-Lease Act 1941.

The battle opened 4 Sept 1939, the first night of the war, when the ocean liner *Athenia*, sailing from Glasgow to New York, was torpedoed by a German U-boat off the Irish coast. The Germans employed a variety of tactics such as U-boats, surface-raiders, indiscriminate minelaying, and aircraft, but the Allies successfully countered all of them, although they suffered some significant reverses such as the sinking of the armed merchant ships *Rawalpindi* (23 Nov 1939) and *Jervis Bay* (5 Nov 1940) by German warships. U-boats remained the greatest menace to Allied shipping, especially after the destruction of the German battleship *Bismarck* by the British 27 May 1941.

Aubers Ridge in World War I, abortive British attack on German lines May 1915 in support of, and diversionary to, the French attack on Lens in the Battle of ◊Artois. Elements of the British 1st and Indian corps attacked on the right flank, while the 8th Division launched the main attack on the left. The British launched their attack 9 May with a 40-minute bombardment at 0500 hrs and at 0525 hrs the first troops advanced, intending to get close to the German trenches under cover of the artillery. Unfortunately, many of the shells fell short of the German lines, causing heavy British casualties and preventing the troops from getting into place. When the bombardment ceased, the Germans took position in their parapets and repulsed the attack; in the one or two places where small parties of British troops were able to reach the German trenches they were cut down by enfilade fire. A German counter-bombardment wrecked the British line and prevented reinforcements reaching the front, and by the afternoon the battle had died out. Allied casualties numbered over 6,000 killed and wounded, while German casualties were just over 3,000.

Augustov successful Russian counterattack after the disaster at ◊Tannenberg at the start of World War I to recapture Augustov, a town in western Poland about 60 km/38 mi north of Bialystok, from the Germans and drive through to East Prussia. German forces under General Paul von Hindenburg defeated a Russian reserve army near Lyck (now Elk) Oct 1914. The Russians fell back and formed a line at Augustov to fight a delaying rearguard action so that fresh Russian forces could concentrate in their rear. When these reinforcements had assembled, the Russians counterattacked and drove the German forces back, recapturing Augustov in a flanking movement 3 Dec. German losses were estimated at about 50,000, and the Russians were able to press their advantage to advance into East Prussia.

Austerlitz French victory over a combined Austrian and Russian force 2 Dec 1805; one of Napoleon Bonaparte's greatest victories resulting in the end of the coalition against France – the Austrians signed the Treaty of Pressburg and the Russians retired to their own territory.

After taking Vienna, Napoleon marched north in search of the Austrian and Russian armies, which were assembled at Olmütz waiting for reinforcements from Prussia. Determined to bring them to battle before fresh troops arrived, Napoleon pressed on and by 1 Dec the armies made contact close to Austerlitz (now Slavkov in the Czech Republic), a village about 22 km/14 mi west of Brno. The Allies planned a flank attack to cut off Napoleon's retreat. Napoleon took advantage of this, protecting his front with a thin screen and falling on the flank of the Russian force as it moved past him. He defeated the flank troops then advanced upon the remainder of the Austro-Russian force, drove them into Austerlitz and seized the road leading to Olmütz. The Austrians and Russians fell back, sustaining heavy casualties as their retreating troops were severely bombarded by French artillery. (See also battle plan 4.)

Badajoz, Siege of costly British victory over Napoleonic forces in the Peninsular War March–April 1812. Badajoz, a Spanish city some 400 km/250 mi southwest of Madrid, was an important fortress on the border with Portugal, which the Spanish surrendered to the French Feb 1811. The British tried but failed to recover the fortress May–June 1811.

The British, under the Duke of Wellington, laid siege to the fortress 17 March 1812 and 6 April launched a full-scale assault; the main force attacked two breaches in the walls while diversionary attacks took place elsewhere. The main assault failed, with 2,000 British dead, and was abandoned. One of the diversionary attacks succeeded in scaling the wall at the second attempt, and a second took one of the bastions. The fortress surrendered the following day; the British troops exacted harsh revenge for the 5,000 casualties they had sustained, looting the town for three days before order was restored.

The breach, which, yawning and glittering with steel, seemed like the mouth of a huge dragon belching forth smoke and flame.

Sir William Napier on the *Siege of Badajoz, History of the Peninsular War*

Bagration, Operation in World War II, major Soviet offensive against German Army Group Centre June 1944; regarded by Soviet authorities as perhaps the most decisive operation of the war on the Eastern Front. The German field marshal Ernst Busch was forewarned of the attack and requested permission to fall back to a better defensive line on the river Beresina, but Hitler refused and ordered the Group to remain in position. The Soviet force consisted of over 40 tank brigades plus supporting troops, heavily outnumbering the Germans in both tanks and artillery. The Germans were encircled and cut off in the Vitebsk, Mogilev, and Bobruysk areas and suffered heavy losses. In the space of four weeks, the Soviets destroyed 25 German divisions, crossed eastern Poland, and advanced 725 km/450 mi, finishing on the line of the Vistula river.

Balaklava Russian attack on British positions during the Crimean War Oct 1854; it was during this battle that the disastrous 'Charge of the Light Brigade' took place. The Russian army broke through Turkish lines 25 Oct and entered the valley of Balaklava, a village and harbour on the Black Sea, Russia, some 13 km/8 mi southwest of Sevastopol. The Russians intended to attack the British supply base in the harbour and relieve the encirclement of Savastopol by attacking British positions from the rear. The battlefield consisted of two valleys divided by low hills; the British cavalry's Heavy Brigade were positioned in the South Valley, while the Light Brigade were in the North Valley. The first Russian advance broke into the South Valley and was immediately driven back over the hill by the Heavy Brigade, forcing the Russians to fall back on their line of artillery.

The Light Brigade were ordered to 'prevent the enemy carrying away the guns'; it seems that this was intended to direct them to the hills where the Russians had captured some Turkish guns. However, the order was badly phrased leading the Light Brigade's commander to assume his target was the Russian guns about a mile away up the North Valley. Following these instructions, he led the infamous 'Charge of the Light Brigade' up the length of the valley between two rows of Russian artillery. Of 673 officers and soldiers, 110 were killed and 137 wounded. A charge by French cavalry saved the Light Brigade from total destruction, and the 93rd Highland Regiment broke up a Russian cavalry attack. The battle ended with the Russians retaining their guns and their position.

Balaton, Lake in World War II, last major German offensive on the Eastern Front 1945. The German 2nd Army and 6th SS Panzer Army attacked the Soviet 3rd Ukrainian Front 5 March 1945, both to preempt a threatened Soviet attack and also to safeguard Hungarian oilfields. The Germans advanced some 32 km/20 mi into Soviet lines but a Soviet counterattack 16 March routed the Hungarian 3rd Army which was guarding the Germans' left flank. This left the German units exposed and the operation was hastily halted. The Germans fell back with losses of over 40,000 troops and 500 tanks and assault guns.

Bannockburn victory of Scots troops under Robert I ('the Bruce') over invading English forces under Edward II 24 June 1314. Edward II had invaded Scotland with a large English army to relieve the siege of Stirling and he met the Scots at Bannockburn, a few miles southeast of Stirling. The Scots were grouped in four units, primarily consisting of pikemen with a few cavalry, and protected their front with pits and stakes. The English bowmen launched the battle but when they were routed by the Scottish cavalry, the first line of English knights rode forward. They floundered in the mud and fell into the pits protecting the Scottish front line. The second line advanced but made little impression, and at that point a large group of Scottish camp-followers appeared over a hill, intent upon watching the battle. The English assumed these to be reinforcements and fled in disorder with heavy casualties: English losses are reckoned at about 10,000 troops against 4,000 Scots.

Bapaume in World War I, the second phase of the British offensive of Aug 1918. The battle was virtually a replay of the 1916 Somme battle, starting from more or less the same positions and following the same general plan. The operation was carried out by the British 3rd and 4th Armies, a total of 23 divisions, commanded by generals Sir Julian Byng and Sir Henry Rawlinson respectively, opposed by German forces consisting of 35 under-strength divisions under generals Oskar von Hutier and Georg von der Marwitz, directed by General Erich von Ludendorff. Supported by tanks and artillery, the British attack began 21 Aug 1918, broke through the German lines and crossed the river Ancre 22 Aug. The Germans abandoned Albert after a flank attack, and on 23 Aug a massed Allied attack on a front 53-km/33-mi long drove the German line back until the Allied forces held the Arras-Bapaume road, so flanking the Thiepval Ridge position.

At 1 a.m. on 24 Aug the British mounted a concentric attack on the Thiepval position, taking it with immense German losses in prisoners and equipment. The advance continued, British troops taking Bapaume and Combles and French troops taking Noyon and Nesle. On 30 Aug, the 2nd Australian Division attacked a very strong German position at Mont St Quentin, finally taking it 1 Sept and thus removing the principal German strongpoint. This allowed other Australian units to take Peronne, and this phase of the operation closed 2 Sept, having pushed the German line back some 8 km/5 mi and captured 34,250 prisoners and 270 guns.

Barbarossa in World War II, German code name for the plan to invade the USSR, launched 22 June 1941. The Germans deployed massive resources for the campaign, organized in three Army Groups. Army Group South (under Field Marshal Gerd von Rundstedt), consisting of 52 divisions, with the 3rd and 4th Romanian Armies, a Hungarian and an Italian corps, and 5 divisions of 1st Panzer Group (under General Ewald von Kleist), advanced southeast from south Poland in the direction of Kiev. Army Group Centre (under Field Marshal Fedor von Bock), consisting of 42 divisions plus 9 Panzer divisions, struck from the Polish border northeast toward Minsk and Smolensk. Army Group North (under Field Marshal Ritter von Leeb) with 7 infantry and 3 Panzer divisions advanced from East Prussia through Lithuania and Latvia toward Leningrad. Some 3,330 German tanks were deployed, with four Luftwaffe air fleets providing total air superiority.

Except for a check to the southern group, initial progress was rapid and immense quantities of prisoners and equipment fell into German hands, while most of the Soviet air force was destroyed on the ground. However, due to interference from Hitler, the impetus of the drive toward Moscow was slowed, so that winter set in before the city could be invested. With the failure to take Moscow, Barbarossa was at an end as the German plan lay in ruins The prime cause of failure was the late start to the operation due to delays caused by the Balkan campaign.

Bardia in World War II, fighting Jan 1941–Nov 1942 between Allied and Axis forces to take a port in eastern Cyrenaica (now Bardiyah) 95 km/60 mi east of Tobruk. Originally fortified by the Italians, the port was captured 3–5 Jan 1941 by 6th Australian Division, who took 38,000 prisoners, 120 tanks, 400 guns, and 700 other vehicles. Used by the British as a supply port, it was recaptured by German troops under Field Marshal Erwin Rommel 9 April 1941, and held until 2 Jan 1942 when it was again taken by British and South African troops. During Rommel's advance to El ◊Alamein June 1942 the town fell into German hands once more, and was finally re-taken by British forces 11 Nov 1942.

Barents Sea in World War II, important British naval victory over German forces north of Murmansk, 30 Dec 1942. A German force, including the cruisers *Lützow* and *Admiral Hipper*, and six destroyers, attacked a British convoy en route to Murmansk. The convoy was protected by six British destroyers and five smaller escort vessels which launched a vigorous counterattack, enabling it to turn away, but then themselves ran into part of the German force. The Germans were unable to tell whether they were British or German vessels due to poor visibility and hesitated long enough for the destroyers to lay a smoke screen. The British ships were severely damaged, and two were sunk, but were saved by two cruisers from Murmansk which sank one German destroyer and damaged the *Admiral Hipper*. The German commander broke off the fight and retired.

The German failure so enraged Hitler that Admiral Erich Raeder was relieved of his post as commander in chief of the German Fleet and most of the German Navy was confined to training exercises in the Baltic, some ships having their guns removed to provide coastal defences for Norway.

Bastogne smaller engagement between US and German forces during the Battle of the ◊Bulge Dec 1944. An important road junction, Bastogne lay in the path of the German advance and was held by the US 101 Airborne Division and Combat Command B of the US 10th Armored Division under Brig-Gen Anthony McAuliffe. It was besieged by German forces 18 Dec 1944 and strongly attacked; the defences were breached in two places 25 Dec. However, the attacks were repulsed and Bastogne was relieved by the US 4th Armored Division the following day, though fierce fighting continued in the area for some days.

Bataan in World War II, unsuccessful attempt by US and Filipino troops under General Douglas MacArthur to defend the peninsular against the Japanese 1 Jan–9 April 1942. Following the surrender of Bataan, MacArthur was evacuated, but Allied captives were force-marched 95 km/60 mi to the nearest railhead in the *Bataan Death March*; ill-treatment by the Japanese guards during the march killed about 16,000 US and Filipino troops.

Battleaxe, Operation in World War II, unsuccessful British offensive in the Western Desert 15 June 1941, intended to relieve Tobruk and recapture

Cyrenaica. Three columns were used in the attack, one advancing toward the Halfaya Pass, one to Capuzzo, and one inland to the Hafid Ridge. The tank attack on Halfaya was ambushed and destroyed by German 88 mm guns, as was the Hafid Ridge advance, though the Capuzzo attack was moderately successful. A German counterattack 16 June did more damage to British armour, and the British withdrew to their start line on the following day.

Bautzen French victory in the Napoleonic Wars over a combined Russian and Prussian force May 1813, at Bautzen, about 40 km/25 mi northwest of Dresden. Napoleon Bonaparte, intent upon punishing the Prussians for deserting his cause, led 115,000 troops against the 100,000-strong combined army under Marshal Gebhard von Blücher and Count Wittgenstein 20–21 May 1813.

Napoleon planned to make a frontal attack to fix the troops on his front, while sending Marshal Michel Ney, approaching with another body of troops, against the enemy's right flank. Three French corps crossed the river Spree 20 May and took Bautzen and a ridge of hills. The combined armies counterattacked 21 May and succeeded in pushing the French back some distance but were then struck by Ney. Although the Russians and Prussians put up a powerful fight, they were incapable of dealing simultaneously with both frontal and flank attacks and the frontal attack, led by Marshal Nicolas Soult, broke through the centre while Ney was steadily advancing from the flank. The combined force had no alternative but to retreat, which they were able to achieve in good order, largely because Napoleon had no cavalry to harry them.

Beachy Head (French *Bévéziers*) English naval defeat in the Channel 30 June 1690 by a French force sailing to London in support of a proposed Jacobite rebellion. The English army at the time was almost entirely occupied in Ireland where William III was opposing King James II. Taking advantage of England's weakness, Louis XIV of France prepared a large fleet to attack London, raise a Jacobite rebellion and invade England. The main English fleet went off to seek the French but missed them; the remainder, reinforced by a Dutch squadron, totalled some 55 sail and 25 fireships against the French fleet of 80 sail and 30 fireships.

Admiral George Byng, later Viscount Torrington, advised protecting the Thames and awaiting the return of the rest of the fleet, but Queen Mary ordered him to give battle. The fleets met off Beachy Head and after severe fighting the wind dropped and both fleets were becalmed. Unable to move, the English were at the mercy of the heavier French armament and sustained heavy casualties. Eventually a breeze sprang up and the remnants of the English fleet were able to retreat into the river Thames leaving the French in control of the Channel.

Byng was court-martialled but acquitted; he said '...while we had a fleet in being they would not dare to make an attempt' and from this came the strategic doctrine of the 'fleet in being' whereby the existence of a powerful fleet becomes a deterrent in itself.

Beda Fomm catastrophic Italian defeat at the hands of the British during the North African Campaign in World War II 7 Feb 1941. Elements of the British 7th Armoured Division had cut across the desert and set up a road block in which the retreating Italian 10th Army was ambushed. Over 25,000 prisoners, 100 tanks, 216 guns, and 1,500 other vehicles were captured.

Beersheba British victory over Turkish armies in World War I 31 Oct 1917. Beersheba formed the left anchor of a Turkish defensive line extending some 50 km/30 mi to Gaza and General Sir Edmund Allenby planned to attack this flank, where the open desert allowed room to manoeuvre. An attack on 27 Oct against Gaza fixed Turkish attention on the other end of the line and on 31 Oct a night attack was made against Beersheba. Two divisions mounted a frontal attack, while a mounted force mainly composed of ANZAC troops moved across the desert to make another attack from the flank. The frontal attack succeeded in taking both lines of defence, while the 4th Australian Light Horse made a cavalry charge from the flank and captured Beersheba. About 2,000 Turkish troops were taken prisoner.

Belgrade Austrian victory over overwhelming Turkish forces 16 Aug 1717 in the war between Turkey and the Holy Roman Empire. About 180,000 Turks, entrenched around the city, were attacked by some 40,000 Austrians under Prince Eugène who launched his assault at night in order to compensate for his lack of numbers. The Austrian right wing became detached, but Eugène was able to get them back into their proper place and drove the defenders out of their lines, capturing the city. The Turks lost about 15,000 killed and wounded and 166 guns, while Austrian losses were about 5,500.

Belgrade was for centuries an outpost of the West as a bastion against the Turks and other forces from the East and was the site of three major battles of Christian forces against the Turks. The other two were in *1456* when Mehmet II besieged the Hungarians under John Hunyadi, but failed to overcome the defenders and retired after 40 days; and *Oct 1789* when the Turks had again occupied the city and, after a brief siege, were driven out by the Austrians.

Belleau Wood US victory over the Germans, June 1918, during the Allied drive to expel the Germans from northern France toward the end of World War I. After their success at ◊Château-Thierry, the Americans then attacked German positions in Belleau Wood 6 June 1918. The initial German posts were driven back, but strong German defences then turned the battle into a tree-by-tree advance by the US Marine Brigade. The Marines spent almost three weeks clearing the wood, every yard of which was bitterly contested. The last German positions were taken 12 June, but sporadic fighting continued until 25 June before the wood could be considered secured.

Beresina partial victory of Russian forces over the French army retreating from Napoleon Bonaparte's abortive attempt on Moscow Nov 1812. Two Russian armies attacked the French as they crossed the Beresina river 28 Nov: one army fell on Napoleon who had already crossed the river while the other attacked Marshal Claude Victor's force which formed the rearguard and was just approaching the river. Napoleon managed to beat off the attack on his force, but Victor's troops were less fortunate: the Russians extracted a heavy toll of mainly stragglers and camp-followers, claiming some 36,000 killed.

Berlin final battle of the European phase of World War II, 16 April–2 May 1945; Soviet forces captured Berlin, the capital of Germany and seat of government and site of most German military and administrative headquarters. Three Soviet Army Groups, commanded by Marshals Georgi Zhukov, Ivan Konev, and Konstantin Rokossovski, together with two tank armies, a total of some 1,595,000 troops, forced a bridgehead over the river Oder, some 70 km/45 mi east of the city, and converged on Berlin. They were confronted by the remains of the German 9th Army and the final battle opened 16 April with a barrage fired by 20,000 Soviet guns. The subsequent Soviet advance was fiercely resisted by the Germans, principally the 56th Panzer Corps. A second attack then developed from the south and the third Russian Group attacked from the north 30 April, the first Soviet shells falling in Berlin 21 April. After further heavy bombardment by massed artillery, which virtually destroyed the city, and bitter street fighting, the Soviet flag was flown from the Reichstag building 1 May.

Hitler committed suicide 30 April as the Soviets closed in and General Karl Weidling surrendered the city 2 May. Soviet casualties came to about 100,000 dead; German casualties are unknown but some 136,000 were taken prisoner and it is believed over 100,000 civilians died in the course of the fighting. After the war, Berlin was divided into four sectors – British, US, French, and Soviet – and until 1948 was under quadripartite government by the Allies.

Berlin in World War II, series of 16 heavy bombing attacks on Berlin by the RAF Nov 1943–March 1944. Some 9,111 bomber sorties were flown during the course of the campaign and immense damage was done to the city. However, almost 600 bombers were lost during the battle, into which the Germans threw all their air defence capability.

Bhamo in World War II, Chinese victory over Japanese troops Dec 1944. Bhamo, a town in northern Burma (now Myanmar) 193 km/120 mi south of Myitkyina, was occupied by the Japanese Jan 1942 during their initial advance through Burma. Chinese troops of the New 1st Army attacked the town 10 Nov 1944 as part of a drive to open communications between China and Burma. The Japanese garrison resisted until the night of 14–15 Dec when some 900 troops managed to break out and escape, and the town was occupied by the Chinese.

Biak in World War II, hard-fought Allied campaign May–June 1944 to recapture the island from the Japanese who were using it as an air base. US and Australian troops attacked the island, off the north coast of New Guinea, 27 May 1944. The Japanese garrison put up strong resistance and the island was not secured until 29 June, with 2,700 Allied casualties and 9,000 Japanese.

Bladensburg during the War of 1812, unsuccessful American attempt to check the British advance on Washington Aug 1814. As the British under General Robert Ross advanced upon Washington, an American force under General William Winder took up a position protecting the only bridge over the river Anacostia which gave access to the city. The bridge was taken in a swift attack, and once the British got their main force across the river they launched a devastating attack on the main American position, defeating them utterly. Ross resumed his advance and entered Washington later that day, 24 Aug 1814.

Blenheim decisive British victory over the French in the War of the Spanish Succession, 13 Aug 1704. Although the war was to continue for a further eight years, Blenheim marked the turning point at which the power of France was first broken.

Brigadier Rowe proceeded within thirty paces of the pales about Blenheim before the enemy gave their first fire, by which a great many brave officers and soldiers fell, but that did not discourage their gallant commander from marching directly up to the very pales, on which he struck his sword before he suffered a man to fire.

Dr Hare's *Journal* describing an incident in the *Battle of Blenheim*

The French planned to send an army to unite with the Bavarians and then march down the Danube to capture Vienna. To preempt this, the British under the Duke of Marlborough and the Austrians under Prince Eugène of Savoy decided on a joint attack on Bavaria. Several groups of German troops joined the Austro-British force during its advance and the opposing armies met at the village of Blindheim, better known as Blenheim, about 25 km/18 mi northwest of Augsburg.

The French had fortified the village, where they based their right flank with their line extending some 5 km/3 mi along a ridge protected to the front by marshy ground bisected by a stream. The Allies marched overnight to gain the element of surprise and attacked at about noon on 13 Aug 1704. Eugène attacked the Bavarians on the French left flank, while Marlborough attacked Blenheim directly, without immediate success. Assuming that the attacks against the flanks would also have weakened the French centre, Marlborough drove a massive force – 90 squadrons of horse, 23 battalions of infantry, and supporting artillery – straight through the centre of the French line. Eugène moved his advance in turn, taking the French in their flank and splitting them from the Bavarians so that both could be dealt with separately. Marlborough then completed the move against Blenheim and captured most of the garrison, although most of the Bavarian forces were able to escape.

Blitz, The (anglicization of *Blitzkrieg*) in World War II, British name for the German air raids against Britain 1940–41 following the failure of the Battle of ◊Britain. It has been estimated that about 40,000 civilians were killed, 46,000 injured, and more than a million homes destroyed and damaged in this period, together with an immense amount of damage to industrial installations.

The first raid was against London 7–8 Sept 1940, and raids continued on all but 10 nights until 12 Nov. The Germans then began to target industrial cities such as Coventry (14 Nov), Southampton, Birmingham, Bristol, Cardiff, Portsmouth, and Liverpool, with occasional raids on London. In spring 1941 the air defences began to take a larger toll of the attackers, due to improvements in radar for night fighters and for artillery control. The raids fell away during the early summer as Luftwaffe forces were withdrawn from the west in preparation for the invasion of the USSR.

Bolimov inconclusive World War I battle between German and Russian forces, forming part of the third German attack on Warsaw Feb 1915; mainly significant as the first battle in which gas was used as a weapon of war.

The German artillery fired several thousand shells filled with xylyl bromide, a lachrymatory gas, but the liquid failed to vaporize because of the extreme cold and so the gas had no effect whatever on the Russian defenders. The Russians discovered that gas had been used, and took steps to issue rudimentary masks to their troops thereafter, as well as alerting Britain and France to the new tactic. However, it was not immediately followed up and the incident was forgotten and so the use of gas at ◊Ypres still came as a surprise.

Borodino battle between French and Russian forces 7 Sept 1812 during Napoleon Bonaparte's invasion of Russia, one of the bloodiest battles of the Napoleonic years.

Napoleon, with 137,00 troops and 585 guns, had advanced as far as Borodino, on the river Koloc, about 110 km/70 mi west of Moscow where a Russian force of about 110,000 had taken up a strong position behind temporary fortifications. After a powerful artillery bombardment the French attacked and captured some Russian field works, which were promptly recaptured. The battle moved back and forth indecisively for some hours before Napoleon mounted a major assault with artillery and cavalry which made considerable inroads into the Russian lines. The Russians counterattacked repeatedly until late in the afternoon when, exhausted, they fell back to a ridge behind their original position; the French, equally exhausted, also fell back to their starting point.

The Russians lost 15,000 dead and 25,000 wounded; the French lost about 28,000, including 12 generals. Although the Russians were still a coherent force, they were in no condition to fight another battle and Napoleon was able to continue his advance on Moscow.

Bosworth final battle of the Wars of the Roses 22 Aug 1485, at which Richard III, the Yorkist king, was defeated and slain by Henry Tudor, Earl of Richmond, who became Henry VII.

Richard's oppressive reign ensured that Henry, landing in Wales, gathered an army of supporters as he marched into England to meet Richard's army which was drawn up on a hill at Bosworth, about 19 km/12 mi west of Leicester. A third, smaller, army led by Lord Stanley stood off from both sides, undecided upon which to join. Henry opened the battle by advancing up the hill and charging into the opposition. Lord Stanley now made his decision and fell on the rear of King Richard's position, causing the King's force to break and flee. Richard was unhorsed in the rush and beaten to death as he lay. As the battle ended, Lord Stanley crowned Henry as king; Henry later married Edward IV's daughter Elizabeth, uniting the houses of York and Lancaster to bring the Wars to an end.

Bougainville US campaign in World War II to recover the most northerly of the Solomon Islands from the Japanese. About 965 km/600 mi from Australia, now part of Papua New Guinea, Bougainville was taken by the Japanese March 1942 and became an important refuelling and supply base for their operations against ◊Guadalcanal and the other Solomon Islands. It was garrisoned by about 35,000 Japanese troops, principally in the south end of the island.

The US 3rd Marine Division landed at the northern end of the island 1 Nov 1943 and established a secure beachhead, reinforced by the US 37th Infantry Division. Thereafter the Japanese, in spite of ferocious counterattacks, were largely neutralized and contained. In early 1944 the US troops were replaced by Australians who proceeded to hunt down the remaining Japanese and had secured the island by April 1944. An estimated 8,500 Japanese were killed in fighting on the island and a further 9,000 died of illness and malnutrition.

Bourgebus Ridge unsuccessful British attack July 1944 on a small ridge southeast of Caen which was held by German troops amply equipped with anti-tank weapons. It was attacked 18 July by three British armoured divisions, which were beaten off with severe losses of both troops and tanks. Nevertheless, the attack had the effect of making the Germans reinforce this area, weakening their hold on the western part of the Normandy beachhead where the main Allied breakout took place.

Bourlon Wood, attacks on in World War I, British operations against a section of the Hindenburg Line Nov 1917 and Sept 1918. The wood lay

5 km/3 mi west of Cambrai and was carefully organized by the Germans as a defensive position.

In the *First Battle of Cambrai* 20 Nov 1917 British tanks reached the edge of the wood but by that time the infantry were too worn out to act in support. The wood was cleared 23 Nov by a force of tanks aided by infantry of the 40th Division but they were driven out the following day by a German counterattack. The wood was finally captured 27 Sept 1918 by the Canadian Corps aided by the 7th Tank Battalion in an attack from both sides of the wood. The Canadians took some 10,000 prisoners and 200 guns.

Bouvines decisive French victory over an Allied army collected by the Emperor Otto IV of Germany and King John of England 27 July 1214. The battle, one of the most decisive in medieval Europe, had wide political ramifications: it so weakened Otto that it ensured the succession of Frederick II as Holy Roman Emperor and confirmed Philip II (Augustus) as ruler of the whole of northern France and Flanders; it led to the renunciation of all English claims to the region.

Otto was to invade France from the Netherlands, where he had allies, while John invaded from the southwest. However, Otto was late starting and John refused to wait for him, marching his army back to Bordeaux. The French, meanwhile, marched toward Flanders, Otto finally marched south, and the two armies met at Bouvines, a village between Lille and Tournai in northern France. Otto's army, with a small English contingent, numbered perhaps 30,000 while the French strength was about the same; each massed their foot soldiers in the centre and placed their cavalry on the flanks, with reserves behind. The French gradually gained the upper hand and the Allies were routed with many troops taken prisoner.

Boyne William III's defeat of the exiled James II and his French allies near Drogheda, Ireland 1 July 1690; it was the final battle of the War of English Succession, confirming a Protestant monarch.

After obtaining aid from Louis XIV of France, James landed in Ireland where he had numerous supporters. King William also landed an army in Ireland, collected more forces from Londonderry, and marched south with about 36,000 troops. James' forces had taken up a position on the south side of the river Boyne, and William launched the attack by sending a force to cross the river some miles upstream so as to turn the Irish flank. The French turned to oppose this attack, and William then sent his cavalry across the river in a frontal assault on James' position. After fierce fighting the Irish foot soldiers broke but their cavalry continued to fight for some time before being routed. James fled to Dublin while his army largely became fugitives; any hopes of James' restoration to the English throne were finally dashed.

Brandywine British victory during the War of American Independence 11 Sept 1777. The British, under General Sir William Howe, moved on Philadelphia from New York, sailing a force of 14,000 men to the head of the

Elk river. An American force under General George Washington marched to meet him and took up a strong defensive position on the fords of the Brandywine river. Howe made a feint against Washington's front while sending a detachment under Lord Cornwallis to cross the stream higher up and swing round to take the American position from the rear. The plan worked: the Americans lost 1,400 troops and were dislodged from their position. The British were unable to pursue due to exhaustion, but Howe was able to resume his advance and captured Philadelphia about two weeks later.

Breitenfeld in the Thirty Years' War, victory of a joint Swedish-Saxon force under King Gustavus Adolphus over Imperial forces under Count Tilly 17 Sept 1631. Gustavus was seeking alliances with Brandenburg and Saxony before advancing south, but while he negotiated Tilly's troops sacked Magdeburg, which he had promised to relieve. Saxony joined the Swedes and Gustavus marched out to find Tilly.

The two forces met at Breitenfeld, about 10 km/6 mi from Leipzig, and the battle began with an artillery duel, followed by an Imperial cavalry charge which was intended to turn the Swedish right flank. The Swedes advanced to meet the charge and were able to drive off the attack. On the other flank the Saxons were driven off in disorder, exposing the Swedish left flank, which was immediately attacked by Tilly's infantry. A desperate struggle followed, but once the cavalry charge had been disposed of, the Swedes from the left flank advanced to the positions vacated by Tilly's advancing troops, captured their guns, and began firing them into the rear of the Imperial advance. This caused the advancing troops to break and Tilly's force was soon in full retreat. (See also battle plan 3.)

Breskens Pocket in World War II, Allied campaign Oct 1944 to dislodge German troops enclosed in the area south of the Scheldt river opposite the Walcheren islands. After the fall of Antwerp, the German 6th Division was enclosed and isolated in the pocket which contained a major coast defence fort commanding the entrance to the river. It was attacked by Canadian forces 6 Oct, but German resistance was strong and the attack was reinforced by the Canadian 4th Armoured Division and British 52nd Lowland Division. The pocket was finally taken 2 Nov and 12,500 prisoners were captured.

Brest-Litovsk, capture of in World War I, German victory over the Russians Aug 1915. After the German capture of Warsaw the Russians fell back slowly, harried by German thrusts from several directions. Eventually the fortress of Brest-Litovsk was isolated by General August von Mackensen in the east and General Max von Gallwitz in the north. Siege artillery was deployed, but the Russian High Command decided not to hold the position and 16 Aug gave orders to evacuate the civil population. As the German forces closed in from the west and south, the Russians withdrew and abandoned the fortress 25 Aug 1915. All its guns and most of its stores were successfully removed before the German occupation.

Britain, Battle of World War II air battle between German and British air forces over Britain 10 July–31 Oct 1940.

At the outset the Germans had the advantage because they had seized airfields in the Netherlands, Belgium, and France, which were basically safe from attack and from which southeast England was within easy range. On 1 Aug 1940 the Luftwaffe had about 4,500 aircraft of all kinds, compared to about 3,000 available to the RAF. The Battle of Britain had been intended as a preliminary to the German plan for the invasion of Britain, *Seelöwe* (Sea Lion), which Hitler indefinitely postponed 17 Sept and abandoned 10 Oct, choosing instead to invade the USSR (see ◊Barbarossa).

The Battle of Britain has been divided into five phases: 10 July–7 Aug, the preliminary phase; 8–23 Aug, attack on coastal targets; 24 Aug–6 Sept, attack on Fighter Command airfields; 7–30 Sept, daylight attacks on London, chiefly by heavy bombers; and 1–31 Oct, daylight attacks on London, chiefly by fighter-bombers. The main battle was between some 600 Hurricanes and Spitfires and the Luftwaffe's 800 Messerschmitt 109s and 1,000 bombers (Dornier 17s, Heinkel 111s, and Junkers 88s). Losses Aug–Sept were, for the RAF: 832 fighters totally destroyed; for the Luftwaffe: 668 fighters and some 700 bombers and other aircraft.

Brusilov Offensive in World War I, major Russian assault against the southern sector of the Eastern Front June 1916 in order to relieve pressure on the Western and Italian Fronts by drawing German forces east. The offensive met this immediate objective but also had far broader effects: it cost the Russians almost one million casualties, which demoralized the army and aided the revolutionary cause; it brought Romania into the war on the Allied side, resulting in the eventual conquest of Romania by German forces; and the decimation of Austro-Hungarian forces made the German Army the dominant partner among the Central Powers thereafter.

General Alexei Brusilov commanded the Russian 7th, 8th, 9th, and 11th Armies, advancing on a line from the Pripet Marshes to the Romanian border. The Austro-Hungarian 4th Army was almost totally destroyed, and the Austro-German 'Southern Army' was forced to retreat as a result. The attack achieved its purpose, since Field Marshal Paul Hindenburg had to withdraw troops from many areas, including Italy, to bolster the defences in Galicia and Bukovina. Although an Austro-Hungarian counterattack checked the Russian advance north, Brusilov pushed forward in the south as far as the Carpathian mountains before his attack came to a halt due to exhaustion of his troops, poor supplies and lack of support from other Russian forces.

Bulge, Battle of the (or *Ardennes offensive*) in World War II, Hitler's plan, code-named 'Watch on the Rhine', for a breakthrough by Field Marshal Gerd von Rundstedt aimed at the US line in the Ardennes 16 Dec 1944–28 Jan 1945. Hitler aimed to isolate the Allied forces north of the corridor which would be created by a drive through the Ardennes, creating a German salient or 'bulge'. There were 77,000 Allied casualties and 130,000 German, including Hitler's last powerful reserve of elite Panzer units. Although US troops were encircled for some weeks at ◊Bastogne, the German counteroffensive failed.

Three armies were deployed in the operation – Sepp Dietrich's 6th Panzer; the 5th Panzer; and the 7th Panzer – together with a 'Trojan Horse' force of English-speaking Germans in US uniforms, under Otto Skorzeny. The offensive opened 16 Dec along a 113 km/70 mi sector of the front, aiming at the US 1st Army and General Omar Bradley's 12th Army Group. Initial progress was good as the Allies were unprepared for action along a section of the front hitherto so quiet it had been nicknamed 'the Ghost Front' and bad weather grounded Allied air support.

All I had to do was cross the river, capture Brussels, and then go on to take the port of Antwerp. The snow was waist-deep and there wasn't room to deploy four tanks abreast, let alone six Panzer divisions. It didn't get light till eight and was dark again at four and my tanks can't fight at night. And all this at Christmas time!

Sepp Dietrich, commander of 6th Panzer Army during the *Battle of the Bulge*

However, the Germans failed to capture vital fuel dumps and the dogged Allied defence of St Vith and Bastogne seriously set the operation back. The Allies quickly recovered from the initial shock and, while north of the Bulge General Bernard Montgomery blocked the German advance at the Meuse, to the south Bradley's forces also struck back, with General George Patton breaking through to relieve Bastogne 26 Dec. By the end of Dec the weather improved, allowing the Allied air forces to play a part in the battle and by 3 Jan 1945 the Allies took the offensive; by 16 Jan the Bulge had been eliminated.

Bull Run two Confederate victories in the American Civil War; named after the stream in West Virginia, about 50 km/30 mi west of Washington DC, where they took place.

21 July 1861 Union troops under General Irwin McDowell opened the battle with a determined attack on Pierre Beauregard's Confederates. This initial assault was firmly resisted by General Thomas Jackson's Virginia brigade, earning him the title 'Stonewall Jackson'. The battle swayed back and forth and then Confederate reinforcements under General Joseph E Johnston arrived at a critical moment, turned the balance, and the Union troops fled the field in disorder.

29–30 Aug 1862 McDowell was replaced by a new general, John Pope, who boasted about what he was going to do to the Confederates, and General Robert E Lee sent Stonewall Jackson north to assess the strength of the Union forces. Lee discovered that the Union commander, Maj-Gen George McClellan, was sending Pope reinforcements, and so he took General James Longstreet's corps and set off north. Jackson initially harried Pope with cavalry and then met him head-on at Bull Run. Jackson held firm and, again in the nick of time, Lee and Longstreet appeared with reinforcements. Lee urged Longstreet to attack but Longstreet took so long over his dispositions that night fell before he was ready and it was not until the following morning that he finally went into action. When he did, all was forgiven; he fell upon Pope's force and scattered it. As with the first battle, this second engagement ended with the defeated Union forces running pell-mell for the safety of Washington, leaving 14,000 dead and wounded behind them.

Bunker Hill first battle of the American War of Independence 17 June 1775 on Breed's Hill and Bunker's Hill, just outside Boston, Massachusetts. The British commander, General Thomas Gage, decided to occupy these two small hills which had a commanding position over Boston. He was pre-empted by a party of about 1,200 American militiamen who seized Breed's Hill on the night of 16 June and erected a stockade which protected them from the fire of the British warships in the harbour.

The following morning General Gage ordered a 2,000-strong force of infantry to clear the hill. They advanced and were met by a strong fire; they re-formed, advanced again, and were again reduced in numbers. A third attack was then arranged on rather more tactical lines and this succeeded in taking the top of the hill and driving off the Americans, who retired in good order, having lost about 450 casualties. The British suffered 226 killed and 828 wounded. The battle, though it took place on Breed's Hill, has always been called Bunker Hill, since this was actually the higher and more important of the two hills.

Burlington Heights engagement between British and American forces in the vicinity of Detroit 5 May 1813 during the War of 1812. A small British force under Col Proctor was attacking an American position on Burlington Heights when it was attacked by a second American force of about 1,300 troops under General Henry Clay. The initial American charge broke through the British lines and captured their guns, but Proctor rallied his troops, counterattacked, and drove off Clay's force with about 1,000 casualties.

Busaco battle in the Peninsular War between English and Portuguese armies under the Duke of Wellington and the French under Marshal André Masséna 27 Sept 1810.

Masséna had invaded Portugal and Wellington was falling back before him toward the lines of Torres Vedras, protecting Lisbon. Upon reaching the heights of Busaco, a ridge about 45 km/28 mi northeast of Coimbra, Wellington decided to offer resistance. The French had little opportunity for tactical surprise and merely made a series of head-on assaults against the British line. They were beaten off with heavy losses, the engagement was quickly over, and the British resumed their retreat, leaving the French to follow. Wellington had bought a little more time and reduced the enemy's force.

C

Calabria World War II naval action between British and Italian forces 9 April 1940. The British Mediterranean fleet of three battleships, an aircraft carrier, and five cruisers, escorting a convoy to Alexandria, met an Italian force of two battleships and sixteen cruisers which was itself escorting a convoy to North Africa. Both sides opened fire and the British hit the Italian battleship *Giulio Cesare* at a range of 24 km/15 mi. The Italians laid a smoke screen and turned away, leaving the British force undamaged.

Cambrai two battles between British and German forces in World War I at Cambrai in northeast France:
20–27 Nov 1917 the first battle in which tanks were used in large numbers, and in which the usual preliminary artillery bombardment was not employed. The British attacked with 330 tanks and 2 infantry corps, accompanied by a specific rather than general artillery bombardment of German defensive positions by 1,000 guns. Considerable gains were made, with 10,500 prisoners and 142 guns taken, but the tank force suffered heavy losses and the infantry were exhausted. Due to the lack of fresh troops in reserve, the German counterattack could not be resisted, so that by 27 Nov the British were back almost where they had started and the battle was broken off.
26 Aug–5 Oct 1918 by 1918 Cambrai was protected by the formidable Hindenburg Line and was attacked as part of the British general advance. Specially lengthened Mark V tanks, which could span the broad trenches of the Line, were used. Preceded by a strong artillery barrage, the attack broke through the Line, eventually making a 65 km/40 mi gap and Cambrai was captured 5 Oct 1918.

Camden probably the greatest British victory in the War of American Independence 16 Aug 1780, near Camden, South Carolina. The Americans, taking the offensive, had sent an army to South Carolina, where the British were present in some strength with their headquarters at Camden. Lord Cornwallis collected his troops and attacked; though much inferior in strength, his force was of disciplined regulars, while the American force was largely composed of untrained militia, and the Americans were comprehensively defeated. They lost over 1,000 killed and wounded and about the same number of prisoners as well as a large quantity of stores, and at the time it seemed that the American cause was doomed.

Camperdown decisive British naval victory in the French Revolutionary Wars over the Dutch fleet 11 Oct 1797, off the Dutch coast; the battle effectively marked the end of significant Dutch naval power.

A large Dutch fleet had been blockaded in the Texel by five British warships which had bluffed Jan de Winter, the Dutch admiral, into thinking that the British fleet lay over the horizon by making spurious signals. A storm forced the blockaders back to England and de Winter broke out with 16 warships and sailed for the river Maas. The British admiral Adam Duncan also mustered 16 ships and sailed to intercept the Dutch course. Duncan signalled for an attack in line, but the foul weather obscured the signals. Eventually Duncan signalled for the British ships to sail between the Dutch, so placing themselves between the Dutch and the shore. All engaged with broadsides as they passed through and the fighting became general, the Dutch ships being defeated one by one. Nine surrendered and the rest fled with considerable damage.

Cannae Carthaginian victory over the Romans in the 2nd Punic War 2 Aug 216 BC near Apulia, Italy. A classic use of encirclement tactics, Cannae was one of the most terrible defeats ever suffered by a Roman army. Despite being heavily outnumbered (40,000 troops to the Romans' 80,000) the Carthaginian general Hannibal allowed the Roman consul C Terentius Varro to advance against his position. He allowed the Romans to push back his centre then used his superior cavalry to break the Roman formations on the flanks. As the Carthaginian centre gave way, Hannibal swept his heavy infantry forward and his cavalry attacked the Romans in the rear: the Carthaginians completely encircled and destroyed the Roman army. The Romans were said to have lost about 50,000 troops as against the Carthaginian casualties of fewer than 6,000. (See battle plan 1.)

Cape Esperance in World War II, US naval victory over the Japanese 11–12 Oct 1942. A Japanese cruiser squadron of three cruisers and two destroyers was ordered to cover the landing of reinforcements on ◊Guadalcanal, after which it was to bombard Henderson Field airstrip. A US squadron of four cruisers and five destroyers was escorting a troop and supply convoy approaching the area.

The two sides met off Savo Island; the US force opened fire first, severely damaging two Japanese cruisers and sinking one destroyer. The US destroyer *Duncan* got involved with two Japanese ships and became the target of not only their fire but that of other US ships attempting to deal with the Japanese in the dark by radar. The vessel caught fire and was abandoned; it sank the following day. The US force then pursued the Japanese out of the area and sank another cruiser and two destroyers.

Cape Matapan in World War II, British naval victory over an Italian force 28 March 1941. The Italian force, consisting of one battleship, eight cruisers, and nine destroyers, set out to disrupt British convoys between

Alexandria and Greece. However, the British were forewarned and Admiral Sir Andrew Cunningham set out to protect the convoys with three battleships, an aircraft carrier, four cruisers, and thirteen destroyers. The two fleets met south of Crete and the British cruisers immediately opened fire and then withdrew, hoping to draw the Italians on to the main British fleet. However, having just suffered a minor air attack, the Italian commander realized the British had a carrier and quite possibly larger vessels in the area and ordered his fleet to turn for home.

Cunningham ordered air and torpedo strikes against the Italian flagship *Vittorio Veneto* which hit the stern but had little effect. A third torpedo attack struck and halted the cruiser *Pola*. The Italians detached two cruisers and four destroyers to assist the *Pola* then withdrew to base. The British found the *Pola* and its escort on radar, closed with them in the darkness, and opened fire at a range of 2,750 m/3,000 yds, sinking five Italian ships.

Cape Spartivento inconclusive World War II naval engagement between British and Italian forces 27 Nov 1940. An Italian fleet of two battleships, six cruisers, and fourteen destroyers attempted to intercept a British convoy escorted by a battleship, a battle cruiser, an aircraft carrier, five cruisers, and ten destroyers. The British commander ordered the convoy to turn away and then took his fleet toward the Italians. The leading cruisers of both sides opened fire but the Italian commander then saw the aircraft carrier *Ark Royal* in the British force. Fearing air strikes against Italy's only two serviceable battleships, he turned about and fled for Naples.

Cape St George World War II naval action between five Japanese and five US destroyers 25 Nov 1943 off New Ireland. The US force was led by Capt Arleigh Burke who typically went straight into action, sinking three Japanese destroyers and putting the other two to flight.

Caporetto in World War I, joint German-Austrian victory over the Italian Army Oct 1917. At the end of Sept 1917 the Italian offensive against the Austrians in the Isonzo area ended, but in the summer the German Staff had planned an offensive in the area and during Oct the Austrians were joined by substantial German reinforcements. The Italians were expecting an attack from the north but a massive German force was assembled in great secrecy at the southern end of the Italian front and on 24 Oct, after a heavy artillery bombardment, General Karl von Bülow broke through the Italian lines west of the Isonzo and headed for Caporetto. Heavy fighting continued throughout the following day, with delays in sending reserves weakening Italian resistance. As the Germans penetrated deeper, so the flanks of the remaining Italian line were threatened and had to fall back. By 26 Oct Caporetto had fallen and masses of Italian troops were in headlong retreat. Eventually General Luigi Cadorna authorized a full retreat, which continued some 95 km/60 mi to the line of the river Piave before the Italian defence could be stabilized.

The sudden collapse of the Italians took von Bülow by surprise and he was unable to bring up reserves or take advantage of the situation. As it was, the Austro-German forces merely moved slowly forward in the wake of the Italians, taking Gorizia, Cividale, and Udine as they did so. Von Bülow's forces crossed the river Tagliamento, the advanced Italian line, 3 Nov 1917 and broke through Italian outposts but their advance was halted by the Piave line.

Carrhae disastrous Roman defeat by the Parthians 53 BC. The Roman consul M Licinius Crassus was overeager to make his name as a general to counterbalance the reputations of Pompey and Julius Caesar, and consequently allowed himself to be drawn too deep into Parthian territory by a Parthian cavalry force under Sillaces. The Parthians drew up for battle then withdrew, drawing the Romans after them; they repeated this tactic until the Roman column was severely extended, then turned, enveloped the head of the column, massacred them, and moved back to the next part of the column. All but 500 of the 6,000-strong Roman force was wiped out; the remainder, including Crassus, were captured along with their standards, a grave blow to Roman pride. Crassus was executed and his head delivered to the Parthian king Orontes.

The disaster preyed on Roman minds until the emperor Augustus recovered the standards and surviving prisoners by judicious use of diplomatic pressure 20 BC.

Carso four major battles 1916–17 between Italian forces under General Luigi Cadorna, pressing an attempt to seize Trieste, and Austrian forces trying to stop them.

Sept 1916 the Italians gained some ground before being stopped by a concentration of Austrian heavy artillery and bad weather.

Oct 1916 Cadorna resumed his attack and made a steady advance, repulsed Austrian counterattacks, and established a new line before the onset of a severe winter prevented further movement.

May 1917 the Italians drove the Austrians from their trench lines from Kostanjevica to the Adriatic shore. After a further advance, they were brought to a standstill by a shortage of ammunition. The Austrians were well stocked due to the collapse of the Russian front, and after a powerful bombardment, they counterattacked 1 June. They met with only limited success and the battle died out. Cadorna had gained a great deal of territory, and taken 16,500 prisoners and a quantity of guns and stores.

Sept 1917 the Italians had been gradually creeping forward throughout the summer and were preparing a major attack on San Gabriele, but the Austrians discovered this and mounted a spoiling attack 4 Sept. The battle lines swayed back and forth but eventually the Austrians prevailed and drove the Italian forces out of their forward positions to a second, rearward, line where the battle died out and the Italians consolidated their position.

Cassino in World War II, series of costly but ultimately successful Allied assaults Jan–May 1944 on heavily fortified German positions blocking the Allied advance to Rome. Cassino is in southern Italy, 80 km/50 mi northwest of Naples, at the foot of Monte Cassino.

It was attacked by the British 10th Corps, US 2nd Corps, and the French Corps 17 Jan–12 Feb 1944 but these assaults were all repulsed. The Allies thought the Germans had fortified the monastery above the town and so it was heavily bombed 15 Feb. Following this attack, the 4th Indian Division made some progress attacking Monastery Hill, and the 2nd New Zealand Division captured the town railway station but lost it three days later. An air raid combined with an artillery bombardment thoroughly wrecked the town 15 March, after which the railway station and Castle Hill were captured in three days of intense fighting.

The final battle began 11 May 1944 when 2,000 guns bombarded the German positions, the Polish 2nd Corps isolated Monastery Hill, the British crossed the river Liri to cut the road west of Cassino, and US and French corps attacked south of the river. The German positions were taken despite being vigorously defended and by 18 May the town and monastery were in Allied hands. Both sides sustained heavy losses in the operation.

Cauldron, the in World War II, British failure to contain Axis forces under Field Marshal Erwin Rommel 1942. The Cauldron was an area in the Libyan desert south of Gazala into which Rommel withdrew his forces after initial reverses in the Battle of ◊Gazala 10 May 1942. After a long delay, the British general Maj-Gen Neil Ritchie attacked the Cauldron 5 June but by that time Rommel had reorganized and re-supplied his forces. He defeated Ritchie, broke out of the Cauldron, and defeated the British at the Battle of Knightsbridge.

Cedar Creek decisive battle of the Shenandoah Valley campaign of the American Civil War 19 Oct 1864; 17,000 Confederates under General Jubal Early attacked and were defeated by 30,000 Union troops under General Philip Sheridan.

Sheridan had conducted a campaign up the valley during the autumn, defeating Early at Winchester and Fisher's Hill. Unwilling to advance further with winter approaching, he then withdrew down the valley and took up a position at Cedar Creek, 32 km/20 mi south of Winchester. Early pursued him and, calculating that the Union troops would be relaxed, made a dawn attack while Sheridan was absent in Washington. The attack struck the flank and rear of the Union position, forcing a headlong retreat. General Horatio Wright, commanding in Sheridan's absence, was beginning to stabilize the Union line when Sheridan returned, took command, and, seeing that the Confederates were more concerned with looting the abandoned Union camp than following up their victory, launched a counterattack which completely shattered Early's force and put an end to any further Confederate activity in the Shenandoah Valley.

Chaeronea Macedonian victory over the confederated Greek army (Athenians and Thebans) 338 BC; this battle marked the end of Greek independence and its subjection to Philip II of Macedon. The 30,000 foot soldiers of the Macedonians held the Athenian section while 2,000 cavalry, led by Alexander the Great, charged the Thebans, who broke and ran, with the exception of their famous 'Sacred Band' who fought to the last. The cavalry then wheeled to take the Athenians in the flank and rear while the Macedonian foot made their advance. The Thebans were annihilated and 6,000 Athenians were killed.

Champagne two battles in World War I between French and German forces, mainly intended to relieve pressure on the Russians by drawing German troops away from the Eastern Front.

Dec 1914–March 1915 both sides were heavily entrenched and the battle was simply a series of limited attacks and counterattacks at intervals throughout the winter. Artillery support was, for the period, enormous: the French fired over 100,000 shells in one 24-hour period in Feb. At the end of the battle, the French had advanced 450 m/500 yds.

Sept–Oct 1915 an initial French assault gained 4 km/2.5 mi to the north in the first day, but the units in the south of the line were less effective, allowing the Germans to withdraw troops to reinforce their northern defences. They held the French advance long enough for reserve troops to be brought from other parts of the front. When the French resumed their attack 26 Sept the German forces drove them back, and a third French attempt on 4 Oct was also stopped. The battle died away at the end of Oct 1915 without further gains. The French army lost 120,000 killed and taken prisoner, and 260,000 wounded, while German losses were estimated at 140,000.

Chancellorsville in the American Civil War, comprehensive victory of General Robert E Lee's Confederate forces over Joseph Hooker's Union troops 1 May 1863.

The Union forces, intending to attack Richmond, Virginia, swung west and crossed the Rapahannock and Rapidan rivers with a view to outflanking Lee. Lee had foreseen the move and positioned cavalry scouts to detect it, and as soon as he had confirmation, moved his forces west to confront Hooker. The two armies met at Chancellorsville, on the edge of a heavily wooded area known locally as 'The Wilderness'. This gave Lee an advantage since the close country prevented effective use of Union artillery. At the start of battle, Hooker had his lines in open country, with open fields of fire which could have slaughtered the Confederates, but he lost his nerve and pulled his line back to the shelter of the Wilderness.

He left his right flank open, and Lee sent Thomas ('Stonewall') Jackson's corps around the open flank by a concealed route to fall on the encampments in the rear of the Union position. Within an hour of his attack,

Jackson had shattered the Union right, but shortly afterward was mortally wounded. Lee attacked frontally, as much to prevent Hooker from turning on Jackson as for direct gain. Losing Jackson slowed down his corps until Lee sent Jeb Stuart to take command and, if possible, drive in and split Hooker's army in two. This was achieved the next day, and Hooker withdrew to a defensive position. Lee was forced to divert his attention to another Union force under General Julian Sedgwick which was moving out from Fredericksburg, but having disposed of this, turned back for a final blow at Hooker. But Hooker had had enough and on 5 May withdrew across the Rapahannock river to safety.

Chancellorsville was a remarkable victory; Lee had defeated a force three times the size of his own. But the loss of Stonewall Jackson meant the loss of perhaps his best general; without Jackson he could never have won at Chancellorsville, and without him in the future it was unlikely that anything as daring would succeed again.

Charleroi World War I battle between French and German forces 21–24 Aug 1914. The poorly equipped and organized French 5th Army, which had concentrated around Charleroi on mobilization, was the main French force involved. In addition there were some 25,000 Belgian troops at Namur and about 30,000 French reservists at Maubeuge in the process of being clothed and equipped. Three German armies, the 1st (under General Alexander von Kluck), the 2nd (under Field Marshal Karl von Bülow), and the 3rd (under General Max von Hausen) were all moving in the direction of Charleroi and the French were in danger of being encircled and destroyed. The French commander, General Charles Lanrezac, was ordered to take the offensive but, appreciating that he would walk into a German trap, stood fast, waiting for the Germans to cross the Sambre, when he could attack them in strength. Unfortunately, his Corps commanders ignored his orders and made independent attacks. However, the German operations were equally badly co-ordinated, so that the French were able to fall back in good order, though this exposed the flank of the British Army and led to the retreat from Mons. This fighting retreat by the British and French held up the German advance and gave time for the French to rally troops ready to fight the battle of the Marne.

Lanrezac was severely criticized at the time, but when the full picture was understood it was realized that his actions had saved the 5th French Army from total destruction and bought sufficient time to prepare a counter-blow.

Château-Thierry in World War I, US victory May–June 1918. During the German attack on the ◊Marne, the US 2nd Division and additional infantry regiments relieved French troops and immediately counterattacked the Germans north of Château-Thierry. Due to the destruction of a bridge behind them, the US troops were unable to retire when ordered to withdraw and fought their way down the Marne valley to the next bridge, where they then crossed; they had been in action continuously for 72 hours. They then prevented the Germans from crossing, after which the battle died away for a few days. It was revived by the action at ◊Belleau Wood 6 June 1918.

Chattanooga American Civil War battle between 64,000 Confederate troops under General Braxton Bragg and 56,000 Union troops under General Ulysses S Grant 23–25 Nov 1863. The Confederates' failure to take Chattanooga put an end to their hopes of invading Tennessee and Kentucky.

After the Confederate victory at the battle of ◊Chickmauga the Union general William Rosecrans had retired to Chattanooga, Tennessee, which was promptly besieged by the Confederates. The Union made great efforts to relieve Rosecrans; reinforcements were sent and General Grant waited until all were in place before launching his attack with an assault on Orchard Knob, to the right of Bragg's position. This led to Bragg withdrawing forces from Lookout Mountain, a peak on the extreme right of the Confederate lines which commanded most of the area. The advance of the Union forces through fog gave rise to the title 'The Battle above the Clouds' for this engagement. An attack against Bragg's centre by General William Sherman was less successful but eventually a flanking movement led by General George Thomas brought the Union forces round to unseat Bragg from his position. The Confederates broke and fell back into Georgia, protected by a stubborn rearguard action led by General Patrick Cleburne.

Chemin des Dames road in the *département* of Aisne, France, from Craonne to Malmaison across the crest of the Craonne plateau. Its possession was fiercely contested throughout World War I.

After their defeat on the Marne Sept 1914, the Germans occupied the area and it was the scene of intermittent fighting thereafter. In April 1917 General Robert Nivelle decided on an offensive to capture the road, the plateau, and the Aisne valley beyond. After a prolonged and fierce battle the French finally captured the road and plateau by the beginning of Nov 1917. During the ◊German Spring Offensive 1918 the French were driven from their position and the road passed back into German hands. Finally, in the Allied advance Sept 1918 the road was retaken by General Charles Mangin's 10th Army.

Chesapeake French victory over a British fleet during the American War of Independence off Chesapeake Bay 5 Sept 1781. The British army under Lord Cornwallis was at Yorktown, with Washington marching an army of 12,000 toward him, and the French fleet had delivered reinforcements to Lafayette's army, putting 8,000 troops between Cornwallis and the sea. A British fleet of 19 ships under Admiral Sir Charles Graves arrived off the Bay and the French sailed out to give battle. Graves' signals were confusing and he was unable to lay his ships in parallel line with the French, so that his leading ships were badly damaged while his rearward ships were unable to engage in the fight. Graves withdrew, and the French manoeuvred to keep him at sea without renewing the battle, allowing more reinforcements to arrive in the Bay. With no relief from the navy and no chance of relief by land, Cornwallis surrendered 19 Oct.

Chickamauga Confederate victory in the American Civil War over Union forces under General William Rosecrans 19–20 Sept 1863. Rosecrans had driven the Confederates under General Braxton Bragg out of middle Tennessee, forcing him to abandon Chattanooga and withdraw into northern Georgia where he gathered his army around Lafayette and waited for reinforcements from Virginia. . Rosecrans mistakenly thought the Confederates were in a disorganized retreat and advanced. He soon discovered his error and hurriedly prepared a defensive position behind Chickamauga Creek, about 24 km/15 mi south of Chattanooga.

The Confederates attacked the Union flanks 19 Sept, and on the following day the battle became general. Part of the Union army was routed, but General George Thomas rallied the troops and conducted a firm defence for six hours, beating off several attacks before retiring in good order to Chattanooga. The Confederates besieged the town which was eventually relieved by the battle of ◊Chattanooga. General Thomas was thereafter known as the 'Rock of Chickamauga'.

Chilianwala battle between British and Sikh forces during the Second Sikh War 13 Jan 1849. Although the British eventually recovered the situation and were not actually defeated, their organization was confused to the point of disaster and this episode may be regarded almost as the infantry equivalent of the more famed Charge of the Light Brigade.

That unfortunate battle where British courage was a more distinguishing feature than either the strategical or tactical skill of the general commanding.

Sir Garnet Wolseley on *Chilianwala*

The British, under Viscount Gough, set out to find the Sikh main army and finally encountered them at Chilianwala in the Punjab, about 48 km/30 mi northwest of Gujarat. Sikh artillery opened fire immediately and Gough ordered a division of infantry, composed of the 24th Foot and Indian troops, to attack the enemy guns. They advanced, and the order to charge was given far too soon, so that they continued their advance with bayonets in the face of 20 guns. The 24th outstripped their Indian companions, broke the Sikh line and took the guns, but at fearful cost; of about 1,000 troops, there were 515 casualties, of whom 238 were dead including 13 officers. Elsewhere, a cavalry force assembled under Brigadier Pope was reduced almost to a shambles by his confusing orders; he eventually got his men facing the right way, but then, instead of ordering 'Threes Right' ordered 'Threes About', so that the cavalry turned about and galloped away from the battle. This debacle was halted by a chaplain, who rallied the troops, got them turned about and sent them back into battle. On the right flank an infantry division managed to save the day by breaking the Sikh lines, capturing guns and stores. Night fell, and under cover of darkness the Sikhs withdrew.

Chosin Reservoir during the Korean War, joint North Korean-Chinese attack on United Nations forces Nov–Dec 1951. The 1st US Marine division, with British Marine Commandos attached, was advancing north in the Chosin reservoir area, in northwest Korea about 80 km/50 mi north of Hungnam. It was attacked 27 Nov by 12 Chinese divisions reinforced with North Korean troops. The UN force was in mountainous country with only one poor road of supply, which was vulnerable to attack and also liable to be blocked by heavy snow at any time, and their only course was to fall back to a concentrated position at Hagaru, at the southern end of the reservoir complex. The Chinese followed up their attack, and the UN force began a fighting retreat south from Hagaru 6 Dec which ended four days later at Hungnam, a supply port on the Sea of Japan, from which the survivors were evacuated by sea. Hamhung was then bombarded to destroy the supply dumps left behind.

The US Marines suffered 4,418 casualties in the battle and 7,313 from other causes, principally frostbite. Chinese losses were later calculated at about 37,500.

Clontarf Irish victory over a Norse invasion force on Good Friday, 23 April, 1014. Details of the battle are scant, but the Norsemen were completely defeated by Brian Boru, King of Ireland, with a loss said to be 6,000 dead. Brian Boru and his son were both killed in the battle; Brian, being too old to fight, was slain in his tent.

Cold Harbor in the American Civil War, defeat of Union forces under General Ulysses S Grant by Confederate forces under General Robert E Lee 1–3 June 1864, during the operations surrounding the siege of Richmond. By this time, the Confederate forces were close to exhaustion and this battle stands out as one of the final Confederate victories toward the end of the civil war. Grant was advancing south with 19 divisions, including 3 cavalry, and Lee, anticipating his movements, occupied the village of Cold Harbor, about 16 km/10 mi northeast of Richmond, with 14 divisions, also including 3 cavalry.

The two armies met 1 June and Grant wished to attack immediately but it was late in the day before his army was in position. When they did eventually attack some ground was gained, but a Confederate counterattack drove the Union forces back almost to their start line. Grant's plans for an attack early on 2 June were again delayed, and it did not begin until 5 p.m., which allowed the Confederates the entire day to strengthen their defences. Grant put two divisions into an attack but this was not a success and he withdrew them and made further changes in his dispositions, finally launching his main attack at 5 a.m. on 3 June. The Confederate defence was unbreakable, and by 7 a.m. the Union had taken 8,000 casualties. At 2 p.m. Grant ordered the attack to be called off, having made no impression on the Confederate front and failed to complete an attempted flanking attack. For nine days the armies lay confronting each other, until 12 June Grant began a side-stepping movement to the east in order to swing round the Confederate lines and cross the River James.

Union casualties 1–12 June totalled over 12,500, while Confederate losses were less than 3,000. The morale of the Union army was severely damaged by this reverse and in later years Grant admitted that this was the only battle he ever fought which he would not fight again under the circumstances.

Colenso British defeat in the South African War by Boer forces 15 Dec 1899. The British sent a force under General Sir Redvers Buller to relieve ◊Ladysmith, then under siege by the Boers. Attempting to cross the Tugela river about 32 km/20 mi south of Ladysmith, Buller ran into a strong Boer defensive position. After an artillery bombardment he attempted to cross the river but was driven back with severe losses in troops and guns and had to withdraw.

This loss, together with defeats at ◊Magersfontein and Stormberg 10–11 Dec, became known as 'Black Week' for the British army, which suffered 7,000 casualties in the three battles. Buller was to make seven more attempts before succeeding in crossing the Tugela and relieving Ladysmith.

Colmar Pocket World War II defeat of Germans by Allied forces advancing through France early 1945. The pocket was an area in the Vosges Mountains of France where the German 17th Army was trapped by the French taking Mulhouse and US troops taking Strasbourg Nov 1944. Both French and US troops set about clearing the area Jan 1945; numbers of German troops were able to escape across the Rhine into German-held territory, but they left some 36,000 casualties behind them.

Coral Sea in World War II, US naval operation which prevented the Japanese from landing in southeast New Guinea and thus threatening Australia. It was the first sea battle to be fought entirely by aircraft with no engagement between the US and Japanese warships.

The Japanese were attempting to move on Port Moresby and Tulagi but the plan was discovered by US intelligence. A US fleet led by the carrier *Yorktown* was dispatched to the area and attacked the landing force at Tulagi. A series of confusing engagements followed as aircraft from both sides attempted to attack the main carrier force of the other, picking off the many small flotillas that had broken off from the main force. The two sides finally located each other 8 May and each launched air strikes. Although the Japanese inflicted greater damage, sinking one US carrier and two other major warships, the US fleet scored a strategic victory in preventing the Japanese invasion of New Guinea.

Corinth in the American Civil War, Confederate attempt 3–4 Oct 1862 to recover Corinth, a town in Mississippi about 130 km/80 mi west of Memphis, which they had abandoned May 1862 after the battle of ◊Shiloh. The town was held by 23,000 Union troops under General William Rosecrans when it was attacked by a 22,000-strong Confederate force under General Earl van Dorn 3 Oct. Rosecrans' forces were well entrenched, but the initial Confederate attack drove them out of their forward line. The attack was resumed on the following day, but was unable to make any further gains, after which a Union counterattack put the Confederates to flight. Van Dorn lost 6,423 killed and wounded and 2,250 prisoners; Union casualties were 2,359.

Coronel World War I German naval victory over a British squadron 1 Nov 1914. At the outbreak of war, the German naval squadron on the China station under Admiral Maximilian von Spee began commerce raiding in the southern Pacific. In Oct 1914 a small British squadron under Admiral Sir Christopher Cradock, sent in search of von Spee, encountered the Germans off Coronel, on the coast of Chile. Cradock was outgunned and outnumbered and was completely defeated, losing two cruisers and 1,500 crew. He was lost along with his flagship.

Corregidor Japanese operation in World War II to sieze and hold a US fortified island in the entrance to Manila Bay in the Philippines. The US Army fortified the island 1905–12 to form the major coastal defence protecting the entrance to the Bay, with 35 guns of calibres ranging from 3 in to 12 in distributed among 14 batteries.

After the defeat of the US forces on ◊Bataan, the island was besieged by the Japanese and suffered heavily from artillery fire and aerial bombing. Japanese infantry landed on the night of 5 May 1942 and the garrison surrendered on the following day. The island was retaken in a combined air and sea attack by US forces 16 Feb 1945.

Corunna battle between French and British forces in the Peninsular War 16 Jan 1809. Sir John Moore, the British commander in Portugal, had occupied Salamanca and then marched his force out to cut French communications with Madrid. Napoleon foresaw this move and assembled an army under Marshal Nicolas Soult to counter the British. Moore, realising his danger, decided to retreat, but toward Corunna in northwest Spain rather than back on his tracks to Lisbon. After a number of rearguard actions, he arrived at Corunna 12 Jan 1809; a fleet arrived to evacuate casualties 14 Jan.

The remainder of the army then prepared to give battle to Soult's force which had now appeared outside the town. On 16 Jan the British forces were arrayed in lines outside the town and the French occupied the heights further out, from which they launched a series of attacks, all of which were beaten off. By nightfall the French were retiring in confusion while the British had advanced their lines for a considerable distance. However, Sir John Moore had been mortally wounded during the battle and command devolved on Sir John Hope. Hope saw there was little chance of resuming the campaign since his army was ragged, starving, and demoralized, and so withdrew his force during the night, embarked them, and escaped.

Coulmiers first French victory of the Franco-Prussian War 9 Nov 1870. Orléans was occupied by the Prussians and held by a force of about 20,000 Bavarian troops under Baron von der Tann-Rathsamhausen when two French columns (about 70,000 troops) under General Claude d'Aurelle de Paladines approached. Von der Tann marched his force out of the city to take up a blocking position at Coulmiers, about 19 km/12 mi to the northwest. He had no idea of the strength of the French and the force of their attack surprised him. The Bavarians resisted for most of the day, in freezing rain, but the superior French numbers persuaded von der Tann to withdraw under cover of the darkness and foul weather. The French held their positions during the night and did not realise that they had won the until next morning when they marched into Orléans and took up possession.

Courland, Campaign in clashes between German and Russian forces, April–May 1915. The Germans crossed the Niemen river in three dispersed columns advancing toward Shavli (now Siauliai). Having captured Shavli they moved on to Libau (now Liepaja) but were met by a strong Russian force which threw them back. A fourth column, moving along the coast, took Libau 8 May, but a flanking movement by Bavarian cavalry to attack the main railway from Petrograd was routed by Russian cavalry. This caused the German line to fall back, pursued by the Russians who gained another victory before the Germans finally stabilized their line, though they retained their hold on Libau. The German advance was resumed in July, when they were able to drive the Russians back 80 km/50 mi in 3 days. By 1 Aug they had captured Mitau (now Jelgava) and the Russians then fell back toward Dvinsk (now Daugavpils), leaving the whole area in German hands.

Courtrai (also called the 'Battle of the Spurs') Flemish defeat of a far better equipped and trained French force 11 July 1302 near Courtrai. Philip IV of France had annexed Flanders and when the people rose in revolt a French army marched into Flanders and met a large Flemish force near Courtrai, Belgium. While the French army was composed of mounted knights with a front of archers and other foot soldiers, the Flemings were entirely on foot and armed with whatever came to hand, largely bills but also agricultural implements.

The French knights rode forward to scatter this rabble but became stuck on the mud, whereupon the Flemings fell on them and killed almost all. They then turned on the bowmen and scattered them. The carnage among the knights was so great that 700 pairs of gilded spurs, taken from their bodies, were hung in the cathedral of Courtrai, hence the battle's alternative name. It was of great significance at the time for demonstrating that infantry could, under some circumstances, deal with unsupported cavalry.

Crécy first major battle of the Hundred Years' War between English and French forces 26 Aug 1346 at Crécy-en-Ponthieu, about 18 km/11 mi southeast of Abbeville. The English victory reinforced the lesson of Courtrai that infantry were well capable of dealing with cavalry.

Edward III of England landed in Normandy in support of his claim to the French throne and advanced toward Paris. Philip VI of France raised an army and set out to meet him. Edward swerved away from Paris toward the Somme, while Philip's forces, on the east bank of the river, prevented any crossing. Eventually Edward found an unguarded ford, crossed the river and drew his army up for battle on a hill between Crécy and Wadicourt.

Edward's forces were arranged in three divisions, all dismounted, with Welsh archers and spearmen in the front ranks. The French arrived in the afternoon; their Genoese crossbowmen opened the battle, but rain had slacked their bowstrings and they were rapidly annihilated by the Welsh bowmen who had unstrung their bows and kept the strings dry. The French knights, impatient for victory, then rode forward but, clustered together by the confined battlefield, they were rapidly picked off by bowmen and spearmen. The battle then resolved itself into a series of charges – some historians say as many as 15 – by the French knights against the English lines, but they were eventually beaten off and before nightfall were in retreat.

Crete in World War II, costly but successful German operation to capture the island of Crete from the Allies May 1941. After the evacuation of Greece, the island held about 32,000 British and Commonwealth troops and about 10,000 Greek infantry, with little artillery or transport. The Germans had complete air superiority and were able to bomb the island at will as a prelude to an airborne attack 20 May. German paratroops landed in several areas and severe fighting ensued; an attempt at landing seaborne reinforcements was thwarted by the Royal Navy. The Germans managed to capture Maleme airfield and were then able to reinforce by air, and by 28 May it was decided that the island could no longer be held and evacuation of Allied troops began.

Some 3,600 British and Commonwealth troops were killed and about 12,000 taken prisoner; German losses came to 6,000 killed and wounded and some 220 aircraft lost. The Royal Navy also suffered heavy losses in men and ships while the German 7th Air Division sustained over 50% casualties. Hitler was so appalled at this casualty rate that he forbade any further major airborne operations

Crusader, Operation in World War II, British operation in Libya Nov–Dec 1941 to relieve the besieged garrison of Tobruk and destroy the

Afrika Korps. The plan was for three British columns to swing south through the desert and around the Axis defensive lines; one column would then swing round behind the Axis line and keep them occupied, while the centre column went for Tobruk and the southern column headed west to engage the German armour.

The initial actions were confused and hard-fought: while the Tobruk garrison was fighting its way out, countered by a German force at ◊Sidi Rezegh, the Germans were themselves under attack from the south from a British force, which in turn was defending its rear against an attack by the Afrika Korps. Other British, German, and Italian units were also milling around the area, simultaneously fighting or evading each other. Amid this confusion, Rommel decided to take his armour and drive east toward the British bases, hoping this would unnerve General Sir Alan Cunningham and cause him to withdraw his troops. It may well have done, but General Sir Claude Auchinleck also considered the possibility, and replaced Cunningham with his deputy Chief of Staff Maj-Gen Neil Ritchie.

However, the absence of German armour from the main action allowed the New Zealand Division to make the junction with the Tobruk garrison, which threatened to cut off Rommel's retreat if he delayed. He had to abandon his plan and was forced to retire to El Agheila, losing his garrisons at Bardia, Halfaya Pass, and Sollum. Axis losses in 'Crusader' amounted to 38,000 troops and 300 tanks, while British losses came to 18,000 troops and 278 tanks.

Ctesiphon in World War I, unsuccessful British attempt to dislodge Turkish forces 22 Nov 1915. After the British capture of Kut, the Turks retreated up the Tigris river toward Baghdad, entrenching at Ctesiphon some 40 km/25 mi from the city. A force of about 9,000 troops under General Sir Charles Townshend attacked 22 Nov and after a severe fight took the trench line. Short of ammunition, they withdrew to the captured trenches overnight but next day were forced back by the Turks and retreated to Kut with 1,600 prisoners. British losses during the battle and retreat were 4,567 men, over half Townshend's force.

Culloden final defeat of Jacobite rebels 16 April 1746 at Culloden Moor about 11 km/7 mi east of Inverness. The Jacobites under Prince Charles Edward, the 'Young Pretender' had returned from their foray into England, defeated the English at Falkirk, and returned to the Inverness region where they occupied the town and surroundings. They encamped on Culloden Moor to await the pursuing English army under the Duke of Cumberland.

Although both sides were numerically equal (about 8,000 strong), the English were a drilled and disciplined force, while the Jacobites were a ragbag mixture of French, Irish, and Scots arguing among themselves and virtually untrained. The English front line opened the battle with a volley of musketry, after which the Jacobites charged and broke through the first

English line but were caught by the musket fire of the second line. They retired in confusion, pursued by the English cavalry which broke the Jacobite lines completely and shattered their force. About 1,000 were killed and a further 1,000 were captured, together with all their stores and cannon.

Custozza Austrian victory over the Italians 24 Jun 1866. Italy had allied with Prussia against Austria and set out to recover Venice. An army led by Victor Emmanuel and the Marquis de La Marmora advanced east to confront an Austrian army advancing west from Venice under command of the Archduke Albert. The two met at Custozza, some 20 km/12 mi southwest of Verona, where the Italians put up a spirited defence against successive Austrian attacks. Had La Marmora used his reserves, he would probably have won the battle, but he was outmanoeuvred by the Archduke, and after about nine hours of combat the Italians collapsed. In spite of this, the war eventually ended with Austria having to cede Venice to the Italians.

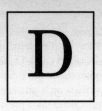

Dakar in World War II, joint British-Free French operation to capture the French naval base at Dakar in order to persuade the French African colonies to join de Gaulle against the Vichy government. In July 1940 the French battleship *Richelieu* was stationed at Dakar (now in Senegal, West Africa) with other French warships. A British naval force arrived 7 July and, wishing to deny the Germans the use of the French warships, presented them with an ultimatum: join the British against Germany; sail to a British port; sail, escorted, to the French West Indies or the USA, there to be disarmed; or be attacked in harbour. The French rejected the ultimatum and on the following day the *Richelieu* was attacked and damaged by British torpedo bombers.

A full naval force was then assembled and sailed for Dakar Sept 1940, but the French governor of the colony refused all approaches from de Gaulle and it was realized that invasion would be futile. British and French warships exchanged fire, and French coastal batteries joined in, resulting in damage to both sides, and the operation was then called off. It was not known until much later that as it was abandoned, the French governor was contemplating surrender.

Dardanelles, attacks on the in World War I, unsuccessful Allied naval operations against the Turks 1915. The Dardanelles is a narrow channel between Asiatic and European Turkey, forming a passage between the Mediterranean and the Sea of Marmora and thence to the Black Sea. Winston Churchill first suggested attacking the Dardanelles in order to defend Egypt at the War Cabinet 25 Nov 1914. On 2 Jan 1915 the Russian government asked for some military diversion to relieve pressure on the Eastern Front, but Lord Kitchener said he had no troops available. Instead a naval attack was mounted 19 Feb 1915 by eight warships, which fired at the various coastal defence batteries and put landing parties ashore to wreck some of the forts. On 18 March an attempt was made to run warships through the channel but four were lost to gunfire and mines and others damaged. The Allies lost some 750 sailors while the Turks lost fewer than 200.

After this debacle the idea of a purely naval attack was abandoned, and instead planning began for a military action against the ▷Gallipoli peninsula. The only real impact of the naval attack was to alert the Turkish army so that they had time to reinforce and fortify the area before the Gallipoli landings.

D-Day 6 June 1944; the day on which Allied forces landed on the coast of France to commence Operation Overlord, the invasion of German-occupied Europe. Five beaches – codenamed Utah, Omaha, Gold, Juno, and Sword – were selected as the landing points for the British 1st and 30th Corps and US 5th and 7th Corps. The operation was preceded by a month-long bombing campaign to disrupt communications, preventing reinforcements from moving quickly into the threatened area, and was accompanied by airborne landings to secure the flanks and destroy vital bridges and gun positions.

The landings commenced at 0630 hrs, and by midnight 57,000 US and 75,000 British and Canadian troops and their equipment were ashore and the beachheads were being linked into a continuous front. The German response to the landings was hampered by the damage done to their communications, by a rigid command structure which required a personal directive from Hitler before any significant move could be made, and by the belief that the landing was a feint and that the major Allied attack would come in the Pas de Calais region, a belief fostered by Allied deception operations. Allied casualties during the day amounted to 2,500 killed and about 8,500 wounded. Allied air forces flew 14,000 sorties in support of the operation and lost 127 aircraft.

Delhi episode in the Indian Mutiny 1857 when mutineers captured Delhi before it was retaken by the British. When the Mutiny broke out 10 May at Meerut, some 65 km/40 mi northeast of Delhi, there were no British troops in Delhi and the mutineers were able to overcome the local garrison, murdering the British officers and civil administrators. General Sir Henry Barnard brought the Delhi Field Force, about 6,000 British troops, to besiege the city 6 June, but was unable to seal it off. The mutineers were constantly reinforced until they outnumbered the British by about seven to one and outgunned them by four to one.

No further troops were available as they were occupied quelling uprisings elsewhere, so the Field Force launched an attack by itself 14 Sept, scaling the walls and entering the city. Six days of savage street fighting followed, but the mutineers, badly led and with no central command, began to desert their cause and by 20 Sept the entire city was under British control once more.

Demyansk World War II airlift to sustain some 100,000 troops of the German 16th Army who were trapped in the Soviet town, about 370 km/230 mi northwest of Moscow, during a Soviet offensive Jan 1942. They were re-supplied and reinforced by air, about 65,000 tons of supplies and over 30,000 troops being flown in and over 25,000 casualties evacuated. This was the first major airlift ever carried out, and it kept the trapped army fighting until it could be relieved by a German counterattack May 1942.

Desert Storm victory Jan–Feb 1991 of United Nations-sponsored coalition forces, primarily US troops, over Iraqi forces which had invaded Kuwait Aug 1991. The Gulf War of 1992, known to the Americans as 'Desert Storm' and to the British as 'Operation Granby', was more a campaign than a battle; indeed, there was no battle in the accepted sense of the word.

Following the invasion of Kuwait 2 Aug 1990 by some 500,000 Iraqi troops, the United Nations Security Council passed a series of resolutions demanding Iraq withdraw its forces. Coalition forces built up in Saudi Arabia throughout late 1900, eventually totalling 725,000 troops, of whom 500,000 were US troops with smaller contingents from many other nations including most of the Arab Gulf states. When Iraq failed to comply with the final deadline for withdrawal 15 Jan 1991, coalition forces launched a massive aerial bombardment of Iraqi cities. After six weeks of aerial bombardment the ground war began 24 Feb and coalition forces quickly rolled Iraqi troops back before them, penetrating deep into Iraq. The ground war lasted only 100 hours in total and was an overwhelming victory for the coalition forces which were vastly superior to the Iraqis, in numerical, technical, and tactical terms. Political considerations prevented the military from following up their comprehensive victory with the complete annihilation of Iraqi forces and it was widely considered that the Iraqi leader Saddam Hussein had been allowed to stay in place, albeit much chastened, in order to avoid destabilizing the strategically crucial Middle East region.

Desert Storm was the first large-scale demonstration of modern technological warfare, in which guided missiles, 'smart' munitions, night vision equipment, infra-red sensors, Global Positioning Systems, cruise missiles, free-flight rockets with multiple warheads, anti-missile missiles, and modern data communications systems were deployed. The result was a foregone conclusion: some of the most technical and competent troops in the world, most highly trained for thirty years to confront the Soviet Army should it venture westward, were deployed against a Third World army, with limited military ability, technical capacity, and inadequate command. Though the Iraqis had a leavening of modern weapons they were scarcely competent in their use, and none were of much value against the technology ranged against them, and the Iraqi army had barely recovered from the lengthy and debilitating conflict with Iran (1980–88).

Dettingen battle between the English and Hanoverians on one side and the French on the other during the war of the Austrian Succession 27 June 1743 in Bavaria, about 16 km/10 mi northwest of Aschaffenburg. This was the last battle in which a British sovereign led his troops in person.

An English force in support of the Austrians advanced on Aschaffenburg and the Main river, on the far side of which a French army had assembled. The Austrians were not inclined to engage the enemy, and so the English commander, Lord Stair, withdrew toward Dettingen only to find the French had arrived there first. By this time King George II had arrived and took command of the Allied army of 42,000 English, Austrian, and Hanoverian troops. The French army, about 50,000 strong, held the river bridges and were protected by marshy ground in front and guns behind them. But the French commander, the Duke de Noailles, grew impatient and instead of awaiting an attack on his well-sited position, ordered his cavalry to charge the English infantry. Despite initial successes, the charge was eventually repulsed and King George led his cavalry in a countercharge which broke the French and sent them fleeing into the river with heavy losses.

Excepting three or four generals, the rest of them were of little service; our men and their regimental officers gained the day, and not in the manner of Hyde Park discipline.

Colonel Russel of the Life Guards,
remarks in a letter to his wife on the *Battle of Dettingen*

Dien Bien Phu in the Indochina War, decisive battle Nov 1953 at a French fortress in the French colony of Tonkin (now in north Vietnam) near the Laotian border. French troops were besieged 13 March–7 May 1954 by the communist Vietminh and the fall of Dien Bien Phu resulted in the end of French control of Indochina.

After several years of indeterminate guerrilla warfare with the Vietnamese, the French commander, General Henri Navarre, decided to draw the Vietminh out of the jungle into a pitched battle on ground chosen by the French. The French built up a series of interlocking strongpoints at Dien Bien Phu which occupied a strategic position in a valley on the principal Vietnamese supply route from Laos. However, the French underestimated the military ability of the Vietminh and made no attempt to occupy and defend the hills surrounding the base. General Vo Nguyen Giap, the Vietminh commander, planned to isolate and destroy each strongpoint in turn, and brought up 72,000 troops and 200 guns and mortars. He occupied the heights which the French had neglected, giving him complete command of the area, and proceeded to demolish the strongpoints one by one. The airstrip inside the base, which the French depended on for all their supplies and reinforcements as well as the evacuation of casualties, was soon rendered useless by constant artillery and mortar fire. From then on, the French could only send in supplies by parachute drops and many of them fell into Vietminh hands. The French made some progress with counterattacks and regained some of the strongpoints around the valley, forcing Giap to suspend operations while he amassed more troops and ammunition and regrouped his forces. He then began a formal siege, with sappers digging trenches forward to the French perimeter. From these trenches, covered by artillery fire, he launched a massive attack 1 May, and on 7 May the French commander and 11,000 troops surrendered. This defeat signalled the end of French control of Indochina; peace terms were negotiated in July and the colony was divided into North and South Vietnam along the 17th parallel of latitude.

Dieppe Raid in World War II, disastrous Allied attack Aug 1942 on the German-held seaport on the English Channel about 305 km/190 mi northwest of Paris. The limited-objective raid was partly designed to obtain practical experience of amphibious landing techniques and German defences, but mostly to placate Stalin who was agitating for a Second Front in Europe. The raid was a dismal failure which cost the Allies heavily in casualties and strained relations between Canada and Britain for some time, although a number of valuable lessons about landing on hostile beaches were learned and applied in the ⟡D-Day landings 1944.

Some 5,000 Canadian troops and 1,000 commandos took part in the landings 18–19 Aug. Eight beaches were targeted, four being used to land commandos to deal with flanking coastal defence batteries and four for the main assault parties in Dieppe itself. Apart from the commando landing on the right flank, which silenced the German coastal battery, the remainder of the operation was a failure. The Germans were in a well-defended position which was difficult to reach and were fully alert, so that the troops and tanks were scarcely able to gain a foothold. By 9 a.m. it was clear that the operation had failed and withdrawal was ordered, but it took three hours to remove the last of the survivors. The Canadians lost 215 officers and 3,164 troops, the commandos 24 officers and 223 troops, the Royal Navy 81 officers, 469 sailors, and 34 ships, and the RAF lost 107 aircraft. In contrast, the Germans lost only 345 killed and 268 wounded.

Dogger Bank World War I naval engagement between substantial British and German forces which met by accident 24 Jan 1915 at Dogger Bank, an extensive sandbank in the middle of the North Sea. A German force of 4 battle cruisers, 4 light cruisers, and 22 destroyers which had left Germany to attack the English coast met the British Grand Fleet of 6 battle cruisers, 8 light cruisers, and 28 destroyers which had left Scapa Flow on the same day to carry out a sweep of the North Sea at 7.20 a.m. 24 Jan. The British put on speed to overhaul the German line, the first shots were fired at about 9 a.m., and the two fleets exchanged shots for about three hours. The German battle cruiser *Blücher* was sunk by gun and torpedo fire, while the British flagship *Lion* was hit in the engine-room and halted. Admiral David Beatty transferred his flag to a destroyer, but when the German fleet approached Heligoland the British disengaged due to the danger of attack by submarines and minefields. British casualties amounted to 6 killed and 22 wounded; German casualties came to about 1,000 killed and 300 wounded. Several ships on both sides were damaged.

Doiran-Struma Front, Campaign on the in World War I, joint Greek and British operations against Bulgarian forces on the Greece–Bulgaria border in Salonika 1918. Apart from a minor Bulgarian attack 1917 this front had lain dormant until the British attacked a Bulgarian salient thrusting toward Greece Sept 1918. This led to more fighting and eventually the British and Greek forces launched a heavy attack enveloping Lake Doiran and capturing the town. At about the same time, the French launched an attack on another part of the front, so the British attack was renewed in order to prevent the Bulgarians reinforcing the areas threatened by the French. Both attacks moved forward with success, crossing the Bulgarian border and reaching Petric 30 Sept 1918 when Bulgaria surrendered and the advance stopped.

Dolomites, Campaign in the in World War I, fighting between Austrian and Italian forces 1915 in the Dolomite mountain range as the Italians attempted to sever strategic Austrian railway links to the north of the mountains. The Dolomite mountain range was the scene of heavy fighting and became an almost continuous front throughout the war, from Cortina d'Ampezzo in the west to the Predil Pass on the east. The ◊Trentino front lay to the west and the ◊Isonzo Front to the south.

When the Italians entered the war 1915 they made a general advance into the mountains, trying to cut off strategic Austrian railway links on the northern side. Fighting in extremely difficult conditions, and making full use of their elite Alpini mountain troops, the Italians made considerable gains and fended off strong Austrian attacks. However, they were never able to break through the Austrian defences to reach the railway lines and the whole front eventually settled down to a static line.

Dresden in the Napoleonic Wars, French victory 1813 with 80,000 troops over an Allied army under Count Schwarzenburg of Austria composed of almost 200,000 Austrian, Prussian, and Russian troops. The Allied army advanced on Dresden which had been captured by the French, forcing Napoleon Bonaparte to hurry back from Silesia to take control. On the evening of 26 Aug the Allies began a heavy artillery bombardment of the city and then attacked with six columns of infantry. The French repulsed the attack at every point and as night fell, the Austrians withdrew. During the night more reinforcements reached Napoleon and in the morning he launched an attack against both wings of the Allied army: General Joachim Murat of Naples and his cavalry went against the left flank, while Marshal Michel Ney, with the guards infantry, attacked the Russians on the right. The fighting raged all day and as night began to fall, Schwarzenburg realised he could make no further progress and ordered a withdrawal. The Allies lost some 38,000 troops; the French about 10,000.

Drina inconclusive World War I battle between Austrian and Serbian forces Sept 1914. Fighting broke out when the Austrians crossed the river Drina to invade Serbia 8 Sept. In the north the Serbs were gathered in strength and repulsed the attack, but in the south the Austrians had more success and made a considerable advance. On 14 Sept the Serbs counterattacked and after hard fighting drove the Austrians back to the river Drina, whereupon both sides, exhausted, dug in and the battle died away.

Dunajetz series of battles in World War I as Austro-German forces made gains at the expense of the Russians 1915. A large German force was assembled around Cracow April 1915 for an intended attack on Galicia. The Russians held a line on the Dunajetz river with about 4 corps against the Germans' 12 until a strong Austrian attack in the Gorlitz area in early May broke through the Russian lines on a 16 km/10 mi front. While the Russians were attempting to stem this breach, the force on the Dunajetz river attacked, intending to break through in the direction of Tarnow. They had little success, failing to cross the river, until the Russian collapse in the south worsened and the Russian forces in the north were forced to fall back to avoid exposing their flank. The advance continued on the entire front, the Russians fighting every inch of the way but by 11 May they had been driven back to a line on the San river, where they were finally able to consolidate and stop the German drive. The Germans captured upward of 100,000 prisoners during their advance but were unable to bring the Russians to a decisive battle and destroy them.

Duppel successful German assault in the Prusso-Danish War March 1868 which opened the way for the invasion of Denmark. Duppel was a fortified position in Schleswig-Holstein, then occupied by the Danes, where a previous German attack had been halted 1848. The principal fort was protected by a chain of 10 earthwork redoubts which the Germans now besieged having learned from their earlier defeat. Artillery bombardments appeared to do little damage, since the earthworks simply absorbed shell-fire and no effective breaches were made in the defences.

After almost three weeks, an astute German observer noted that the Danish commander was in the habit of withdrawing his troops from the foremost redoubt at dawn, so as to protect the troops from the daily shell-fire, returning them in the evening. The Germans waited until they had left and then launched a sudden attack which turned into a race to see who could occupy the redoubt first. The Germans won the race, the line of redoubts was breached, and the Danish garrison surrendered.

Dvina in World War I, inconclusive series of engagements between German and Russian forces 1915–16. The river Dvina formed a natural barrier before Riga and the first battle Aug–Sept 1915 swayed back and forth across the river but died away with both sides in their original positions. The second battle flared intermittently Jan–Aug 1916 as a series of attacks by German forces under Field Marshal Paul von Hindenburg were repulsed by the Russians under General Alexei Kuropatkin. Before either side could gain an advantage, the Galician front flared up and both commanders turned to that, leaving the forces on the Dvina more or less where they had been in 1915.

Dvinsk in World War I, series of German attacks 1915–16 on Dvinsk, a strategic rail and road junction in Russia (now in Latvia and known as Daugafpils), as part of the battle for the ◊Dvina. The Germans mounted three successive attacks, each in increasing strength, but all were driven back by the Russian defenders.

The second battle began 19 Jan 1916 and lasted for most of the year in a series of attacks and counterattacks. However, the success of the ◊Brusilov Offensive in Galicia diverted the attention of the commanders and the Dvina front settled into trench warfare. The front remained in that state until the collapse of the Russian armies 1917.

E

East Africa Campaign in World War II, British conquest of Italy's colonies in Africa 1940–41. Although Italy declared war on Britain 10 June 1940 the relatively isolated garrisons in its African colonies – Eritrea, Abyssinia (now Ethiopia), and Italian Somaliland – restricted themselves to a brief foray into the Sudan and Kenya and overrunning British Somaliland.

The British decided to take the initiative with two offensives: one from the south, entering Italian Somaliland from Kenya; and one from the north, entering Eritrea from the Sudan. The southern offensive began Jan 1941, capturing Mogadishu, capital of Italian Somaliland, by 25 Feb and quickly securing the rest of the country, forcing the Italians to abandon British Somaliland and fall back into Eritrea. The British swung toward Abyssinia, capturing Addis Ababa 6 April 1941 and forcing more Italians into Eritrea. The northern attack then began to take effect, putting further pressure on Eritrea, while a guerrilla force trained and commanded by Maj-Gen Orde Wingate caused unrest in the more remote areas of Abyssinia and Eritrea. Both British offensives then converged in Eritrea and trapped much of the Italian army, which surrendered 19 May. The remainder of the campaign was simply a matter of cleaning out individual pockets of Italian resistance and the final surrender came 3 July 1941.

Eastern Solomons World War II naval action between US and Japanese forces 23–24 Aug 1942; although the battle itself was indecisive, the US object of preventing Japanese troops reaching ◊Guadalcanal was achieved. The US Navy learnt of a Japanese fleet escorting troop reinforcements to Guadalcanal and deployed Task Force 61 in the area. Both fleets had aircraft carriers and the Japanese had sent one of theirs ahead of the main body of the fleet to act as a decoy. A US reconnaissance plane spotted the main Japanese fleet but a strike force sent to intercept it failed to find it due to rain cloud cover. The following day another reconnaissance plane found the lone Japanese carrier and the strike force was sent out again, but was then partially diverted when another observation plane found part of the Japanese main fleet. The decoy carrier was sunk but only a few aircraft reached the main body of the fleet and did little damage. At the same time the Japanese had found the US fleet and the arrival of their strike force coincided with the return of some of the US strike force who combined with the 50 US fighters protecting the fleet, leading to considerable aerial confusion. In an inconclusive exchange, some US ships were damaged, but not seriously, and both fleets then withdrew. Meanwhile land-based US aircraft had found the transports which the Japanese were supposed to be escorting, sank one, severely damaged an escort cruiser, and drove the other two transports to shelter in the Shorland Islands where the troops had to be reloaded into destroyers for another attempt at reaching Guadalcanal.

Eben Emael in World War II, daring assault May 1940 by German glider troops to capture a Belgian fort. Eben Emael was strategically placed at the junction of the Albert Canal and Maas river, north of Liège, to guard a vital crossing-point and was considered to be impregnable as any assault would have to be made across either the river or the canal. It was attacked 10 May 1940 by a squad of 85 German glider troops who landed on top of the fort and used special explosive charges to put the gun turrets out of action, but were unable to get into the fort itself as they were pinned down by crossfire from neighbouring forts. The following day German troops crossed the canal by boat to relieve the glider force, who had suffered relatively low casualties (6 dead and 15 wounded), and the fort surrendered. The gliders were quickly removed so for several years it was believed that the assault had been made across the canal.

Ebro principal battle of the Spanish Civil War 24 July–18 Nov 1938, in the vicinity of Gandesa, about 40 km/25 mi south of Lerida; it effectively destroyed the International Brigades and put an end to any hope of Republican victory. A Republican army under General Juan Modesto had advanced across the river Ebro against the Nationalists, hoping to force a way through and link Catalonia with the rest of Republican-held Spain. The advance carried them almost to Gandesa, where they were stopped by fresh Nationalist troops under General Francisco Franco. Franco counterattacked 1 Aug and gradually drove the Republicans back. There was a pause while Franco strengthened his force and re-grouped, until 30 Oct when he launched a powerful attack which drove the Republicans back across the Ebro. The battle ended 18 Nov, by which time the Republicans had lost about 30,000 dead, 20,000 wounded, and 20,000 prisoners, while the Nationalists lost 33,000 killed and wounded.

Eckmühl in the Napoleonic Wars, French victory 22 April 1809 over 76,000 Austrians under the Archduke Charles, at Eckmühl, near Ratisbon (now Regensburg) Bavaria. The Austrians occupied Ratisbon but found Napoleon Bonaparte had cut their line of communication with a force of some 90,000 troops. In the hope of restoring it, the Archduke led his army out of the town and occupied a position on a hill at Eckmühl and prepared for battle. Napoleon attacked, cut the Austrian army in two and reduced it to a shambles, driving them across the river Danube and back to the safety of Ratisbon. Napoleon granted Marshal Louis Davout the title Prince of Eckmühl 1811 for his part in the victory.

El Alamein see ◊Alamein, El.

Elephant Point the only paratroop operation of the British Burma campaign in World War II. Elephant Point was a peninsula commanding the sea entrance to Rangoon and the 2/3rd Gurkha Parachute Battalion dropped here 1 May 1945 and eliminated the Japanese defences, so clearing the way for an amphibious landing in Rangoon by 26th Indian Division.

Empress Augusta Bay World War II naval engagement between US and Japanese forces Nov 1943 in a bay on the western coast of ◊Bougainville, Solomon Islands. A Japanese naval squadron of four cruisers and six destroyers was sent to attack the US troop and supply transports in the bay which were protected by four cruisers and eight destroyers deployed across its mouth. The Japanese approached at night but were detected by US radar and the commander had just begun turning his fleet into line when the Americans opened fire. One Japanese cruiser was sunk immediately, two destroyers collided, a third was rammed by a cruiser and sank, and the remainder of the squadron was reduced to a shambles and forced to withdraw. Only one US destroyer sustained any damage.

Epéhy in World War I, successful British assault 12–25 Sept 1918 on outposts and advanced positions of the Hindenburg Line, which the Germans had fallen back on following the battles of ◊Bapaume and ◊Arras. The objective consisted of a fortified zone some 5 km/3 mi deep and almost 32 km/20 mi long, together with various subsidiary trenches and strongpoints. British troops of the 3rd and 4th armies (under General Sir Julian Byng and General Sir Henry Rawlinson respectively) and French troops of the 1st Army (under General Marie-Eugène Debeney) attacked elements of the 2nd and 18th German armies. Fighting was fierce, in difficult country, and was broken into a series of battles against limited objectives. By 25 Sept the entire area was in Allied hands; 11,750 prisoners and 100 guns had been captured, but British casualties totalled 72,000.

Erzerum, capture of in World War I, Russian victory over the Turks 16 Feb 1916. The capture was a remarkable feat of arms, conducted in severe winter conditions, in mountainous country, and against well-prepared fortifications. The Russians under General Nikolai Yudenich had advanced from the Caucasus Mountains into Armenia, forcing the Turks to retreat before them and take up positions on a strongly fortified ridge in front of Erzerum. The Russians split into two wings and moved to outflank the Turkish position 26 Jan; the Turks fell back and lost various fortified positions. The Turkish defence collapsed 15 Feb and Yudenich entered Erzerum the next day. The Russians captured 13,000 prisoners, 300 guns, huge quantities of ammunition and stores, and the Turkish loss was estimated at 60,000 killed and wounded. The town remained in Russian hands until re-occupied by the Turks 11 March 1918.

Eylau in the Napoleonic Wars, battle 8 Feb 1807 between 79,000 French troops under Napoleon Bonaparte and 73,000 Prussians and Russians under Marshal Levin Benningsen. Benningsen was retreating toward Königsberg (Kaliningrad) after his defeat at Pultusk, but with Napoleon in pursuit, he decided to make a stand at Eylau, East Prussia (now Znamensk, Russia), about 38 km/24 mi east of Königsberg.

The battle began in a snowstorm: Napoleon attacked with two infantry corps and six divisions of cavalry, all the troops he had to hand since the rest of his army was still moving up. The attack was beaten back and was followed by a Russian counterattack; Napoleon countered this with his 7th corps which had now arrived on the scene. Blinded by snow, enfiladed by artillery, and attacked by infantry the 7th Corps broke and fled when a sudden charge of Russian cavalry descended upon them. As a final hope, Napoleon threw in 18,000 of General Joachim Murat's cavalry against the Russians, who were scattered, ridden down, and destroyed piecemeal. As more French troops arrived throughout the day, Napoleon pressed his attack against Benningsen, who retired into Königsberg, having lost 18,000 troops and 24 guns.

Falaise Gap in World War II, defeat of German forces caught between advancing Allied forces Aug 1944. The gap consisted of the area between Argentan and Falaise, southeast of Caen, France. The Canadian 1st and British 2nd Armies were advancing south from Caen, while the US 1st and 3rd Armies were advancing east and north in their breakout from Normandy. The two forces threatened to trap the German 7th Army, 5th Panzer Army, and Panzergruppe Eberbach, leaving them only the narrow gap between the two towns as an escape route. The Germans were decimated by artillery fire from three sides and constant air attacks. The gap was finally closed 19 Aug, leaving only a pocket of resistance until it too was overrun two days later. German losses were heavy – of the estimated 80,000 troops in the pocket, some 20,000 escaped, 10,000 were killed, and 50,000 surrendered, while losses of equipment included 567 tanks and assault guns, 950 artillery weapons, and 7,500 vehicles.

Falkland Islands World War I British naval victory over German forces 8 Dec 1914. After the British defeat at ◊Coronel, Admiral Sir John Fisher sent a powerful squadron of two battle cruisers, five other cruisers, and two armed ships into the South Atlantic under the command of Admiral Sir Frederick Sturdee. They arrived in the Falkland Islands 7 Dec 1914 and began coaling; the old battleship *Canopus*, armed with 12-in guns, was already in the area, acting as a floating defence battery for the islands. The German commander Admiral Maximilian von Spee knew nothing of this force and had sailed around Cape Horn intending to bombard the Falklands in passing before proceeding around the Cape of Good Hope to arouse the disaffected Boers of South Africa.

Von Spee approached the Falklands early on the morning of 8 Dec and sent the *Gneisenau* to bombard the islands but it was fired at by the *Canopus*; believing this fire to come from coastal defence guns of unknown strength, the ship turned away. Von Spee then saw, over the masking shoreline, the tripod masts of the British battle cruisers and realised he had sailed into a trap. His squadron set off eastward at full speed but the British force had already raised steam and rapidly overhauled them. Battle opened at 12.51 p.m.; at 4.17 p.m. the *Scharnhorst* sank from the effects of British gunfire, and at 5.55 p.m., severely damaged, the *Gneisenau* was scuttled in deep water, with the loss of over 800 of the crew. Two other German ships were sunk; one escaped but was later caught and sunk. Von Spee's squadron was entirely destroyed with a loss of 2,100 crew. The British lost no ships, though some damage was done, and suffered only 5 killed and 16 wounded.

Festubert World War I battle between British and German forces May 1915. In order to assist the French, who were attacking in Artois and Arras, the British 1st Army was ordered to make an attack against the Aubers Ridge. A short bombardment 9 May did little or no damage to the German trenches and the British assault was repulsed with over 12,000 casualties. The attack was repeated 15 May after a much longer artillery bombardment and broke through the German lines in two places. In spite of a counterattack, these two inroads were linked up and a gain of about half a mile was eventually made before the battle died out and fresh trench lines were dug. Total British losses amounted to 3,620 dead, 17,484 wounded, and 4,321 missing.

Five Forks last major battle of the American Civil War 1 Apr 1865; the victory of 28,000 Union troops commanded by Maj-Gen Philip Sheridan and Brig-Gen Gouverneur Warren over 19,000 Confederates under Maj-Gen George A Pickett broke General Robert E Lee's flank guard, forced him to abandon Richmond, and led to his surrender eight days later. Lee's main Confederate force was besieged in Richmond and Petersburg by Union forces led by Ulysses S Grant. However, the siege was incomplete, and Grant's endeavours to send raiding parties around Richmond to cut rail and road communications had so far been held off by Confederate forces.

Grant now decided to change his tactics and simply send an army around the southern flank of the Confederate position to destroy whatever Confederate force he found, so as to force Lee to either evacuate Richmond or surrender. Warren's corps was given the task of cutting a vital road in order to isolate the Confederate field army from Richmond, but Warren, a slow mover, still had his various units spread out and unconnected when the Confederates attacked. Feeding the Union's brigades into the battle one by one merely resulted in their destruction one by one and eventually they broke and ran, communicating their panic to those behind. The disorder in the Union ranks was eventually stemmed and the Confederate drive was halted. Grant ordered Sheridan to take Warren's troops and deal with this Confederate force, which had fallen back to a prepared position at Five Forks, about 16 km/10 mi southwest of Petersburg. Sheridan's dismounted cavalry, together with Warren's infantry, struck the Five Forks position in the late afternoon and destroyed the Confederate force, taking 4,500 prisoners and scattering the remainder.

Flanders collective term for the series of actions at the end of World War I which constituted the British advance in Belgium and northern France Sept–Nov 1918 more usually divided into the battles of the ⟡Yser and ⟡Ypres. The overall plan conceived by Field Marshal Sir Douglas Haig was to develop a series of attacks along the entire length of the British front from Dixmude to the Ypres salient. To do this a massive army group was assembled, consisting of the Belgian Army with three divisions on the Allied left; the French 6th Army with four divisions in the centre; and the British 2nd Army plus the 2nd and 19th Corps, on the right. The group was under the overall direction of the Belgian king Albert I, and his Chief of Staff was General Jean Marie Degoutte of the French army.

The attack began 28 Sept 1918 with no preliminary bombardment but with a creeping barrage covering the assault. By 1 Oct the Allies had gained 13 km/8 mi of ground and all the German defensive lines had been taken. Between 1–14 Oct another British corps was brought in, communications were reorganized, supplies dumped, and preparations made for the next attack, which began 14 Oct. By 17 Oct Ostend had been cleared of Germans and on 19 Oct Bruges was liberated. The advance reached the Dutch frontier 20 Oct and the pressure turned eastward to push the Germans back into Germany. By 11 Nov the Allies had reached a line running from the Dutch frontier at Terneuzen, to Ghent, along the Scheldt river to Ath and thence to St Ghislain where the line linked up with Haig's main group of armies.

Fontenoy French victory in the Austrian War of Succession over an Allied army of about 50,000 British, Dutch, and German troops under the Duke of Cumberland 11 May 1745. The Allies were aiming to relieve Tournai, Belgium, then under siege by the French, but at Fontenoy, about 8 km/5 mi southeast of Tournai, they came up against a strong French position held by 70,000 troops under Marshal Maurice de Saxe, which blocked their advance. The attack opened with an abortive Dutch assault on the French centre. The British and Hanoverian infantry then advanced and a general melee ensued, culminating in a sudden attack by an Irish brigade under French command. The Allied square defence broke but they were able to retire in good order, although they lost some artillery.

Fort Donelson in the American Civil War, victory of Union forces led by General Ulysses S Grant over Confederate forces under Brig-Gen Gideon Pillow and Brig John Floyd 15 Feb 1862. Fort Henry, on the Tennessee river, and Fort Donelson on the Cumberland river about 19 km/12 mi away, were two vital Confederate defences. Fort Henry was badly sited on low ground and was almost inundated by the river flooding and so fell to Grant's attack quite easily. He then moved overland to attack Donelson, to which most of Henry's garrison had fled. An initial attack by Union gunboats failed; their commander took them too close to the fort and was severely punished by the Confederate guns for his over-enthusiasm.

However, the Confederate commander was not confident of holding the fort and formed a striking column to sally out and break open a route through the Union lines, by which the remainder of the garrison could escape. The sally began well, taking one Union division by surprise and swinging it back on the rest of the Union line, but Grant sent a reserve corps under General Lew Wallace to deal with the Confederate column and ordered a frontal attack on the earthworks around the fort in order to draw defenders away from the attempted breakout. By the end of the day the Confederate column was back inside the fort, the Union lines were redrawn, and a renewed attack was planned for the following morning.

During the night, Pillow decided that surrender was his only course but as no Confederate general had yet surrendered to a Union force, he was apprehensive of what might happen to him if he fell into Union hands. He passed command to Floyd and made his escape from the fort. Floyd did likewise, passing the command to General Simon Bolivar Buckner, who sent a message to Grant asking his terms. 'Immediate and unconditional surrender ... I propose to move immediately upon your works' was the famous reply, and Buckner and 15,000 troops surrendered the following morning.

Fredericksburg in the American Civil War, Confederate victory 11–15 Dec 1862 over Union forces under General Ambrose Burnside on the Rapahannock river close to Fredericksburg, Virginia. The Union force, 125,000 strong, was advancing south on Richmond, and Fredericksburg was the obvious place to cross the river. As the northern side of the river gave the Union artillery good command of the town and vicinity, Confederate general Robert E Lee took up a position with 85,000 troops on Marye's Heights, a range of low hills about two miles from the river. Here the Confederates constructed fieldworks and artillery emplacements commanding the ground between them and the river.

The Union army threw pontoon bridges across the river and captured the town of Fredericksburg 12 Dec. The remainder of the Union forces followed, and on 13 Dec the Union army advanced in massed formation toward the Confederate lines. The battle opened with an artillery duel, but this died away as the infantry approached their objectives. As they got within range, the Confederates poured a devastating fire into the ranks and 9,000 Union troops fell on the slopes of the hills. A second assault by the Union 'Grand Division' of 27,000 troops from Fredericksburg met with a similar fate and Burnside lost heart and withdrew his forces back across the river, leaving 13,000 dead and wounded. Confederate losses were under 5,000, most of them lightly wounded. Since a counterattack by Lee was impossible due to the river, and Burnside was reluctant to make a further attempt, both armies went into winter quarters and the battle ended.

It is well war is so terrible. We should grow too fond of it.

Confederate general Robert E Lee, on seeing the slaughter at the *Battle of Fredericksburg*

Friedland French victory in the Napoleonic Wars over the combined Prussian and Russian armies 14 June 1807 at Friedland (now Pravdinsk, Russia) 42 km/26 mi southeast of Königsberg (now Kaliningrad). Napoleon was marching toward Königsberg, and Marshal Levin Benningsen, the commander of the Allied army, marched out to meet the French. He encountered a French corps under General Jean Lannes at Friedland which pinned him in place until Napoleon Bonaparte's main force came up. Lannes allowed the allies to cross the river so they were trapped with their backs to the river with the bridges of Friedland their only possible route of escape.

The battle finally began late in the day when Marshal Michel Ney attacked Friedland, but he was thrown back by a furious Russian cavalry charge. Artillery was concentrated on the Russians and Marshal Claude Victor's corps thrown in to assist Ney. Combined with a charge of French dragoons, this turned the Russians back and routed them, and Ney chased them through Friedland and across the river. The Allies lost 20,000 killed and wounded, the French slightly over 9,000. Ten days later, Tsar Alexander and Napoleon met on a raft in the middle of the Niemen river and signed the Treaty of Tilsit.

Froeschwiller (also known as the battle of Wörth or Reichshofen) first major battle of the Franco-Prussian War 6 Aug 1870 around the village of Froeschwiller, about 50 km/31 mi southwest of Saarbrucken. It proved the rising power of breech-loading artillery to dominate a battle, and the futility of cavalry in the face of breech-loading small arms and artillery. Despite these lessons, it was to take many more years before they were universally understood.

Bavarian and Prussian troops crossed the frontier into France 4 Aug, taking the town of Wissembourg. The French withdrew, and for a time the two armies lost contact with each other. Marshal Marie MacMahon decided to prepare a strong defensive position on the Froeschwiller ridge with troops of the 1st and 7th Corps, and instructed 5th Corps, then further north, to join him. As the 5th Corps was spread out along the frontier it could not be collected in time to be of any use so MacMahon had only 48,000 troops instead of the 76,000 he had hoped for.

On the evening of 5 Aug, Prussian patrols arrived on the river Sauerbach at Wörth to see French patrols on the other side. They opened fire and the French retired into the woods. Next morning, other advancing German units bumped into the French positions and the battle began without any formal orders as these individual contacts began to spread and intensify. Prussian artillery was brought up and rapidly dominated the French artillery, while German commanders called for reinforcements. On the southern flank of the French position, the German 11th Corps made a major attack which swept all before it. In desperation the French commander launched a cavalry charge which found itself confined in farmyards, vineyards, and the village of Morsbronn, where the Prussians were able to shoot them down with impunity; nine French squadrons were totally destroyed for no Prussian loss. The German 5th Corps attacked further north and after desperate fighting managed to drive the French back. On the northern flank the Bavarian corps sustained severe losses as they came out of a forest into an open area well covered by the French infantry, but overcame the initial setback and began pressing south, putting the French under pressure in three directions. After an unsuccessful counterattack with his reserves, MacMahon realised that further resistance was futile, as his regiments were melting away; at about 4 p.m. the Prussians stormed into the village of Froeschwiller while the surviving French made their escape as best they could, leaving 11,000 dead and wounded and 9,200 prisoners behind. German casualties were about 11,000 killed and wounded.

Fuentes d'Onoro in the Peninsular War, indecisive battle 3–5 May 1811 between the British and French at Fuentes d'Onoro on the Spanish/Portuguese border 25 km/15 mi west of Ciudad Rodrigo. The Duke of Wellington was blockading the fortress of Ciudad Rodrigo with 32,000 troops and Marshal André Masséna marched to relieve it with 45,000 troops. Although inferior in numbers, Wellington decided to fight and posted his troops behind a stream flowing through a deep ravine. One French division attacked 3 May but was thrown back after hard fighting. After a day's pause, Masséna threw his full strength into an attack 5 May in an attempt to outflank the British right, but Wellington had assumed he would try this and had extended his front for 11 km/7 mi. The French persisted nonetheless and gradually turned the flank, splitting the British army in two. To prevent more disasters Wellington fell back to a fresh defensive position while his Light Division, in square formations, fought a rearguard action against French cavalry. A new line was formed and the French were eventually driven off by artillery fire. Wellington reputedly said that had Napoleon Bonaparte been there 'we would have been damnably licked'.

G

Gaba Tepe, landing at in World War I, unsuccessful Australian operation at ◊Gallipoli April 1915. On 24 April the ANZAC corps landed at 'Z Beach', about 3 km/2 mi north of the hill known as Gaba Tepe. The first wave drove the Turks from the immediate area of the beach, allowing further Anzac troops to land. This force then moved through broken country until it established a line anchored on Gabe Tepe. The Turkish force, about 20,000 strong, attacked this line but were beaten back by the entrenched Anzacs, supported by naval gunfire. The position was entrenched, ammunition and supplies were landed, and the Anzac force was reinforced by the Royal Naval Division. Reinforcements were landed 6 Aug and, in conjunction with an attack at the southern tip of the peninsula, the beach-head was enlarged, but no further progress was made and the surviving force was evacuated from Suvla Bay 20 Dec 1915.

Galicia World War I offensive by Russian troops 1915–16 in Galicia, the largest province of Austria; today it covers most of the Slovak Republic and parts of Poland and Russia north and east of the Carpathian mountains. At the end of 1915 the Russians began an offensive towards Czernowitz (now Cernovcy) in order to forestall a possible Austro-German move against Romania and to further their own plan of an advance toward the Caucasus. At the same time General Alexei Brusilov began an offensive in the area of the Pripet Marshes, capturing Chartoryisk (Cartorijsk) and drawing off Austro-German forces from Galicia. The southern offensive made good progress and captured a bridgehead over the river Dniestr at Uscieczko (Kostrizevka) 9 Feb 1916. Having gained this, they drew their trench lines and there was little change until the start of the ◊Brusilov Offensive June 1916.

I asked him about the landing at Gallipoli, but he could tell me nothing about it. All he knew was that he had jumped out of a bloody boat in the dark and before he had walked five bloody yards he had a bloody bullet in his foot and he had been pushed back to Alexandria almost before he bloody well knew he had left it.

Compton Mackenzie on *Gallipoli*, in *Gallipoli Memories*.

Gallipoli in World War I, abortive Allied campaign to make inroads into Turkey. At the instigation of Winston Churchill, Allied troops made an unsuccessful attempt Feb 1915–Jan 1916 to force their way through the Dardanelles and link up with Russia. The campaign was fought mainly by Australian and New Zealand (ANZAC) forces, who suffered heavy losses. An estimated 36,000 Commonwealth troops died during the nine-month campaign.

Gaugamela during the Asiatic campaign of Alexander the Great, Macedonian victory over the Persians 331 BC, about 80 km/50 mi northeast of Nineveh (now Al Mawsil, Iraq). This battle broke the rule of Darius and gave Alexander the whole of Asia Minor.

Alexander, at the head of a force of about 47,000 Macedonians and Greeks, was confronted by about 120,000 Persians under Darius. He personally led his right wing in an attack against the junction of the Persian centre and left wing, separating them and then taking the Persian centre in its flank. The Macedonian left was also pressing the Persians hard; Darius' forces gave way between the two Macedonian wings and a rout ensued with Darius forced to flee. Alexander's force pursued them hard, with considerable slaughter, before the last of the Persians managed to escape.

Gaza in World War I, unsuccessful British attacks on Turkish-held town of Gaza March–April 1917. During the Allied invasion of Palestine, a British force under General Sir Charles Dobell advanced along the coast from Rafa and mounted an attack on Gaza 26 March 1917. The attack was three-pronged: an infantry division attacked from the south while Anzac forces and cavalry attacked from the east and north. The attack was at first partially successful, and Anzac troops entered the town. However, the Turks put up a strong defence, the British force had no water for its horses, Turkish reinforcements were coming up to the rear of the enveloping British forces, and General Dobell had to withdraw. On 17 April he made a second attack, but to the the interval Gaza had been heavily reinforced and fortified, and in spite of support from tanks the British were beaten off with losses of about 7,000 troops. When night fell the battle was broken off and was not renewed the next day. General Dobell was relieved of his command as a result of the failure.

Gazala German victory over British forces in North Africa May–June 1942; the most severe defeat inflicted on the British during the entire desert campaign of World War II. Gazala was a coastal town in Libya, about 95 km/60 mi west of Tobruk; in 1942 the front line ran south from the town to the oasis of Bir Hacheim.

Field Marshal Erwin Rommel launched a powerful attack against Gazala 26–27 May 1942, using two Italian corps as a diversion at the northern end of the line while the Afrika Korps and another Italian corps swung around the southern end of the line and then northeast toward Tobruk. In spite of the surprise the British fought back well; Rommel sustained heavy losses and was trapped in a corner between a minefield and a British defensive 'box'. With no supplies or fuel and no apparent chance of receiving any, Rommel was contemplating surrender until the Italian Trieste Division managed to open a route through the minefield and get a supply column to him. Indecision and arguments in British headquarters also gave Rommel valuable time so that eventually, re-supplied and rested, he was able to break out of the Cauldron area 1 June and overwhelm the British 'box'. The British responded with uncoordinated and careless attacks 5 June which Rommel easily defeated and then resumed his offensive drive toward Tobruk. He defeated several British formations as he encountered them and the British forces were forced to abandon their positions and fall back to the El ◊Alamein line in Egypt.

German Spring Offensive in World War I, Germany's final offensive on the Western Front 1918. The collapse of Russia allowed the Germans to bring all their best troops from the Eastern Front to reinforce the Western Front, giving them a strength of about 1.6 million troops and 16,000 guns against an Allied strength of 1.4 million troops and 16,400 guns. The Germans made a concerted effort to conclude the war before the arrival of US troops, launching the *Second Battle of the ◊Somme* 21 March 1918. They attacked the weak British sector between Cambrai and the Oise river, held by the 5th Army, and drove the British back a considerable distance. They launched a second attack on the Armentières front 9 April, overwhelming the Portuguese Corps and driving a deep wedge into the British front, capturing the Messines Ridge. On 27 May a third attack was launched against four weak British and four tired French divisions on the Aisne, between Soissons and Reims, which reached the Marne in the region of Château-Thierry. The Germans extended this front and came to within 72 km/45 mi of Paris.

By this time, however, their troops were beginning to flag, and a barrage of mustard gas, the first time the French had used this tactic, halted a further attack 12–13 June. The Germans paused to consolidate their gains and were then further delayed by bad weather, so it was not until 15 July that Ludendorff launched 35 divisions across the Marne to envelop Reims; his attack was held and driven back in the *Second Battle of the ◊Marne*. During this time Foch had been preparing a large French-US force, well supported by tanks, for the Allied counterattack which began May 1918 in the ◊Château-Thierry area. The assault was successful and marked the end of the German campaign and the commencement of the Allied advances which ended the war.

Gettysburg Confederate defeat by Union forces 1–3 July 1863, at Gettysburg, Pennsylvania, 80 km/50 mi northwest of Baltimore; one of the decisive battles of the American Civil War. Gettysburg was the high point of the Confederacy: it was the farthest intrusion into Union territory ever made, but General Robert E Lee's failure to secure a decisive victory condemned the Confederacy to a prolonged struggle in which its forces were unable to regain the strategic initiative.

After ◊Chancellorsville, Lee, with a force of 72,000 troops, decided to advance north into Union territory: his army was starving and needed to operate in an unravaged area which could provide food; and such an advance would draw the Union forces away from the South to protect Washington. Lee therefore marched up the western side of the Blue Ridge mountains and sent General J E B ('Jeb') Stuart's cavalry to the east to act as scouts. Unfortunately, Stuart set off to find a Union force so he could perform some feat of arms to compensate for a near-defeat he suffered some days previously. He eventually rounded up a Union wagon train and began leading it slowly back toward Lee but failed to carry out any scouting, leaving Lee blind to Union movements. When Lee reached Chambersburg, he found that two Union corps were a few miles away across the mountains and that General Joseph Hooker had been replaced as commander of the Union Army of the Potomac by General George Meade, a more dangerous adversary.

Lee sent General Ambrose P Hill's corps over the mountains to reconnoitre and report on the Union forces' strength; they advanced into Gettysburg hoping to find supplies they could appropriate. A Union cavalry patrol discovered them and Meade began moving his 82,000-strong army toward Gettysburg. The two forces met close to the town and fighting broke out more or less immediately: as units of both sides appeared on the scene they were fed into positions and joined the battle. The Union forces eventually passed through the town and took up a strong position on Cemetery Hill. Lee ordered General Richard Ewell's corps to attack it 'if practicable' but Ewell lost his nerve and never attacked. Lee moved his troops on to Seminary ridge, across the valley, and ordered an attack the following morning.

Confederate general James Longstreet suggested simply outflanking Meade and placing the army between Meade and Washington but Lee dismissed the idea. Longstreet procrastinated the next day and failed to support Ewell during the morning attack, only making his move in the early afternoon; even then, as soon as Lee was out of sight, he came to a halt. By the time Lee got him moving once more the Union lines had moved so that Longstreet's corps was outflanked; but even knowing this, Longstreet continued with his advance according to Lee's original plan, turning the attack into a shambles. Night fell, the armies rested, and the following day Lee planned another concerted attack, Again Longstreet failed to move, allowing Ewell to make his attack and be beaten back. Instead, he decided on an artillery bombardment to soften up the Union lines, but due to the powder smoke most of the shells went over the Union position. Ammunition began to run low, and General George A Pickett, waiting with his division to make a frontal attack when Ewell and Longstreet had done their part, was warned that unless he made his assault now, there would be no covering fire available. Longstreet ordered Pickett to advance, without informing Lee that the ammunition situation was critical. 'Pickett's Charge' went into history; his division poured from a ravine and was blown to shreds by concentrated Union artillery fire. At the same time Hill made an attack on the Union lines which was driven off by the appearance of a strong Union reserve. This was enough, and the two armies retired to their lines. During the night, Lee saw that there was no hope of victory, disengaged his troops, and set off back to Virginia

Gibraltar, siege of in the American War of Independence, unsuccessful combined French and Spanish siege of the British-held fortress of Gibraltar 1779–83. The French and Spanish fleets entered the bay of Gibraltar June 1779, while attacks were also made by land approach with extensive siege works. Admiral Sir George Rodney managed to drive off the combined fleets long enough to permit supply ships to reach the harbour Jan 1780, and another major resupply took place 1781; from time to time small ships managed to run the blockade, but starvation came very close at various times, although a British sortie Nov 1781 partially destroyed the siege works threatening the north. Throughout the siege, there were regular artillery exchanges. The final Spanish attack took place Sept 1872 with an army of 40,000, aided by the combined French and Spanish fleets. The attack was accompanied by an intense artillery bombardment, to which the defenders replied with red-hot shot, damaging many of the warships and floating batteries. Great losses were inflicted on the attacking force and the siege was finally raised 6 Feb 1783.

Givenchy inconclusive World War I battle between British and German forces 16–22 Dec 1914. In early Dec 1914 an Allied force was opposing strong German defences around Givenchy, a French village in the Pas-de-Calais. In order to relieve pressure on the French, then fighting at Arras, orders were given to attack and pin down the Germans so that they could not reinforce Arras. Indian troops of the Lahore division attacked 19 Dec and captured two lines of German trenches but were then driven out by a fierce counterattack. On 20 Dec the Germans, strongly reinforced, mounted a sudden attack against the Indian trenches which were inundated due to rain, and broke through to occupy part of the village. Two British battalions in reserve were called up and recaptured the village in the evening. The battle continued and several salients were driven into the British line, until Field Marshal Sir Douglas Haig brought up reinforcements from the 1st Army 21 Dec, relieved the Indian division, and forced the Germans back to their original line. The battle died out the following day with all participants back where they had started, at a cost of about 4,000 British and 2,000 German casualties.

Glorious First of June naval battle between the British and French fleets off Ushant 1 June 1794; the first major naval action of the French Revolutionary Wars. Following the French Revolution, the harvest failed and France faced starvation. The British were blockading the French coast and a convoy of 116 ships of grain from the United States had to be escorted to safety in French harbours. Admiral Sir Richard Howe was sent out with the British fleet to intercept the French, and came up with the main French fleet 28 May. After a few minor skirmishes, the two fleets cleared for action 1 June; Howe's plan was to attack the enemy in line, then break through the French line, prevent their retreat, and fight to a finish on their lee side. Due to vagaries of wind and current, this could not be executed as precisely as Howe would have wished, but the plan was generally followed, and the battle became a matter of pairs of ships hammering at each other until one was vanquished. The British captured six French ships and sank one before the action ended. Both sides claimed a victory; the British because they had damaged the French fleet and there was no major naval action for the next two years; the French because their fleet, damaged as it was, was not destroyed, and the vital grain convoy had reached France in safety.

Gondar in World War II, final defeat of Italian forces in Ethiopia 1941. Gondar, an exceptionally mountainous area about 320 km/200 mi southwest of Asmara and north of Lake Tana, was held by the Italian general Nasi with about 40,000 troops, the last large body of Italian troops in Ethiopia. Access to the town was by two passes, both held by Italian garrisons which were starved into surrender in June and Sept respectively. Two brigades of the 12th African Division then converged on Gondar which held out until African troops gained the heights which commanded the Italian positions and the Kenya Armoured Car Regiment actually penetrated the outskirts of the town. Nasi requested terms 28 Nov 1941 and the garrison surrendered.

Goose Green in the Falklands War, British victory over Argentina 28 May 1982. British troops landed at and around Port San Carlos on the western side of the West Falkland island 21 May and prepared to advance to Port Stanley, some 80 km/50 mi to the east. An Argentine force was known to be at Goose Green, to the south of San Carlos, and since this posed a threat to the flank of the British advance, troops of the Parachute Regiment, with a battery of 105 mm guns in support, were sent to deal with it. Due to a shortage of helicopters at a critical time, not all the battery of guns and its ammunition was able to get into position, and with this limited support the Parachute troops made an attack on foot. A brisk firefight resulted, in which the commanding officer of the Parachute troops was killed while leading a charge, for which he received a posthumous Victoria Cross. The Argentine garrison was overrun, the survivors taken prisoner, and the advance on Port Stanley was free to move.

Gorizia, capture of in World War I, Italian victory over Austrian forces Aug 1916. The town of Gorizia was then part of the Austro-Hungarian empire and its position made it a strategic obstacle since it closed the road to Trieste, a prime Italian objective. The Italian offensive on the ◊Isonzo of 1915 made little headway but Italian forces were able to drive out the Austrians Aug 1916 after an intense artillery bombardment and, after a three-day battle, occupied the town. This enabled them to outflank other Austrian positions holding up the general advance. The Italians held Gorizia until the Austro-German offensive of autumn 1917 forced them to withdraw on 28 Oct. They eventually recovered it late 1918 and it became part of Italy after the war.

Granson during the Burgundian Wars, defeat of 36,000 Burgundians under Charles the Bold by 18,000 Swiss troops 1476. The town (now called Grandson) is at the southeast end of Lake Neuchâtel and was captured by the Swiss 1475. In Feb 1476 the Duke of Burgundy recaptured it and massacred the entire garrison. By way of revenge the Swiss advanced on the town again and Charles the Bold, attempting to decoy the Swiss out of the mountains and into open country, ordered a retreat. The Swiss followed closely and attacked his rearguard, whereupon Charles panicked and fled with the rest of his army. The Swiss pursued, completely destroyed his camp, and scattered his army.

Gravelotte (St Privat) Prussian victory in the Franco-Prussian War 18 Aug 1870; the battle took place on a ridge between the villages of the same names, about 10 km/6 mi west of Metz. The French general François Bazaine, marching to Verdun, had been checked by the Prussians at ◊Vionville, and the road to Verdun was now closed. He therefore decided to fall back on a line between St Privat and Rozerieulles where his army could rest while vital stores, ammunition, and rations were brought up from the fortress of Metz. The army was demoralized and made little attempt to place itself in a defensive posture; the troops simply went to sleep as soon as they arrived in the new location.

Meanwhile the Prussians under Count Helmuth von Moltke were advancing north, trying to find where the French had gone. In fact they were advancing across the front of the French and were wide open to a flank attack; but Bazaine was not the sort of general capable of taking such an opportunity. Eventually Prussian cavalry discovered the French position, though there was some miscalculation over the position of the northern end of the line, and the armies gradually wheeled into position to begin the battle. The fight was bitter, with the French having the positional advantage, but eventually the Prussians were able to turn the French right flank at St Privat, the north end of the line, which led to a general rout and Bazaine's entire force falling back into the fortress of ◊Metz, where they were subsequently besieged. It was a strategic victory for the Prussians, but it cost them over 20,000 casualties, while the French lost around 13,000. With Bazaine's army safely locked up in Metz, the Prussians were now able to concentrate upon Marshal Marie MacMahon's army which they destroyed at ◊Sedan.

Great Marianas Turkey Shoot World War II air battle during the naval Battle of the ◊Philippine Sea 20 June 1944. A Japanese fleet of 6 aircraft carriers with 342 aircraft set out to trap a US fleet between itself and land-based aircraft from Guam. The US fleet, equipped with 15 carriers and 956 aircraft, was aware of the plan and sent out their own aircraft, catching the Japanese some 80 km/50 mi away from their target. Over 300 Japanese were shot down and only a handful reached the US fleet, causing little or no damage.

Guadalcanal important US operation in World War II on the largest of the Solomon Islands for control of the area 1942–43.

land campaign discovering that the Japanese were building an airfield on the island, the US 1st Marine Division landed there 7 Aug 1942, scattered the small Japanese garrison, and completed the airfield, which received its first US aircraft 20 Aug. The Japanese sent reinforcements to recapture the airfield and began naval and air attacks against the beachhead. Both sides built up strength throughout constant fighting until the Marines were relieved 8 Dec by US 14th Corps which drove the Japanese off the island, finally declaring it secure 7 Feb 1943. US casualties came to 1,600 killed, 2,400 wounded, and 12,000 hospitalized by disease; Japanese losses were 14,000 killed, 9,000 dead from disease or starvation, and 1,000 captured.

naval actions while the land battle for Guadalcanal raged, both sides were attempting to reinforce their troops by sea and prevent the other side from doing likewise, resulting in almost constant minor skirmishes and two major naval engagements.

The *First Battle* began 12 Nov 1942 when the Japanese sent 2 battleships, a cruiser, 14 destroyers, and transports carrying 13,500 soldiers to the area; 5 US cruisers and 8 destroyers were sent to intercept them off Savo Island. The resulting battle was a confused affair but it ended with 4 US destroyers sunk, 2 cruisers so badly damaged that they sank later, and the rest of the US fleet damaged, whereas the Japanese lost a cruiser and 2 destroyers. However, they withdrew and postponed the reinforcement for 24 hours until they could assemble more cruisers to bombard the airfield. Then 3 cruisers and 2 destroyers arrived and carried out a heavy bombardment, destroying 18 US aircraft but without doing much damage to the airstrip. As they withdrew they were harried by US aircraft which sank 7 of the 11 Japanese troop transports.

The *Second Battle* followed almost immediately. The Japanese ordered a further bombardment of the airfield and tried landing the remaining reinforcements 14–15 Nov. They were met by a US force of 2 battleships and 4 destroyers about midnight and a confused battle ensued in which 3 US destroyers were sunk and 1 damaged, while the US battleship *South Dakota* was severely damaged. However, the Japanese were severely punished by the US 16-in guns and the destroyers and transports withdrew at high speed out of danger, having managed to land no more than 2,000 troops. Although these actions were inconclusive, they convinced the Japanese that there was no future in sending naval units to their doom for the sake of one island, and they evacuated 7 Feb 1943.

Guam in World War II, US operation to recapture the island from the Japanese 1943. Guam is at the southern end of the Marianas group, about 1,600 km/1,000 mi north of New Guinea. It was occupied by the Japanese 10 Dec 1941 and used as a naval and air base. US forces invaded 21 July 1943 and by 10 Aug the entire island was in their hands. US losses amounted to 1,744 killed and 5,970 wounded; the Japanese lost 18,250 killed and 1,250 captured. Some of the Japanese garrison fled to the interior of the island – the last of them did not surrender until 1960.

Guise (also called the Battle of St Quentin) battle between French and German forces 29–30 Aug 1914. The retreating French 5th Army under General Charles Lanrezac had fallen back to Guise when it was ordered to attack St Quentin some 25 km/15 mi away, in order to relieve pressure on the British at ◊Mons and buy time for the French 6th Army to assemble near Paris. The attack was mounted, but the force's open flanks were immediately threatened by German attacks, forcing Lanrezac to abandon the St Quentin objective and concentrate instead on a frontal holding battle against whatever forces the Germans sent. He met and drove back an attack from General Karl von Bülow's army, but the danger of his flank being turned by General Alexander von Kluck's forces was such that he could not pursue his victory. He had no choice but to break off and re-start his retreat. Nevertheless, his action caused some 6,000 German casualties and upset the German plans.

Guilford Court House in the War of American Independence, costly British victory March 1781 over American forces at Guilford Court House, a few miles northwest of what is now Winston-Salem, North Carolina. The 1,300 British troops, under Lord Cornwallis, attacked a stronger American force under General Nathaneal Greene which was in a well-prepared defensive position. By a series of attacks on individual strongpoints the British eventually put the Americans to flight, leaving their guns, stores, and wounded behind. However, the British sustained 548 casualties, almost half Cornwallis' force, leaving him too weak to pursue the enemy or carry out further operations for some time.

Gujarat in the Second Sikh War, massacre of 50,000 Sikhs under Shir Singh by 25,000 British troops under Lord Gough 21 Feb 1849. After the battle of ◊Chilianwala, Gough waited for reinforcements and, with his strength up to 24,000 troops, marched for Gujarat in the Punjab, about 160 km/100 mi southeast of Rawalpindi, in order to attack the main Sikh army, estimated to be 60,000 strong. He found them drawn up outside the fortified town and opened his attack with an artillery bombardment lasting two and a half hours. The British infantry then advanced and after some fighting the Sikh ranks broke and ran. They were pursued by cavalry for several miles, and the result was the complete annihilation of the Sikh army and the capture of all its guns and baggage. The remainder of the Sikh armies surrendered at Rawalpindi 10 March and the war was ended. The British casualties at Gujarat amounted to 96 killed and 700 wounded; this battle was the first in which surgeons used anaesthetics in the field to carry out amputations.

Haarlem during the Netherlands War of Independence, siege of Haarlem, capital of the province of North Holland, by 30,000 Spanish troops 11 Dec 1572. The garrison numbered only 4,000 troops but they were not only able to beat off successive assaults but mounted a sortie which captured a large quantity of food from the besiegers. However, the Dutch fleet, attempting to bring supplies, was defeated by a Spanish fleet 28 May 1573. Facing starvation, the city, with its garrison now reduced to only 1,800 troops, surrendered 12 July 1573. The entire garrison and several hundred civilians were massacred by the Spanish, who had lost 12,000 casualties during the siege.

Halfaya Pass in World War II, disastrous British attack June 1941 on German-held pass south of Bardia, on the Libya–Cyrenaica border. The pass gave access from the coastal plains through the escarpment to the inland plateau and thus to the open desert. Secured by Field Marshal Erwin Rommel during his first offensive 1941, it became notorious when attacked by British tanks during Operation ◊Battleaxe 15 June 1941. Rommel had concealed a number of 88 mm anti-aircraft guns in the pass and deployed some of his armour to draw the British into the pass. When British tanks pursued this decoy force they were almost all destroyed by the concealed guns.

Hallue River battle of the Franco-Prussian War 23–24 Dec 1870, 8 km/5 mi northeast of Amiens. With Paris under siege, citizen armies were raised all over France. The northern army, under the command of General Louis Faidherbe, was ordered Dec 1870 to attempt a junction with General Alexandre Ducrot's force, which was expected to break out from Paris and march northeast. Faidherbe marched out and captured a small fortress from the Germans, causing them considerable alarm. Hearing that the German garrison had been withdrawn from Amiens, Faidherbe set off to take the city, but was forestalled by the garrison returning to their posts.

The Prussian 1st Army advanced toward Faidherbe who decided to stand and fight in a loop of the Hallue river, with his left flank protected by the river Somme. He deployed his two best divisions in front, retaining an untried division of *Gardes Nationales* as his reserve. The Prussian army was under strength, with only about 25,000 troops and 108 guns; they attacked centrally with one division while the remainder attempted an unsuccessful flanking movement. The French then counterattacked but with little effect since their effort was spread across the entire front rather than being concentrated at any one point. After camping the night on the battlefield, Faidherbe decided that his troops would be unlikely to perform well for a second day and retired to the safety of Arras. The Prussians did not pursue, being wary of possible ambush and because their presence was required elsewhere to deal with another minor uprising.

My army is 35,000 strong, of whom half fight seriously. They decrease at every encounter. The rest are only useful for making a show on the battlefield.

General Louis Faidherbe after the *Battle of Hallue River* Dec 1870

Hamel, Capture of in World War I, successful US attack on German positions July 1918. On 4 July 1918 the 33rd Illinois National Guard Division decided to celebrate Independence Day by attacking Hamel Wood, near Corbie on the Somme. In co-operation with some Australian troops, and after a severe artillery preparation, the combined force advanced under cover of tanks on a 6-km/4-mi front, the US forces concentrating on Hamel. The joint force advanced 2.5 km/1.5 mi, Hamel and Vaire woods were taken, and 1,500 prisoners, 20 mortars, and 100 machine guns were captured.

Hampton Roads in the American Civil War, inconclusive naval engagement March 1862, the first battle between armoured warships. When the Confederates occupied Norfolk, Virginia, they found a damaged steam frigate, the *Merrimac*. The hull was sound and the engines repairable, so they cut away the upper works and built a new superstructure of 20-in thick pine timber covered by 20-in thick plates of iron. Loopholes were left to allow four 7-in and six 9-in guns to be fired from this protected battery. The resulting craft was named the *Virginia*. Hearing of this threat, the Union government commissioned John Ericsson, a Swedish-born engineer, to devise an armoured vessel. His solution was an armoured raft carrying a revolving turret with two 11-in guns, christened the *Monitor*.

The *Virginia* went into action 8 March 1862 in Hampton Roads, off Norfolk, against a Union fleet blockading the port. Union ships opened fire but the shots bounced off the *Virginia*, which proceeded to ram the USS *Cumberland* and then bombarded the USS *Congress* into submission. Later that day, after the *Virginia* had returned to her berth, the USS *Monitor* appeared, and on the following day both ships came out to give battle. Each captain watched their shots bounce off the other vessel, and although they circled and bombarded for some hours, no decision was reached. *Monitor* ran out of ammunition, and *Virginia* withdrew to make some minor repairs. Although the *Virginia* made a few minor forays after that, it never encountered the *Monitor* again and did relatively little damage. The Union army then captured Norfolk and the Confederates set *Virginia* on fire before abandoning the town. *Monitor* was sunk in a storm while sailing back to New York 31 Dec 1862.

Haslach French victory over the Austrians in the Napoleonic Wars 11 Oct 1805. A 6,000-strong French force under General Pierre Dupont de L'Etang was marching on Ulm when he was stopped by an Austrian force of 60,000 troops under the Archduke Ferdinand which commanded the heights around his route. He immediately occupied and fortified the village of Haslach, about 45 km/28 mi southwest of Strasbourg, which was then attacked by about 25,000 of the Austrians. Dupont managed to hold them off until nightfall, then disengaged and withdrew, taking 4,000 Austrian prisoners with him.

Hastings decisive victory of Norman forces under William, Duke of Normandy (thereafter known as the Conqueror), over King Harold II of England 14 Oct 1066. Harold had just defeated a Norse army at ◊Stamford Bridge when he learned William had landed at Pevensey. Rapidly marching south, he took up a position, on a hill later called Senlac near Hastings, England. He was attacked by Norman archers, foot soldiers, and finally cavalry with no result. Then some of Harold's personal guard left their places to pursue some stragglers, and William ordered some of his troops to simulate panic and flight. The strategy worked as many of the English troops broke ranks to run down the hill after the Normans, who then turned and cut them down. William then resumed his attack on the hill, with his archers shooting into the air. With arrows falling about them, the English opened up, allowing the Norman foot soldiers to get among them. Harold and his two brothers were killed and his army totally destroyed, leaving England open to Norman rule. (See also battle plan 2.)

Hattin crushing defeat of the Crusaders by Saladin 4 July 1187 at a village in Palestine 8 km/5 mi northwest of Tiberias. A column of Frankish Crusaders was marching to the relief of the citadel of Tiberias which was besieged by Saladin. The column was attacked by a Moslem army and brought to a halt at Hattin, a place with no water. Harassing attacks during the night ensured that the Crusaders had no rest, and the lack of water demoralized them. On the following morning they were in no condition to withstand attack; the Moslem army swept around in two wings and completely annihilated the Crusader force and with it the military power of the Kingdom of Jerusalem.

Heligoland Bight World War I British victory over German naval forces 28 Aug 1914. The battle was fought in the Heligoland Bight, the stretch of water between Heligoland island and the German mainland used by the German fleet for exercises. A British force of 2 light cruisers, 33 destroyers, and 8 submarines sailed into the Bight, surprising the German vessels there. These were principally light cruisers and destroyers; as it was low tide, the heavier German warships were unable to leave their bases. The Germans attempted to cut the British fleet off from its return route, but were surprised by a second force of British light cruisers. However, these reinforcements were unable to get close to the Germans because of the British submarines between them. The Germans got over the initial shock of the raid and used their superiority in number of cruisers to begin driving the British out of the Bight. The arrival of the battle cruiser squadron of the Grand Fleet, under Admiral David Beatty, reversed the situation once again and their heavy firepower sank three German cruisers. The rest of the German fleet then turned about and returned to their bases, while the British fleet sailed out of the Bight, having sunk three light cruisers and a destroyer. The success of this attack was a severe blow to German naval morale.

Hohenfriedburg Prussian victory over the allied Austrians and Saxons during the War of the Austrian Succession 3 June 1745 56 km/35 mi southwest of Breslau, Prussian Silesia (now Wroclaw, Poland). Frederick the Great, with a Prussian army of 65,000, had been watching the approach of the 85,000-strong allied force under Charles of Lorraine toward Silesia, while keeping his own army concealed. Seeing his opportunity, he manoeuvred his army and guns into position during the night and at dawn attacked the allied left wing, putting the Saxons to flight before the Austrians could move to their assistance. He then rapidly swung and attacked the Austrians. They put up a strong resistance but a charge of the Bayreuth Dragoons broke their line and the battle was over. The allied force lost 4,000 killed and wounded, 7,000 prisoners, 66 guns, and their regimental colours. The Prussians lost just over 2,000 killed and wounded.

Hong Kong, Capture of in World War II, Japanese capture 1941 of the British colony on the south coast of China comprising the island of Hong Kong and the mainland peninsula of the New Territories. In 1941 the garrison consisted of about 11,000 troops in five infantry battalions, two coastal defence artillery regiments, an anti-aircraft artillery regiment, and support troops. Too far isolated to be a safe fleet base and with poor land defences, the loss of British sea and air superiority made its fall inevitable. The first Japanese patrols crossed the border from China 8 Dec 1941, followed by the main attacking force of 3 Japanese divisions supported by 80 aircraft and a naval squadron. Japanese air attacks soon destroyed what RAF presence there was and then subjected the entire colony to bombing attacks. The British defences on the 'Gin Drinker's Line' were soon breached and they fell back to the island. From there they turned the coastal defence guns to the mainland and bombarded the Japanese, though with little effect since the ammunition was designed for use against armoured warships. Japanese heavy artillery was emplaced in Kowloon and began bombarding the island and the first Japanese troops landed on Hong Kong itself 18 Dec. They drove a wedge between the British forces and gradually subdued the defenders until the garrison surrendered 25 Dec 1941.

Hukawng Valley in World War II, Allied operation to capture this valley in Burma which extends southwest from Ledo on the Indian border in the general direction of Myitkyina. The Chinese 22nd and 38th Divisions under US general Joseph Stilwell advanced down the valley Oct 1943 with the intention of re-opening the Burma Road but were stopped by the Japanese 18th Division. Stilwell was joined Feb 1944 by Brigadier Frank Merrill's 'Marauders' who outflanked the Japanese position while he maintained pressure from the front. The Japanese were manoeuvred out of both positions and Stilwell was able to enter the Mogaung Valley and advance on Mytikyina.

Imjin River Korean War battle; see ◊Solma-Ri

Imphal in World War II, Allied operation 1944 to hold Japanese forces back from an important road junction in the Manipur district of northeast India, 600 km/375 mi northwest of Calcutta; the turning point in the Burma campaign. In 1944, Imphal and ◊Kohima were on the route of the Japanese invasion of India aimed at setting up a defensive line on the Naga Hills to keep the British out of Burma. Field Marshal Sir William Slim countered the Japanese plan by concentrating the 17th, 20th, and 23rd Indian Divisions with a tank brigade around Imphal where they established a defensive perimeter which could be resupplied by air. When the Japanese 15th Army attacked the perimeter, Slim's plan worked, resupply went smoothly, the armour was able to move easily on the plain, and the Japanese attacks were resisted.

British Chindit operations in the Japanese rear also began to have an effect upon their supply lines, exacerbated by the superior Allied air forces which disrupted Japanese communications and freely bombed their positions. Finally, the British 33rd Corps broke through the Japanese blocks at Kohima and were able to join up with the Imphal perimeter. The Japanese, starving and diseased, had by now lost 53,000 troops and fell back to the Chindwin river, abandoning their artillery and transport.

Inchon in the Korean War, amphibious landing by US Marines 15 Sept 1950 at Inchon, 32 km/20 mi west of Seoul, South Korea. North Korean forces, which invaded South Korea 25 June 1950, had advanced down the Korean peninsula and contained US and ROK (Republic of Korea) forces in a tight perimeter around Pusan from which they were unable to break out.

General Douglas MacArthur proposed an amphibious landing at Inchon so as to cut the North Korean supply lines which ran through Seoul and thus weaken their grip on the Pusan perimeter. The US took time to assemble forces and plan, as their troops were unprepared, and the proposed target was exceptionally difficult due to a winding sea approach through islands and an enormous tidal rise and fall. In spite of these and other difficulties, the landings were successful, with only 20 Marines being killed and 176 wounded. The Marine force advanced toward Seoul while reinforcements were poured in through Inchon and by 27 Sept the city had been taken, the communist supply lines broken, and the North Korean forces around the Pusan Perimeter were in retreat.

Indaw World War II British operation to capture a town in Burma about 160 km/100 mi southwest of Myitkyina on the railway to Mandalay, with roads leading west to ◊Imphal and ◊Kohima. An important Japanese supply base in their offensive against India, it was attacked by the Chindits June 1944. This interrupted the supply line to the Japanese front and prevented troops from Indaw being used to reinforce the Imphal battle. The town was finally captured by the British 36th Division Dec 1944.

Inkerman in the Crimean War, British and French victory over Russian forces 5 Nov 1854 on the Inkerman Ridge outside Sevastopol. British troops had occupied the ridge as part of the investment of Sevastopol, and were attacked 25 Oct by a Russian force which they drove off without difficulty. A more serious attack was launched under cover of fog 5 Nov, the Russians reaching the British lines without being seen. The Russians outnumbered the British at their selected point of attack, and were able to seize the hilltop and bring up artillery. However, mist prevented them from opening effective fire, and a rapid counterattack by the British 2nd Division recaptured the hilltop and drove off the Russians.

The Russians then launched a second attack at a fresh objective, the 'Sandbag Battery' which, again, was driven off by the arrival of British and French reinforcements. The fighting lasted about seven hours, during which time the British lost about 2,400 troops, the French about 1,000, and the Russians an estimated 11,000. Due to the fog, most of the action was by small formations, out of sight and command of the senior officers, and so Inkerman is often called 'The Soldiers' Battle'.

Iron Triangle in the Vietnam War, US operation (codenamed 'Cedar Falls') to clear Vietcong (VC) guerrillas from a triangular area some 48 km/30 mi north of Saigon. By 1967 the Triangle had been overrun by VC irregulars, whose presence threatened Saigon and severely limited US and ARVN (Army of the Republic of Vietnam) operations.

Operation 'Cedar Falls' was mounted to clear the area and render it incapable of supporting VC operations. About 15,000 US and ARVN troops were deployed along the sides of the triangle, after which helicopter-borne and armoured forces entered the area, divided it up, and cleared each sector individually. All villages were destroyed and the civilian population removed to more secure areas; some 300 VC were captured and an estimated 250 killed. Once this ground search had been completed, US aircraft sprayed chemical defoliant on the trees so as to remove leaf cover and make the area open to aerial observation and suppressive fire.

Isandhlwana Zulu victory over British forces 22 Jan 1879 about 160 km/100 mi north of Durban. A column led by Lord Chelmsford seeking the Zulu army camped at Isandhlwana while patrols went out to scour the district. A report was received and Chelmsford moved out with half his strength, leaving the camp occupied by six companies of the 24th Regiment, two guns, some Colonial Volunteers, and some native contingents: about 1,800 troops in all.

Late in the morning, an advance post warned of the approach of a Zulu army. Then a mounted patrol found thousands of Zulus concealed in a ravine; as the patrol rode to warn the camp the Zulus followed. The camp commander spread his troops around the perimeter of the camp, but the Zulus broke through; the native contingents fled but were chased and killed. The 21 officers and 534 soldiers of the 24th Regiment were killed where they fought; there were no wounded, no prisoners, and no missing. Only about 50 Europeans and 300 Africans escaped. The invasion of Zululand was temporarily halted until reinforcements were received from Britain.

Isonzo series of battles in World War I between Italian and Austrian forces 1915–17. The Isonzo river rises in the Julian Alps and runs south, more or less following the present-day border of Italy and Yugoslavia, to the Gulf of Trieste. On the declaration of war by Italy, 23 May 1915, the Austrians took up a defensive position on the east bank, facing Italy.

The *first battle* was an Italian attack across the river June 1915 which made some gains and reached a position overlooking the Carso Plateau. Bad weather then prevented any further movement.

The *second battle* began July 1915 with an Italian thrust against the fortifications of Gorizia, followed by an attack in the Carso region. They failed at Gorizia but took a great deal of ground and prisoners in the Carso before the battle died away Sept 1915.

The *third battle* began 18 Oct 1915 with a heavy Italian artillery bombardment along the whole line, followed by another attack against Goriza and further operations in the Carso until winter weather prevented further movement.

The front then lay quiet until Aug 1916 when the *fourth battle* was launched with another attack against Gorizia and its surrounding defences, which fell to the Italians 9 Aug. This was followed by an advance in the Carso region which gained ground in the direction of Trieste. This attack died down by the end of Aug but sporadic fighting continued until Oct 1916.

During the winter both sides made preparations for a spring offensive, and the *fifth battle* opened May 1917 with an Italian thrust against the Austrian line north of Goriza. This made some gains but was then stopped by a powerful Austrian counterattack after which the lines stabilized, despite six further battles, until ◊Caporetto.

Issus Persian defeat by Alexander the Great 333 BC at the ancient port of Issus in Cilicia standing on what is now the Gulf of Alexandretta, about 80 km/50 mi west of present-day Adana, Turkey. Alexander, intent upon securing his line of supply and, if necessary, retreat before his invasion of the Persian Empire met and defeated a Persian force under King Darius III, aided by 30,000 Greek mercenaries, drawn up in a defensive line on the river Pinarus. Alexander, with an army of 35,000 Macedonians, launched his cavalry against the Persian cavalry and routed them. The Macedonian foot soldiers then crossed the river and assaulted the Persian centre, while Alexander personally led his own cavalry against the bodyguard of King Darius, who fled from the field. The Persians followed him in flight and the Greek mercenaries were left to fight what remained of the battle. The Macedonian victory was completed by Alexander's capture of Darius' family.

Ivangorod, attacks on in World War I, part of the German offensive against the Russians in Poland Sept–Oct 1914. Ivangorod (now Deblin, Poland), was a Russian fortress on the east bank of the Vistula river, besieged by the 4th Austro-Hungarian army under General Victor Dankl. The first attack was defeated by a Russian counterattack which severely mauled the Austro-German forces and forced them to retreat to Radom. They remained there until July 1915 when, under the command of General Remus von Woyrsch, they attacked, seized a bridge across the Vistula and invested the fortress. The advance continued around the fortress, linking up with Hungarian and Austrian troops from the south and threatening to cut the only Russian line of retreat. The Russians removed everything they could and abandoned Ivangorod 4 Aug, blowing bridges behind them as they retired.

Iwo Jima in World War II, US capture of Japanese-held island in the Bonin group, about 1,450 km/900 mi south of Tokyo after intense fighting Feb–March 1945. Fortified by the Japanese, it held two airfields, with a third under construction, and was a valuable strategic target for US forces as it would provide a base for land-based bombers to raid the mainland of Japan. It was assaulted by US Marines 19 Feb 1945 after a prolonged air and naval bombardment. The 22,000 Japanese troops put up a fanatical resistance but the island was finally secured 16 March. US casualties came to 6,891 killed and 18,700 wounded, while only 212 of the Japanese garrison survived.

J

Java Sea World War II naval engagement between Japanese and Allied forces 1942. A Japanese fleet escorting the Eastern Invasion Force was intercepted 27 Feb 1942 by a mixture of British, US, Australian, and Dutch warships intent upon preventing them reaching Java. The Allied force of five cruisers and ten destroyers was severely mauled by the Japanese and while attempting to escape they ran into a second Japanese invasion force and were almost totally destroyed. Only four US destroyers, all damaged, managed to escape to the safety of Australia. This victory allowed the Japanese a free run in the waters around Java and they were able to complete their invasion without interference.

Jellalabad Afghan siege of isolated British outpost in Afghanistan 1841. Jellalabad (now Jalalabad) lies about 130 km/80 mi east of Kabul and 1841 was little more than a wide place in the road with a fort, held by about 2,000 troops under General Sir Robert Sale. After the massacre of the British force in Kabul, Jellallabad was surrounded by Afghans; Sale received orders to retire into India, but felt that his chances of passing through the Afghans were slim and decided to defend the fort. The Afghans made repeated attacks which were beaten off, and when rations were running short, a successful sortie captured 300 sheep from the besiegers. Eventually, after five months under siege, Sale mounted an attack against the Afghan forces, captured their main camp, baggage, stores, guns, and horses and the Afghans fled to Kabul.

Jena-Auerstadt comprehensive French victory in the Napoleonic Wars over the combined Prussian and Saxon armies 14 Oct 1806 at Jena, Germany, 90 km/56 mi southwest of Leipzig. Napoleon Bonaparte so broke the Prussian forces that they were unable to prevent him marching on Berlin, and it was recollection of this disaster which led to the complete overhaul and re-organization of the Prussian Army and its subsequent military prowess. Austria had been seeking Prussia's aid in the fight against Napoleon for some time, but it was not until Napoleon was returning to France after ◊Austerlitz that Prussia finally declared war.

Napoleon acted promptly: his army was resting near Würzburg and he immediately marched north. The Prussian commander, the Duke of Brunswick, had begun moving south with 143,000 troops, and a separate force of 44,000 Prussians was moving south under Prince Hohenlohe. These two forces concentrated near Weimar and then moved separately, Brunswick heading for Naumberg and Hohenlohe for Jena. Napoleon split his army in two, placing Marshal Louis Davout with 27,000 men near Auerstadt to intercept Brunswick and holding the rest of his army, about 56,000, near Jena to deal with Hohenlohe. He then intended to swing north and deal with the Brunswick force which Davout would be holding in place. Neither of the Prussian forces was particularly well-trained or experienced, and while Napoleon shattered Hohenlohe's army, Davout routed Brunswick's force. The Prussians and Saxons lost some 40,000 troops and 200 guns, while the French lost about 14,000.

Jutland World War I naval battle between British and German forces 31 May 1916, off the west coast of Jutland. Both sides claimed victory, Germany for having sunk more ships than they lost, and Britain because the German High Seas Fleet never ventured outside harbour for the rest of the war. Early on 31 May the German fleet under Admiral Reinhard von Scheer entered the North Sea from the Baltic, intending to entice British battle cruisers in the area to the Norwegian coast and there destroy them. Leading the fleet were 5 battle cruisers under Vice-Admiral Franz von Hipper; the main fleet consisted of 16 Dreadnought and 6 pre-Dreadnought type battleships accompanied by 11 light cruisers and 72 destroyers. Alerted by German radio traffic, the British Grand Fleet under Admiral John Jellicoe (later Earl Jellicoe) sailed from Scapa Flow with 28 Dreadnoughts and 3 battle cruisers. A further force of 6 battle cruisers and 4 fast battleships under Admiral David Beatty sailed from the Rosyth naval base.

There seems to be something wrong with our bloody ships today, Chatfield.

Admiral Beatty to his aide, during the ***Battle of Jutland***.

Hipper's and Beatty's scouting destroyers saw each other in the afternoon of 31 May and the German force promptly turned away to entice the British to the German fleet. Beatty took the bait and a long-range gunnery duel then took place in which two British battle cruisers were sunk and Beatty's flagship damaged. Beatty himself then turned away to draw the Germans north and bring them against Jellicoe's heavier strength. The fleets met, and a general melee ensued during which another British battle cruiser was sunk. Seeing that he was outgunned, Scheer turned away under cover of smokescreens and destroyer attacks. Jellicoe continued south in the hope of getting his fleet between Scheer and the German bases. Scheer turned back into range, then left four battle cruisers to cover his retreat. Jellicoe, fearful of torpedos in the failing light of evening, decided not to follow and the battle thus came to a somewhat inconclusive end.

Kandahar British victory 1880 over Afghan forces besieging a fort about 160 km/100 mi northwest of Quetta and 440 km/275 mi southwest of Kabul. In March 1880 a British force of about 4,000 troops was besieged in the fort at Kandahar; about the same time another British force was annihilated at Maiwand. A relief column of about 10,000 troops plus an estimated 8,000 camp-followers, 2,300 military horses and mules, and 8,000 pack animals, under General Frederick Roberts, set out from Kabul 9 Aug. On hearing of Roberts' approach, the Afghans raised the siege, and when he arrived at Kandahar 23 Aug he found the garrison in reasonable condition. He then marched after the Afghans and routed Ayub Khan 1 Sept, capturing the Afghan camp and supplies. Although not much of a battle, the forced march from Kabul to Kandahar to rescue the beleaguered force caught the public eye and Roberts became famous for it. He was later ennobled as Lord Roberts of Kandahar and Waterford.

Kasserine Pass in World War II, US defeat by Field Marshal Erwin Rommel's tank corps Feb 1943. The pass was in the Memetcha mountains about 240 km/150 mi west of Gafsa, Tunisia. Held by US II Corps under General Lloyd Fredendall, it was attacked by the German 5th Panzer Army 14 Feb. The US forces were shattered, as were two US counterattacks on the following day. General Harold Alexander (later Earl Alexander of Tunis) quickly moved British and US forces into blocking positions to halt the German thrust before it could get clear of the mountains, and Rommel withdrew so skilfully that the Allies never realized he was gone. Fredendall was subsequently relieved of his command and replaced by General George Patton.

Keren in World War II, Allied victory over Italian forces in Ethiopia 1941. Keren, a town in Eritrea, about 80 km/50 mi northwest of Asmara, was accessible only through a mountain gorge and surrounded by peaks. It was attacked Jan 1941 by the British 4th and 5th Indian divisions, who had to isolate and attack each of the defended mountain outposts before an attempt could be made to break through the gorge with a tank column. The battle took eight weeks and the town was finally taken 26 March.

Khalkin Gol crushing Soviet victory Aug 1939 over the Japanese Kwangtung Army on the border of Manchuria and Outer Mongolia, about 645 km/400 mi northwest of Harbin; the most disastrous defeat ever suffered by the Japanese Army, it is largely unknown in the West as attention was focused on Poland at the time.

The border between Mongolia and China generally follows the Khalkin river, but at this point cuts across a bend in the river, on the Manchurian side, for about 64 km/40 mi. In May 1939 the Japanese Kwangtung Army were probing the Mongolian border to find out just how serious the USSR was about the Pact of Mutual Assistance it had recently signed with Outer Mongolia. The Japanese therefore pushed beyond the border line to occupy the salient and relocate the border on the river. A combined force of cavalry and infantry crossed the line 11 May; the Mongolian border guards called for help and a squadron of Mongolian cavalry drove the invaders back. Three days later the Japanese re-appeared in greater strength, supported by aircraft and occupied the disputed area. A Soviet infantry unit some miles behind came up to the river, and over the next month each side fed more troops into the area and the line of contact moved to and fro over the disputed ground.

By early July, the Japanese had 40,000 troops, 135 tanks, and 235 aircraft engaged. The Soviets now appointed General (later Marshal) Georgi Zhukov to settle the matter, giving him 12,500 troops, 135 tanks, and 225 aircraft. He confined his efforts to merely repulsing the Japanese whenever they moved, but this merely spurred them to greater effort and they increased their forces to 80,000 troops, with tanks, armoured cars, and artillery, and 450 aircraft. Zhukov had 35 infantry divisions, 20 cavalry squadrons, 500 guns, 500 tanks, and 600 aircraft in the area by Aug 1939. On 20 Aug he launched an encircling attack, opening with an intense air strike followed by a two-hour artillery bombardment. By 31 Aug the entire Japanese 6th Field Army was surrounded and virtually destroyed, over 50,000 being killed or captured.

Kharkov series of battles 1941–43 between Soviet and German forces over possession of Kharkov, the fourth most important city in the USSR, about 480 km/300 mi east of Kiev. It was taken by the German 6th Army 24 Oct 1941 with little resistance. In May 1942 a Soviet 'Front' of 640,000 troops and 1,200 tanks set out to recapture the city, but two German armies attacked the flanks and cut off the spearhead, taking about 250,000 prisoners and destroying the remainder. It was re-taken by Soviet troops after their breakout from Stalingrad Feb 1943 but was then recaptured by the German Army Group South 15 March. It was finally liberated by Soviet troops under General Rodion Malinovsky Aug 1943, following the failure of the German offensive against ◊Kursk.

Khe Sanh US victory over Viet Minh forces during the Vietnam War Jan–April 1968. Khe Sanh was a US fire base, close to the Laos border about 96 km/60 mi northwest of Hue. In late 1967 it became obvious that there was a build-up of North Vietnam Army (NVA) forces in the area, so

Khe Sanh was heavily reinforced and massive air support organized to provide a barrier against any NVA advance. A total of about 6,000 US Marines, Rangers, and troops of the Army of the Republic of Vietnam (ARVN) held the base.

In mid-Jan about 20,000 NVA troops began to close around the fire base and the US force occupied a series of heights around the base to prevent the NVA coming too close. By 21 Jan the base was entirely surrounded and besieged, helicopters being the only means of supply. In order to reassure the South Vietnamese of US commitment, especially after NVA victories in the ◊Tet Offensive, General William C Westmoreland, the US theatre commander, decided to fight for Khe Sanh and provided heavy air support. Even so, a nearby smaller base held by Special Forces was overwhelmed by the NVA using light tanks, and heavy artillery bombardment of Khe Sanh drove the defenders underground. A succession of NVA attacks were repulsed, and finally, on 1 April, a US attack to relieve the besieged base began. The column forced its way through and the siege was lifted 7 April.

Kiev in World War II, German victory over Soviet forces and capture of Kiev, a Soviet city on the Dniepr river, about 800 km/500 mi southwest of Moscow. In July 1941 Hitler changed his mind about the strategy of Operation ◊Barbarossa, the German invasion of the USSR, and directed General Heinz Guderian to swing south and help Field Marshal Gerd von Rundstedt to clear the Ukraine, instead of going straight for Moscow. Following this order, Guderian's force swung around the east of Kiev and, meeting von Rundstedt's force, effectively cut off the Soviet South West Front which had been detailed to protect Kiev. The Soviet forces were quickly surrounded and the Germans proceeded to utterly destroy the contents of the pocket, taking 665,000 prisoners, 900 tanks, and 3,719 guns. Although this was a considerable victory, Guderian's diversion from Moscow meant that the winter descended before Moscow could be invested. Kiev remained in German hands until liberated by the 1st Ukrainian Front Nov 1943.

In my opinion the three main milestones on the road to victory were Alamein, Stalingrad and Kohima, and of these Kohima was almost the worst. It was a terrible battle, won entirely by the endurance and courage of regimental officers, NCOs and men.

Lt Gen Sir Brian Horrocks on the *Battle of Kohima*

Kohima one of the most savage battles of World War II as the Allied garrison at Kohima repulsed a wave of Japanese attacks with severe casualties. Kohima was a town in Manipur province, northeast India, about 95 km/60 mi north of ◊Imphal garrisoned by an Indian infantry brigade and a British infantry battalion, with two Indian infantry battalions holding a small defensive box about two miles away. It was attacked by the Japanese 31st division 5 April 1944, isolating the British at Imphal. The British 14th division broke through and relieved the Kohima force 14 April, but were unable to break through the Japanese positions blocking the route to Imphal until the end of May, by which time the Japanese were weakened by disease and starvation and began to retreat.

Kokoda Trail fighting between Japanese and Australian troops 1942. The Kokoda Trail is a track over the Owen Stanley Mountains of New Guinea, from Port Moresby to Buna. Little more than a muddy footpath in parts, the Kokoda Trail is generally agreed to have been the worst terrain and conditions under which any troops fought during the war. A Japanese force advanced south from Buna along it Aug 1942 and reached to within 32 km/20 mi of Port Moresby before being halted by Australian troops. They were held there and eventually withdrew on orders from Tokyo, pursued back along the trail by the Australians who carried the battle to the outskirts of Buna.

Kolombangara World War II naval engagement between US and Japanese forces July 1943. Four Japanese transports escorted by a cruiser and four destroyers were attempting to resupply the Japanese garrison on Kolombangara, one of the Solomon Islands, when they were intercepted by three US cruisers and nine destroyers. The US vessels opened fire, sinking the Japanese cruiser; in reply the Japanese destroyers launched a torpedo attack which crippled one US cruiser. About two hours later the two forces met once more and the Japanese torpedoes crippled the two remaining US cruisers and sank one destroyer. By this time the Japanese had landed their troops and supplies and so they withdrew.

Komandorski Islands World War II naval engagement between US and Japanese forces 26 March 1943. A Japanese naval force was escorting a troop convoy to reinforce the Aleutian Islands when it was attacked by a US squadron of two cruisers and four destroyers. One cruiser on each side was damaged by long-range gunfire, and the US destroyers then closed in with a torpedo strike. The Japanese commander, fearful of the torpedoes and also apprehensive of an air strike from nearby US airfields, withdrew without landing the reinforcements. He was subsequently relieved of his command.

Königgratz (also known as Sadowa) battle between Prussian and Austrian forces during the Austro-Prussian (Seven Weeks') war 3 July 1866. The battle took place around the village of Sadowa, about 16 km/10 mi northeast of Königgratz (now Sadova and Hradec Kralove, Czech Republic) and is consequently known by either name.

After the early part of the campaign, the Austrian army had retired behind the river Elbe. The Prussian 1st and Elbe armies attacked the Austrians at the bridge of Sadowa early in the morning. They were able to drive the Austrians back for a short distance but the Austrian artillery fire prevented any further progress. The arrival of the Prussian 2nd Army in the late morning threatened the Austrian right flank. To meet this threat the Austrians pulled their right wing back so that it faced north, but a bold advance by the Prussians, taking advantage of the cover provided by high corn and the smoke of the Austrian artillery fire, led to their infantry being able to get close to the Austrian lines and then charge home, breaking the line and capturing over 50 guns. The Austrians began to pull back and finally retreated from the field, leaving 40,000 dead and wounded. Prussian losses were about 10,000.

Kosovo Turkish victory over the combined forces of Serbia, Bosnia, and Albania 1398. The Serbian ruler was killed and the Serbian Empire came under Turkish rule. The Plain of Kosovo forms part of Serbia and extends southwest from the river Ibar, about 80 km/50 mi long and 24 km/15 mi wide. It is a focal point for any operations in Serbia. The Serbians had their revenge during the Balkan War of 1912 when they soundly defeated the Turks in several small engagements in this area, and in 1915 it was the scene of the last stand of the Serbian Army before being driven from the country (see below).

Kosovo Turkish victory over a combined Hungarian and Wallachian army 1448. The Turks were held off until the Wallachians deserted and turned on the Hungarians, whereupon the latter were forced to fight their way off the field and retire, leaving 17,000 killed and wounded.

Kosovo, retreat from in World War I, retreat of the Serbian Army before the advancing Austrians Nov 1915. The Austrian army's sweep in north and central Serbia, combined with the Bulgarian army's advance in eastern Serbia, trapped the Serbian army in the Kosovo plain, leaving only the option of retreating southwest to Scutari (now Shkoder, Albania). The suffering on the retreat was terrible, many thousands dying from starvation and cold due to the harsh winter conditions and mountainous route.

Kota Bharu in World War II, Japanese victory over Indian troops holding Kota Bharu, a seaport in north Malaya, 55 km/35 mi north of Singapore. Some 5,300 Japanese troops made a landing there 7 Dec 1941 and were met by the 8th Indian Brigade who held the airfield. The Indian troops put up the best defence they could but lost 320 dead and 538 wounded, while RAF aircraft severely damaged three troop transports. By the end of the following day the Japanese had secured their beachhead, had taken the airfield, and forced the remains of the Indian brigade to retire to the south.

Kovno World War I siege of a fortress town in Lithuania by German troops under Field Marshal Paul von Hindenburg as an off-shoot of his advance against ◊Warsaw. On 8 Aug 1915 German forces arrived outside the fortifications and after a short bombardment attempted to storm the place without success. This was repeated twice, after which heavy artillery was brought up and the town and fortifications were shelled for a week. An infantry attack then captured one of the smaller forts, making a gap in the defences, more reserves were thrust in and the town fell 17 Aug.

Kronstadt World War I Romanian defeat by Austro-German forces Oct 1916. Kronstadt (now Brasov, Romania) was an Austro-Hungarian border fortress town in a highly valuable strategic position covering several routes into Transylvania. Initial advances by Russia and Romania led to its abandonment by the Austrians. As General Erich von Falkenhayn's offensive caused the Romanian armies to retreat in Transylvania Oct 1916, Kronstadt was held by a Romanian force and was attacked by German columns converging upon the fortress. Driven out of the town, the Romanians made a desperate stand on the nearby heights, but were eventually driven off and the town was regained by Austria.

Kunersdorf Russian victory in the Seven Years' War over Frederick the Great 12 Aug 1759 about 20 km/12 mi west of what is now Swiebodzin, Poland. Frederick was attempting to save Dresden from the advancing Russian army, about 90,000-strong. Having somewhat less than half this number, Frederick decided to make an encircling attack from the flanks, but his plans were ruined by his troops getting lost in the forests and failing to coordinate their attacks. He was decisively defeated by the Russians, losing half his army and almost all his artillery, and Dresden fell three weeks later.

Kursk World War II tank battle between German and Soviet forces July 1943; the greatest tank battle in history and a turning point in the Eastern Front campaign. In spring 1943 the Soviet front line bulged out into the German front between ◊Kharkov and Orel. The Germans planned an offensive to pinch off this salient and flatten the front but the Soviets were forewarned by their intelligence service and planned to absorb the German thrust and then counterattack. They prepared for the assault with 20,000 guns, millions of mines, 3,300 tanks, 2,560 aircraft, and 1,337,000 troops; the Germans massed 10,000 guns, 2,380 tanks, 2,500 aircraft, and 900,000 troops.

The battle began 5 July in pouring rain. The northern half of the German force reached a point about 16 km/10 mi into the salient before being stopped; the southern thrust reached its climax 12 July when 700 German tanks battled with 850 Soviet tanks. But the Allies had landed in Sicily 10 July and Hitler demanded the withdrawal of troops from the USSR to reinforce Italy; on the same day the Soviets opened a massive offensive north of the Kursk salient. Hitler terminated the Kursk battle 17 July and the German forces in the area were left to extricate themselves best they could. (See also battle plan 5.)

Kut Al Imara Turkish siege Dec 1915–April 1916 of British-held city in Iraq, on the river Tigris. In World War I, Kut was part of the Turkish empire and was attacked by a British column under General Sir Charles Townshend Sept 1915. After successfully mounting a diversionary attack in the south, Townshend was able to assault the town from the north, and broke in and routed the Turkish garrison. He then advanced to Ctesiphon but was repulsed and fell back into Kut and fortified it.

The Turks attacked Kut without success, but then completely encircled the town and laid siege to it 25 Dec 1915. British relief columns attempted to reach Kut but were beaten back, and Townshend surrendered his force of about 3,000 British and 6,000 Indian troops 29 April 1916. Their treatment by the Turks was barbaric and two-thirds of the British and half the Indian troops died during a forced march to captivity of some 1,900 km/1,200 mi. The town was eventually recaptured by a fresh British force under General Sir Frederick Maude 23 Feb 1917, remaining in British hands for the rest of the war.

Kuwait see Operation ♢Desert Storm.

Kwajalien in World War II, fierce fighting as US troops captured this atoll in the Marshall Islands from the Japanese; it was taken by the US 4th Marine and US 7th Infantry divisions under General Holland M Smith 4 Feb 1944. The Japanese garrison of 8,000 troops fought so fanatically that there were no survivors.

La Bassée World War I battle between British and German forces Oct 1914. The British 2nd and 3rd Corps were between Aire and Béthune, about to swing west and secure Lille. Large German reinforcements had arrived in the area and while the 6th German Army advanced and captured Lille 12 Oct 1914, the 4th German Army arrived and struck at the exposed British flank near ◊Ypres. The British advanced toward Lille in the hope of recapturing it but were held, while the flank attack placed them in danger. Attempts were made in vain to straighten the British line, and a concentrated attack drove the British back until La Bassée and Neuve Chapelle were taken by the Germans. Another heavy German attack swept round Armentières, but was beaten back. By this time, (early Nov) the battle for Ypres had begun. Ypres took priority with both sides, so the battle around La Bassée and Armentières died out and the line stabilized.

Ladysmith, Siege of Boer operation during the South African War 2 Nov 1899–28 Feb 1900. When the war broke out, various detachments of troops in Natal were concentrated in Ladysmith under General Sir George White. He sent out two detachments to assault Boer positions in the district, both of which were defeated. The Boers then closed in and on 2 Nov the last train got out of the town, the telegraph was cut, and the town surrounded. Attempts to relieve the town by a column under General Sir Redvers Buller repeatedly failed. A sortie from the town by 600 troops 8 Dec captured a Boer gun, and the Boers made a determined attack on the town 6 Jan which was repulsed. Eventually, at his 12th attempt, Buller succeeded in reaching the town and ending the siege 28 Feb 1900. British casualties were 420, but there were also 2,000 troops in hospital with various diseases.

Langensalza Prussian victory in the Austro-Prussian War (Seven Weeks' War) 27 Jun 1866 32 km/20 mi northwest of Erfurt, Germany. A Hanoverian army, fighting on the Austrian side, was attacked by a Prussian army, both sides numbering about 12,000. The Hanoverians beat off the Prussians, inflicting losses of about 1,400 killed and 900 taken prisoner, while themselves losing about 1,400. However, the Prussian army was deployed in strength in this area and reinforcements quickly arrived and surrounded the Hanoverians, forcing their surrender.

Laon in the Napoleonic Wars, French defeat at the hands of a joint British-Prussian army 9–10 March 1814. Napoleon had taken up a position at Laon,

140 km/87 mi northeast of Paris and a major fortress, with about 45,000 troops; he was attacked by an Allied army of 85,000 under the Prussian Marshal Gebhard von Blücher. Napoleon's southern wing was driven in, but a counterattack by his Guards restored their line, and after moving troops from his other flank he was able to mount another attack and take the village of Arden before nightfall. The following morning Blücher directed his attack against the weakened northern wing, drove them in and forced them to retreat toward Reims. Napoleon ordered his southern force to advance against the Allies, a move which should have exposed him to certain destruction, but he was saved by Blücher calling off his pursuit of the northern element, missing the chance to take Napoleon in the flank. Holding off the Allies with limited counterattacks, Napoleon was able to retire in good order towards Soissons as night fell, having lost about 6,000 troops.

Laon in World War I, Allied victory over the Germans 1918. Laon was capital of the *département* of the Aisne and a major fortress. It was captured by the Germans 30 Aug 1914 and remained in their hands until late 1918. In Aug 1918 the French 3rd, 5th, 6th, and 10th armies, under General Charles Mangin with US and Italian units attached, advanced against the German forces holding the Laon district on a line from Soissons to Compiègne. Noyon was taken by 30 Aug and the Forest of Coucy was cleared 5 Sept, putting an end to the threat of the 'Paris Gun'. The Laffaux plateau took most of Sept to clear, and finally, after intense artillery bombardments, the French entered Laon 13 Oct 1918. By the end of the operation, the French had advanced 56 km/35 mi over extremely well-defended country and taken some 30,000 prisoners.

Le Cateau two battles between British and German forces in World War I near Le Cateau, a French town in the *département* of Nord, occupied by the Germans throughout the war.

The *first battle* took place 26–27 Aug 1914. The British 2nd Corps had reached Le Cateau during the retreat from Mons. Almost worn out by three days of constant marching and fighting, the corps spread out between Le Cateau and Caudry and began digging in. General Sir Horace Smith-Dorrien, commanding, decided to make a stand; General Sir John French, the commander in chief, was afraid of exposing his flank and was in favour of continuing the retreat, telling Smith-Dorrien that he could expect no support if he stayed. Four German corps fell upon the British line, greatly outnumbering it; the British guns were brought up into the open, among the infantry, so that their visible support would aid infantry morale. The Germans had some 660 guns to the British 246, and gradually obliterated the British batteries. Eventually the Germans forces found an exposed flank and began working around, so that the British were forced to retire. Thanks to the screening action of French cavalry and the rearguard of remaining British guns, most of the troops were able to withdraw. The Germans were sufficiently shaken to delay their pursuit until the next day, thus giving Smith-Dorrien's force a slight respite.

The *second battle* of Le Cateau took place 6–12 Oct 1918 across the same ground, this time as part of the general Allied advance after breaking the Hindenburg Line. Liberally supported by tanks and bombing aircraft, the British forces simply rolled the Germans up in front of them and it was less a battle than a pursuit action.

Leipzig (also known as the Battle of the Nations) in the Napoleonic Wars, French defeat by a combined Allied army 16–18 Oct 1813 near Leipzig, Germany. Napoleon Bonaparte had an army of about 185,000, mostly half-trained conscripts with a contingent of Saxons. He was opposed by 60,000 Prussians under Marshal Gebhard von Blücher and 160,000 Austrians and Russians under Prince Schwarzenburg. A further 150,000 Swedes under Prince Bernadotte were en route to the battlefield.

Napoleon had set up a defensive line on the Elbe but was forced back toward Leipzig by the threat of envelopment by the Austro-Russian force from the south, the Prussians from the northeast, and the Swedes from the north. Schwarzenburg attacked 16 Oct, but after a day of fighting the French held firm. There was indecisive skirmishing 17 Oct, but by 18 Oct all the Allied armies had arrived. The Saxons of Napoleon's army deserted him for the Allied side, abandoning their position and leaving a weakened front. Napoleon then began a fighting retreat and by the morning of 19 Oct about half his army had managed to escape on the road to Erfurt. The three-day battle cost the French some 60,000 killed and wounded and 11,000 prisoners. Allied losses were about 50,000.

Lemberg in World War I, fighting between Austrian and Russian forces 1914–15 at a town in Galicia (later Lvov, Poland, now in the Ukraine). A fortress town and military HQ, the Austrian army fell back to Lemberg when defeated by the Russians at Sokal Aug 1914. Three Austrian armies were advancing eastward to do battle; the 2nd was based on Lemberg, the 1st was about 15 km/9 mi south of Lemberg, and the 3rd was in southwest Poland. The Russians mustered four armies and when the 2nd Austrian advanced, the Russians, under General Alexei Brusilov and General Nikolai Russky, almost encircled it and completely defeated it, while effectively keeping the other two Austrian armies at bay. This defeat led what was left of the 2nd Army to retire and abandon Lemberg to the Russians.

In June 1915, German troops under General August von Mackensen advanced on Lemberg from the south but were repulsed. Keeping the defences diverted, this attack allowed other German forces to swing north and east and thus threaten the rear of the defended zone. After a fierce battle lasting several days the Russians finally evacuated the town and fortress 22 June 1915, and it remained in German hands thereafter.

Leningrad, Siege of in World War II, German siege of Soviet city as part of Operation ◊Barbarossa, the German invasion of the Soviet Union 1941. The German army reached Leningrad 1 Sept 1941 and were prepared to take it but Hitler ordered them to besiege the city in order to achieve a bloodless occupation. Within a week, all land communication was cut off and the city subjected to air and artillery bombardment. Before the year was out, starvation was causing 300 deaths a day although this was partially eased when Lake Ladoga froze so that a truck route could be established to bring in food over the ice. Meanwhile the population laboured in munitions factories, dug defences, and served in the front line.

The siege ended 27 Jan 1944 when advancing Soviet forces drove the Germans out of artillery range. It has been estimated that about 1 million inhabitants of the city died during the 900 days of the siege, either from disease, starvation, or enemy action. Leningrad was awarded the title of 'Hero City' for withstanding the siege.

Lens World War I battle May–Aug 1917 between Allied and German forces, the British attempting to drive the Germans from the area and also make them fear for the safety of Lille and draw troops away from the Ypres front. Lens, a French town in the *département* of Pas-de-Calais, a railway junction and engineering town in a mining area, was the scene of almost constant battle during the war, and the town itself was taken by the Germans Oct 1914. The damage to the town and surrounding area was so great that mining operations could not re-start until 1921.

Canadian troops made a determined attack on the town, gaining the suburbs, but the battle degenerated into house-to-house fighting and little real progress was made. The Germans launched several counterattacks but the Canadians held on to their gains. A final assault was planned, but by this time the enormous British losses in the battle of ◊Ypres meant that the reserves for another attack on Lens were not available, and the Canadians were withdrawn, leaving the Germans in possession. It was finally taken 3 Oct 1918 after German defeats elsewhere led them to abandon the town.

Lepanto Holy League naval victory over the Turks 7 Oct 1571 in the Adriatic Sea off Lepanto (now Navpaktos), Greece; the last major naval engagement to be fought by galleys. The Holy League fleet, with contingents from Spain, the Papal States, Venice, and Genoa, numbered 202 galleys, against an estimated 275-strong Turkish fleet; both fleets were divided into three squadrons. The Turkish centre squadron, after several hours of fighting, was completely defeated by a Spanish squadron. While this battle was in progress the Turkish right flank attempted to move round and take the Christian left flank in the rear, but the manoeuvre failed, and the Venetian squadron drove the Turks into a bay and there destroyed them. The third Christian squadron, the Genoese, decoyed the third Turkish squadron and by skilful manoeuvre managed to keep it occupied without allowing the two sides to close in to fighting range. Once the other two Christian squadrons had defeated their opponents, they turned and came to the aid of the Genoese. After a further battle, the Turkish commander managed to escape with only 20 galleys. The Turks are said to have lost 190 galleys captured, 30,000 killed, 10,000 prisoners, and 12,000 slaves who were freed by the Christians. The Christians lost 7,500 killed.

Leuctra Theban defeat of the Spartans July 371 BC, southwest of Thebes (now Thivai, Greece). The defeat finally ended the 30-year period of Spartan dominance over Greece and the Thebans assumed the hegemony over the Greek states.

The battle is also remembered for the innovative tactics introduced by Epaminondas, the Theban commander, which foreshadowed the famous *phalanx*, later developed so successfully by Philip of Macedon and then Alexander the Great. Until this time, hoplite battles had always been fought by the two sides confronting each other in two long lines; Epaminondas concentrated hoplites 50 deep at one point in the line in a wedge formation and used this local superiority to drive a hole through the Spartan line. As the other Spartans left their formation to come to the aid of their overwhelmed companions, the rest of the Thebans fell upon their disorganized ranks, killing over 1,000 of them.

Leuthen Prussian defeat of Austria during the Seven Years' War 5 Dec 1757 about 16 km/10 mi west of Breslau (now Wroclaw, Poland). The Austrian general, Count Leopold von Daun, returned to Austria in disgrace with only 37,000 of his 90,000 troops, and Austria was forced to yield Silesia to the Prussians.

The Austrians were advancing from Breslau and took position astride the Breslau-Neumarkt road in two lines about 10 km/6 mi long, with cavalry on each flank. Frederick the Great, marching east from Leipzig at the head of a Prussian force half the size of the Austrians, decided to attack. He offered a free discharge to any soldier who felt disinclined to fight, threatened the cavalry with demotion to garrison troops if they faltered, and threatened the infantry with the loss of their colours if they failed to attack vigorously.

Frederick made a feint against the Austrian right flank, drawing cavalry and other reinforcements from their left, and then fell on the left with the majority of his force, leaving only an advance guard to keep the Austrian right occupied. Before the Austrians could reorganize, their left flank was completely destroyed. As they fell back, the Austrian right moved across and began a desperate battle around the village of Leuthen. An Austrian cavalry charge threatened to drive in the Prussians, but Frederick had cavalry reserves in waiting which took the Austrians in flank and rear once they had galloped past. The Prussians renewed their attack and forced the Austrians back against the river Oder. The few bridges across the river could not cope with numbers of Austrian troops fleeing the battle and the

Prussians took 21,000 prisoners and 116 guns. The Austrians lost another 3,000 troops killed, while the Prussians lost only 1,140 killed and 5,200 wounded.

Lexington first battle of the American War of Independence 19 April 1775 18 km/11 mi northwest of Boston. Anticipating a rebellion, the British general Thomas Gage sent 800 troops to seize stores at Concord and arrest John Hancock and John Adams, two prominent American rebels. An advance party under Major Pitcairn encountered a party of about 50 Minutemen, American rebel militia troops, on Lexington Common. They refused to disperse when ordered to do so, and Pitcairn ordered his troops to open fire. Eight Minutemen were killed and the remainder retired. The British party turned back for Concord and was later ambushed; it was only saved by reinforcements sent out from Concord. The total losses in the two actions were 73 British killed and 174 wounded, 49 Americans killed and 39 wounded.

Leyden siege during the Netherlands War of Independence 26 May–3 Oct 1574 in which the Dutch defenders were besieged by Walloon and German troops. The Dutch force was little more than the town guard and a few mercenaries, while the besiegers numbered about 8,000 and had ample artillery. To save the city, the Prince of Orange ordered the sea gates to be opened, bursting the dykes and flooding large areas surrounding the place. Just as the inhabitants were reaching the end of their food stores, a Dutch fleet broke through at the end of Sept, by which time the rising water had driven the besiegers out of position after position. Aided by the sailors from the relief fleet, the townspeople were able to capture the remaining German redoubt, and the siege was broken 3 Oct.

Leyte Gulf the biggest naval battle in history, involving 216 US warships, 2 Australian vessels, and 64 Japanese warships 17–25 Oct 1944; the battle ended with the annihilation of the Japanese navy. When the Japanese realized the USA intended to invade the Philippines 1944, they prepared a complex naval trap at Leyte, an island on the east of the Philippine group. Their four aircraft carriers would be stationed near Leyte as bait for the US fleet while two powerful Japanese fleets would sail through the Philippine islands on different routes to execute a pincer movement when the Americans took the bait.

There were a number of separate actions as elements of these forces met and diverged, but the overall result was the destruction of the Japanese Navy; they lost some 500 aircraft, 3 battleships, 4 carriers, 10 cruisers, 11 destroyers, and 1 submarine. Of the surviving Japanese warships, few if any had escaped damage. In contrast, the Americans lost 3 light carriers, 2 destroyers, 1 destroyer escort, and 200 aircraft. While the naval battle was raging, General Walter Krueger landed the 6th US Army on Leyte island, which was secured 25 Dec 1944.

Liaoyang inconclusive battle between Japanese and Russian forces during the Russo-Japanese War 25 Aug–4 Sept 1904, in Manchuria, about 80 km/50 mi southwest of ◊Mukden (now Shenyang). The battle foreshadowed the tactics of World War I, with the use of massed armies, modern rifles and machine guns, barbed wire, and entrenchments.

The Russians, under General Alexei Kuropatkin, had prepared three strong defensive lines south of Liaoyang: the first was some 88 km/55 mi long, the second 24 km/15 mi long, and the third was a series of forts and strongpoints outside the town. The Russian strength was about 145,000; the Japanese force, under Marshal Iwao Oyama, was about 120,000 strong and divided into three armies, though the Russians believed it to be much stronger.

The 1st Japanese Army, under Count Tamesada Kuroki, attacked from the east, to make a junction with the 4th Army under Nodzu attacking from the south, while the 2nd Army under Oku attacked from the southeast. The attacks began 22 Aug: while Kuroki met with strong resistance, the other two Japanese armies made good progress, and Kuropatkin, believing them much stronger than they really were, was bluffed into retreating to his second line. The Japanese followed up and began their attack on this line 29 Aug. The struggle was at first inconclusive, until Kuroki pushed his army around to the northwest to try and cut the Russian line of retreat to Mukden 31 Aug. After severe fighting, Kuropatkin managed to frustrate this move, but then decided to abandon his position. He retreated to the north and the Japanese entered Liaoyang 4 Sept. The Russians cannot be said to have been defeated, as they retired in good order with their reserves uncommitted and lost only 16,000 troops to the heavy Japanese losses of 25,000. Had Kuropatkin kept his nerve, and had he known the actual Japanese strength, he could probably have defeated them.

Liège at the start of World War I, German siege and capture of the Belgian city of Liège, the principal town of the Liège province and a principal centre of Belgium's defence against German invasion. A notable centre of gunmaking, the city was heavily protected by a ring of forts and had a garrison of about 30,000 men under General Gérart Leman. The defences were attacked by a force of about 100,000 German troops 5 Aug 1914. When a simple infantry assault failed, artillery bombardment began and a small German force managed to penetrate the ring and occupy part of the city. On 12 Aug the 42 cm 'Big Bertha' howitzers were brought up and began reducing the forts one by one. The last forts fell 16 Aug 1914, General Leman was wounded and captured, and on the following day the city was occupied, remaining in German hands throughout the war.

Liegnitz Prussian defeat of the Austrians during the Seven Years' War 15 Aug 1760. Frederick the Great was close to Liegnitz (now Legnica, Poland) with a Prussian army about 30,000 strong. Fearing an attack by Count

Leopold von Daun, leading an Austrian force three times the size of the Prussians, Frederick retreated back to a better position near Parchwitz (now Prochowice). He unwittingly occupied an area which the Austrians had selected as their bivouac for the night, and an Austrian corps, ignorant of the Prussian presence, marched straight into the Prussian lines. It was immediately attacked, losing 4,000 casualties, 6,000 prisoners, and 82 guns.

Ligny French victory over the Prussians 16 June 1805 during Napoleon's 'Hundred Days', at Ligny, a Belgian village 14 km/9 mi northeast of Charleroi. It was Napoleon Bonaparte's final attempt to overcome the Prussian army before he went on to Waterloo to meet the British alone.

Marshal Gebhard von Blücher at the head of a force of 84,000 Prussians and 224 guns near Ligny was attacked by Napoleon with 75,000 French troops and 218 guns. Napoleon's orders to Marshal Michel Ney went astray, and the French met with considerable resistance, but as the Prussians tired Napoleon succeeded in launching a violent attack with a division of heavy cavalry and a reserve division of infantry. This forced the Prussians to retire with a loss of about 12,000, but they survived as an organized force and thus remained a threat to the French.

Linköping (also known as Stangebrö) Swedish victory over the Poles 1598, during the Swedish-Polish wars. Sigismund III, king of Poland, succeeded his father as king of Sweden 1592 and attempted to establish a Catholic ascendancy in Sweden, a policy vigorously opposed by the Lutheran Swedes who elected his uncle Charles as regent of Sweden in place of Sigismund's nominee 1595. When Sigismund eventually set out for Sweden 1598, his army was ambushed and totally destroyed by the Swedes. Charles became King Charles IX of Sweden 1599 and the Polish hold over Sweden was broken.

Lissa during the Austro-Prussian War, Austrian naval victory over the Italians, who were allied to Prussia, 20 July 1866 near the island of Lissa, in the Adriatic about 65 km/40 mi southwest of Split, Yugoslavia. An Italian fleet arrived off Lissa 18 July, intending to capture the island, but found it well provided with coast defence artillery. While holding off the Italians, the garrison commander telegraphed Rear-Admiral Wilhelm von Tegethoff, the Austrian commander in chief, and on the morning of 20 July the Austrian fleet reached Lissa. The Italian fleet had 29 ironclads with 641 rifled guns while the Austrians had 26 ironclad ships and 532 smooth-bore guns, which did not have the range of the superior rifled Italian guns, formed into three arrow-heads. Had the Italians wished, they could have used the advantage of the greater range of their rifled guns to fire upon the Austrians from a distance and hold them off, but instead they chose to engage at close quarters, which suited the Austrians far better.

Tegethoff turned his fleet toward the Italians and signalled to 'Charge the enemy ironclads and sink them!' At that moment the Italian commander, the

Count of Persano, decided to change his flag to another ship; the two vessels stopped while the Admiral was ferried across, leaving a gap in the Italian line through which the Austrian fleet passed, turned about, and began attacking both ends of the Italian line. The battle became ship-to-ship combat, and Tegethoff, seeing the Italian ironclad *Re d'Italia* in difficulties with its steering, rammed and sank it. An Italian gunboat was sunk by gunfire, after which the Italian fleet turned about and ran for home, leaving the Austrians controlling the Adriatic. The ramming incident made naval strategists aware of the possibilities of the ram, and for the next 20 years ramming was the principal naval tactic, even though several other attempts to ram during the battle had failed.

Lódz in World War I, German capture Dec 1914 of Russian-held industrial town in central Poland, 120 km/75 mi southwest of Warsaw. During Field Marshal Paul von Hindenburg's attack on Warsaw Oct–Dec 1914, a German force under General August von Mackensen also attacked Lódz but were held off by fierce Russian resistance. However, the German forces passed on both sides of the town for some distance, making the town a prominent salient. The Russians realised Lódz would be difficult to defend if the German columns moved together on the town and so it was evacuated without loss 5 Dec 1914. The Germans continued to bombard it for most of the following day before they realised the Russians had left. It remained in German hands for the rest of the war.

Loigny-Poupry during the Franco-Prussian War, Prussian victory over the French 2 Dec 1870 at Loigny, 40 km/25 mi east of Chartres. After the Prussians besieged Paris, French military effort relied upon 'Citizen's Armies' raised in the provinces. The Army of the Loire, based on Orléans, set out toward Paris in the hope of meeting a sortie from the besieged city. A section of this army under General Antoine Chanzy attacked a Bavarian force near Loigny, taking them by surprise and driving them out of the village. Two battalions of Prussian troops were rushed up and halted the French attack, while Prussian cavalry swung round the French flank, forcing Chanzy's force to retire.

A new French division under General Paytavin arrived to threaten the Prussian left flank at the village of Poupry and a fresh battle broke out. Fighting raged for the rest of the day before the Prussians finally beat off the French, who lost about 6,500 casualties and 2,500 prisoners. The French commander, General Claude d'Aurelle de Paladines, ordered a retreat to Orléans, but the Prussian commander, Prince Frederick Charles, launched an attack on Orléans. The Army of the Loire was decimated and the survivors merged into other units.

Loos World War I offensive by British and French forces against the Germans Sept 1915 with the aim of recovering the mining district around the towns of Loos and Lens and, if possible, capturing Lille. At the same time as the French offensive in Champagne, it was hoped to divert German forces from there to aid the French.

The German positions were well-fortified, with large numbers of steel and concrete pillboxes and shelters. The British forces included numbers of battalions of the 'Kitchener armies', being used for the first time. This was the first time the British had used gas, but unfortunately the wind shifted and the gas was blown back into the British lines, although the cylinders were rapidly shut off and little damage was done. The attack managed to drive a salient some way into the German lines, but the reserves were badly organized and before they could be brought up a German counterattack drove the British back to their start line. A second attack, south of the Hohernzollern redoubt, managed to gain some 3,200 km/3,500 yds and this was retained. About 250,000 British and a similar number of French troops were engaged in the battle; British losses were about 60,000, among them three generals. French casualties are not known since they were included with other actions at the same time, but they were probably heavier than the British.

Lucknow, Siege of investment of the British garrison and civilians at Lucknow, India, 2 July–16 Nov 1857 during the Indian Mutiny. Sir Henry Lawrence, administrator of the Punjab, foresaw the Mutiny and had moved all British civilians and the small British garrison of about 300 British soldiers and 700 loyal Indian troops into the Residency. The siege began 2 July and two days later Lawrence was mortally wounded by a shell splinter. His place in command was taken by Lt-Col John Inglis who managed to defend the Residency in spite of shortages of food, medical supplies, and ammunition.

A column led by General Henry Havelock managed to fight its way through the rebel lines and enter the Residency 25 Sept but the combined force of the garrison and the relief column was not strong enough to fight its way out again, so the siege continued with even more people compressed into the Residency. The relief column had ample ammunition but little food, making conditions worse. However, the greater strength of British forces inside the Residency allowed sorties to be made to wreck rebel guns, capture houses, and improve the defences.

After a further 53 days a new column of some 5,000 troops led by General Sir Colin Campbell appeared outside the city but he was uncertain of how best to reach the Residency. Thomas Kavanagh, a civil servant, slipped through the rebel lines in disguise to contact Campbell and guide his force in the attack, for which he became the first civilian to be awarded the Victoria Cross. Campbell fought through to the Residency but was not strong enough to subdue the entire city, so he rescued the besieged force and civilians, escorted them out to safety, and then left the city to the rebels. It was finally cleared and captured March 1858.

Lutsk in World War I, fighting between Austrian and Russian forces 1914–17. Lutsk (now Luck, Poland) was a Russian town, one of three Russian fortresses known as the 'Volhyn Triangle'. Captured by the Austrians 31 Aug 1914 after a battle with retreating Russians, the Russians mounted a counteroffensive on the Styr river line Sept 1914, and were able to retake Lutsk 24 Sept. However, lack of supplies and ammunition led them to evacuate it again 28 Sept and it remained in Austrian hands until the ◁Brusilov offensive April 1916. As part of the general Russian gains in this campaign, Lutsk was recaptured 7 June 1916, remaining in Russian hands until they retired from the war 1917.

Lützen in the Thirty Years' War, Swedish victory 16 Nov 1632 over an Imperial army under Albrecht von Wallenstein 45 km/28 mi west of Leipzig, Germany. The Swedish army, about 19,000 troops under King Gustavus Adolphus, was marching from Naumburg when Gustavus heard that Wallenstein, at the head of a similar-sized force, had sent some of his troops off on a foraging expedition. Gustavus turned and advanced on Wallenstein, hoping to seize the opportunity to fall upon a weakened enemy.

Wallenstein's army was drawn up ready for battle. The Swedish cavalry, on the flanks of Gustavus' line, quickly defeated their opposite numbers; meanwhile the infantry, in the centre of the lines, had a long and bitter struggle, in which Gustavus Adolphus was killed, and the Imperial forces began to have some success. Prince Bernhard took command of the Swedes, rallied them, and regained the lost ground and guns. Wallenstein's cavalry then reappeared and battle was joined again; in the subsequent battle the cavalry's commander was killed. Swedish reserves were now thrown in and the Imperial forces were finally defeated. At nightfall, a thick fog descended and Wallenstein was able to disengage using the fog as cover. Although he managed to withdraw his troops from the field, he had to abandon his artillery.

Lützen in the Napoleonic Wars, French victory over an Allied force of Prussian and Russian troops 2 May 1813. Napoleon Bonaparte was moving toward the Elbe with about 200,000 troops and directed his advanced guard to Lützen. The Allied commander, Count Wittgenstein, decided to attack the advance guard with a small detachment, while directing the major part of his army against Napoleon's right and rear. The attack on the head of the French column began about 9 a.m., and Napoleon, hearing Wittgenstein's artillery, immediately realised what was intended. He took charge of his force, detailed off a reserve and withdrew it, leaving the rest to hold off the Allies. Waiting until both sides in the ensuing battle had fought themselves to a standstill, he then sent in a grand battery of 100 guns to blow a hole in the Allied line with case shot, through which he then threw his reserve force. This so disrupted the Allies that during the night their two kings ordered a retirement. The Allies lost about 20,000 troops, the French about half that number.

Madrid in the Spanish Civil War, Nationalist victory 31 Mar 1936 over Republican forces after a prolonged siege. Madrid, held by Republican troops under General Jose Miaja, was attacked Nov 1936 by a Nationalist force under General Emilio Mola, who became famous for his claim that while he had four columns of troops outside the city, there was a 'fifth column' of sympathisers inside Madrid to assist him.

By 21 Nov, the Nationalists had advanced and taken the University City suburb, but after this trench lines were dug and stalemate ensued. The Republicans mounted a counterattack July 1937, but were driven back at a cost of 15,000 casualties. The siege remained in place for the next two years while the Civil War continued elsewhere in Spain, and eventually the various Republican factions began quarrelling among themselves. The Nationalist leader, General Francisco Franco, launched a sudden offensive against Madrid 26 March 1939; resistance collapsed and the city was occupied 31 March, ending the Civil War.

Mafeking, Siege of during the South African War, unsuccessful Boer siege of British-held town Oct 1899–May 1900. The British garrison, about 750 soldiers under Col Robert Baden-Powell, 1,700 townspeople, and about 7,000 Africans, was besieged by a 10,000-strong Boer force under General Piet Cronje. The siege was not pressed very hard, the town was never completely invested, and the only serious attack the Boers attempted failed. Inside the town, Baden-Powell organized the population to keep life proceeding more or less as normal and maintain morale: there were tea-parties, concerts, and polo matches. Eventually a British column led by Col Herbert Plumer and Col Mahon arrived, dispersed the Boers, and relieved the town 17 May 1900. The announcement of the town's relief led to wild scenes of celebration in London and across Britain, far out of proportion to the actual strategic value of the operation, and even led to the coining of a new verb – 'to maffick', meaning to celebrate intemperately.

Magdala British victory 13 April 1868 during the Abyssinian War at Magdala, a fortress on a mountain top (now known as Amba Maryam, Ethiopia) about 190 km/120 mi southeast of Gondar. The Abyssinian Emperor Theodore imprisoned the British consul and other foreign nationals here Jan 1864 and despite persistent requests refused to release them. An expedition sent from Britain under General Sir Robert Napier arrived Jan 1868 with 13,000 British and Indian troops and 36,000 pack animals. Napier was an engineer and was well aware of the need for careful organization; he divided his army into two parts, with a striking force of 5,000 troops and the remainder forming a supply line. After a brisk battle with Theodore's outposts, Napier arrived below the fortress and Theodore released the prisoners but refused to surrender.

The following day, Napier marched up the mountain track with his troops to assault the stronghold. The British only discovered that the sappers had forgotten the gunpowder and scaling ladders when they reached the fort itself, so the fortifications had to be breached by a drummer boy scrambling up the wall and helping his companions up. Nonetheless, the fort was captured with the loss of only 2 dead and 13 wounded and Theodore shot himself. Napier razed the fort, marched back to the coast, and sailed home. On his return to Britain, he was thanked by parliament and ennobled as Baron Napier of Magdala.

Magdeburg during the Thirty Years' War, Imperial victory over the Swedes 20 May 1631 at Magdeburg, Germany. The Swedes besieged and captured Magdeburg 1629. They held the city with a small garrison until an Imperial force under Count Tilly arrived early 1631 and placed it under siege. The garrison held out for five months in the hope of being relieved until May when Tilly heard that a Swedish army under King Gustavus Adolphus was approaching, forcing him to decide between storming the place or giving up the siege. He elected to storm the city and took it in two hours of hard fighting 20 May 1631. His mixed force of Croatian and Walloon mercenaries then sacked the city and massacred most of the population. Magdeburg itself was set on fire, leaving only the cathedral standing.

Magenta Austrian defeat 4 June 1859 at the hands of a mixed French and Sardinian force during the War of Italian Independence at Magenta, about 55 km/35 mi west of Milan. The Sardinians, holding a position north of Alessandria, had already staved off two attacks by the Austrians who had drawn back and taken up a line behind the Ticino river.

On the arrival of their French allies, the Sardinians advanced in a frontal attack, assisted by the French. The battle continued for some time without either side gaining any advantage until Marshal Marie MacMahon led his French troops across the Ticino, to the north of the battle, and then swept down onto the Austrian flank. The flank immediately collapsed and the battle was over before the Sardinians could advance in support. The Austrians lost about 6,500 troops, the French and Sardinians about 4,500.

Magersfontein Boer victory over the British 11 Dec 1899 during the South African War, at a crossing of the Modder river some 65 km/40 mi south of Kimberley, South Africa. A British column was dispatched under General Paul Methuen to relieve the British force which was besieged at Kimberley. The relief column arrived at Magersfontein and noticed that a hill which commanded their route was held by the Boers. The British would have to remove this obstacle before they could continue – an artillery bombardment on the top of the hill was planned, to be followed by a dawn attack. However, the Boers had entrenched at the bottom of the hill, and as the assaulting troops moved forward in close order during the night to prepare for their attack, they came under fire from the Boers, killing the brigade commander and over 50 officers and 700 troops. The assault troops fell back in disorder, and waited throughout the day for the Boers to retire. They did not, and Methuen withdrew his force, having lost over 1,000 troops and 68 officers. Boer losses were estimated at 70 killed and 250 wounded. The Boer victory at Magersfontein combined with the British defeats at ◊Colenso and Stormberg to make this week known as 'Black Week'.

Maida in the Napoleonic Wars, defeat of about 6,500 French under Marshal Jean Reynier by a 5,000-strong British force under General Sir John Stuart, 3 July 1806, near Maida in the toe of Italy, about 20 km/12 mi west of Catanzaro. In one of the backwaters of the Napoleonic Wars, a British force was in Italy supporting the dispossessed royal families of Spain and Sicily and attempting to break the French military control of the Kingdom of Sicily. The British were moving west intending to embark for Sicily when the French forces moved to block their way.

This battle shows an interesting contrast between tactical systems: while the British deployed in line, the French attacked in a column, allowing the full strength of the British to fire volleys into the French mass, while only the first two ranks of the French could respond. After a few of these devastating volleys, the British mounted a bayonet charge and the French broke and ran.

Majuba British defeat by the Boers during the First South African War 27 Feb 1881 at Majuba Hill in Natal, about 16 km/10 mi south of Volksrust. Sir George Colley was appointed British Governor of Natal shortly before the first Boer rising; when the Boer revolt broke out he set about organizing a column to invade the Transvaal. He assembled about 1,000 troops from various regiments, including a small naval detachment, and set out from Pietermaritzburg. His attempt to attack a Boer position at Laing's Nek was a failure, and Colley had to await reinforcements before advancing further. While he was waiting, the Boers began a flanking movement to cut his supply route, so he took a detachment of infantry back down the route to keep it clear but lost half his troops in an ambush.

Colley decided to establish himself on Majuba Hill, which he saw as the key to the situation: the Boers would have to either attack and be defeated, or retire once he had secured this dominant position. He occupied the hilltop with 490 soldiers and 64 sailors after a night march. The following day was Sunday, and the Boers became angry at the British carrying on a war on the Lord's day. They sent about 180 marksmen to climb the hill while covering fire from another 1,000 troops kept the British pinned down. The marksmen gained the summit and within an hour had completely defeated the British force, killing 93 troops, wounding 133, and taking 58 prisoner; Colley was among the dead. The Boers lost one dead and five wounded.

Malaga during the War of the Spanish Succession, British naval victory over the French 24 Aug 1704 off the Spanish coast near Malaga. The French fleet of 53 ships commanded by Admiral the Comte de Tourville was sailing south to reinforce a Spanish fleet attempting to recapture Gibraltar. A British fleet of 45 ships under Admiral Sir George Rooke, who had captured Gibraltar about a month before, intercepted them and a savage battle ensued. Both sides suffered casualties, but neither side lost any ships, and the battle ended in a tactical draw. However, the battle amounted to a strategic victory for the British since they prevented the meeting of the two fleets and the possible reinforcement which might have wrested Gibraltar from British hands.

Maloyaroslavets during Napoleon Bonaparte's retreat from Moscow, inconclusive battle of great ferocity between French and Russian forces 24 Oct 1812 at Maloyaroslavets, about 95 km/60 mi southwest of Moscow. Although the battle was tactically a victory for Napoleon, the Russians had the better of it strategically since it multiplied the French problems in their retreat.

Napoleon had left Moscow 19 Oct and was aiming for Kaluga, about 160 km/100 mi to the southwest. A Russian patrol reported French troops at Forminskoe, about 65 km/40 mi from Moscow, and Marshal Kutuzov, thinking this to be a foraging party, sent General Docturov with about 23,000 troops and 84 guns to deal with it. After he had departed, another patrol alerted him to the fact this it was actually Napoleon's main force, and Docturov decided to take up a blocking position at Maloyaroslavets. By the time he arrived the French had secured the town bridges and Docturov attacked. Fierce fighting continued all day, the town changing hands five times, before some 10,000 Russian reinforcements arrived and enabled Docturov to take the town, though he was unable to capture the bridges. The French threw in reinforcements of their own and drove the Russians out. As night fell, Kutuzov arrived and, deciding that the odds were too great, ordered his troops to fall back on Kaluga. The French realised that their projected route would bring them up against a strongly reinforced Russian force, so Napoleon changed his route, going northwest through Smolensk, a far more difficult route which he had hoped to avoid.

Malplaquet during the War of the Spanish Succession, Imperial victory over the French 11 Sept 1709 at Malplaquet, a French village about 16 km/10 mi south of Mons. The Imperial army, under the joint command of the Duke of Marlborough and Prince Eugène of Savoy, had been camped for two days opposite the French Army, under Marshal Claude de Villars, awaiting orders from the Dutch envoys to attack.

Permission eventually arrived and the battle began 11 Sept at 9 a.m. with an attack by the Prussian and Austrian contingents of the Imperial army. This attack was repulsed and Marlborough sent three English battalions into the battle; the additional pressure of these fresh forces forced the French back. The Royal Irish Brigade then charged the Irish contingent of the French army and routed them, after which the battle spread to involve all units. The Prince of Orange, on the left of the Imperial forces, was driven back by the French. Eugène and Marlborough retaliated with a powerful assault on the French centre and right flank, and after a prolonged struggle the French were forced back and the Imperial forces began advancing. However, the losses on the Imperial side were so great and the troops so fatigued, that they were unable to pursue the French as they retreated. No other battle during this war approached Malplaquet for ferocity and losses; the Imperial force lost over 20,000 troops and the French 12,000, both having begun with about 90,000 troops.

It was the only rash thing the Duke of Marlborough was ever guilty of; and it was generally believed that he was pressed to it by Prince Eugène...

General Keane on the *Battle of Malplaquet* in his *Memoirs*

Maraçesti World War I defeat of Austro-German force by combined Russian and Romanian forces Aug 1917; the greatest battle fought by the Romanian army during the war. After defeating the Russians in Galicia 1916, General August von Mackensen attacked the Russo-Romanian defences on the river Sereth with 12 divisions, heading toward Maraçesti, an important railway junction. He was stopped close to the town by a strong Russo-Romanian force and the battle continued for some days, Eventually, the Russian element of the defences, under the influence of Bolshevik agitators, broke and ran. By this time, though, Romanian reinforcements were arriving and in spite of heavy fighting defeated Mackensen's force and prevented him taking Moldavia.

Marathon famous Greek victory at the start of the Persian Wars Sept 490 BC over the Persian king Darius' invasion force, on the Plain of Marathon about 40 km/25 mi northeast of Athens. The Greeks, a combined force of about 10,000 Athenians under Miltiades supplemented by allied Plataeans, were encamped overlooking the plain, about a mile away from the Persian force which was some five to six times their strength. Taking advantage of the fact that the Persians had their backs to the sea, the Greek strengthened their wings and attacked. The Persians held off the Greek attack on their centre, but Miltiades then wheeled round the Greek wings, crushing the Persian flanks and putting pressure on their centre. The Persians were driven back into the sea and although most managed to re-embark into their ships, about 6,000 lay dead on the field, while Greek losses were under 200.

The victory at Marathon was an enormous boost to Greek morale which was to be of great value when the Persians mounted a much more threatening invasion 10 years later. The battle has been immortalised by the race named after it in memory of the runner, Pheidippides, who reputedly ran to Sparta from Athens to appeal for aid before the battle. He covered the distance of 200 km/125 mi in a day but the Spartans failed to provide any assistance. A more recent legend, that he ran from Athens to Marathon (a distance of about 40 km/25 mi) to fight in the battle, then ran back with the news of the victory before dropping dead, actually gives rise to the name of the modern race but is considered spurious by scholars.

Marengo during the Napoleonic Wars, French victory over the Austrians 14 June 1800 at Marengo, a village in northern Italy 8 km/5 mi east of Alessandria; one of Napoleon Bonaparte's greatest victories, which resulted in the Austrians ceding northern Italy to France. The Austrian army in Italy was about 100,000 strong but was divided, with only a small portion watching for a French advance. Napoleon assembled an army of about 40,000 troops in Switzerland and marched secretly across the St Bernard Pass. He entered Milan 2 June, cutting the Austrian supply and communication route. He then tried to find the main Austrian army and sent off detachments in several likely directions; eventually the Austrians found him when a major force of about 32,000 advanced from Alessandria toward Marengo where the main body of the French army, about 28,000 strong, was camped.

The French were outnumbered and were falling back when Napoleon arrived. He organized the retreat, falling back slowly and in good order, and the Austrians felt that the battle was as good as won. However, Napoleon had sent for reinforcements and at about 3 p.m. General Louis Desaix de Veygoux arrived with a fresh division of troops to attack on one flank, while cavalry attacked on the other and Napoleon massed what artillery he had in the centre to hold the Austrian advance. The Austrian force broke and fled the field, losing about 9,000 troops; French losses were about 4,000, including General Desaix.

Mareth Line German defensive line in North Africa running from the sea close to Mareth to the Matmata Hills, about 50 km/30 mi away. It followed the Wadi Zigzau, a dried river bed which made an excellent defence against tanks. Field Marshal Erwin Rommel retired to this line March 1943, and frontal attacks by the British had no effect on him. He was finally manoeuvred out of the position by a force of New Zealand troops which made a wide flanking movement around the Matmata Hills accompanied by the British 1st Armoured Division. A hastily organized blocking operation by 21 Panzer Division managed to hold off the threat for long enough to allow Rommel and the rest of his forces to retire from the line into Tunisia.

Marignano during the Italian Wars, French victory over the Swiss 13–14 Sept 1515 at Marignano, a village close to the Swiss-Italian border. A Swiss force of about 22,000 fell on the French camp, which held some 32,000 troops, forced the defensive lines, and fought all day without reaching any decisive result. The armies disengaged at nightfall and fell to again next morning, with the Swiss gradually gaining the upper hand. The situation was reversed by the arrival of a Venetian force to assist the French and the Swiss were forced to withdraw, having lost over 12,000 troops. The French lost about 6,000 troops but gained the Duchy of Milan.

Market Garden in World War II, unsuccessful operation by British and US forces to cross the Meuse, Waal, and Neder-Rijn rivers in Holland Sept 1944. British airborne forces were to capture vital bridges at ◊Arnhem to open the way for an armoured thrust from the south. When the airborne operation failed, the armoured force was unable to reach Arnhem and the whole operation collapsed.

Marne in World War I, two unsuccessful German offensives in northern France. In the First Battle Sept 1914, the German advance was halted by French and British forces under the overall command of Joseph Joffre; in the Second Battle July–Aug 1918, the German advance was defeated by British, French, and US troops under the French general Henri Pétain, and German morale crumbled.

First Battle of the Marne 6–9 Sept 1914: three German armies were swinging round from Belgium to sweep through France and encircle Paris in accordance with the Sohlieffen Plan. After some initial uncertainty, Marshal Joffre realised what the German strategy was and ordered the French 1st and 2nd Armies to hold the Germans around Verdun and Nancy. Meanwhile, he formed two new armies, the 6th and 9th, in preparation for a counterattack and drew back his left flank to entice the Germans further south. The French 6th Army under General Joseph Galliéni moved against the exposed flank of General Alexander von Kluck's 1st German Army which halted its southward drive and turned aside to deal with Galliéni. This opened a 48 km/30 mi gap between the 1st German Army and the 2nd Army under Field Marshal Karl von Bülow. Joffre now threw his counterattack force against von Bülow who retired, forcing von Kluck to retire in order to avoid being totally surrounded, and the German advance was halted and turned back. Although tactically inconclusive, the first battle of the Marne was a strategic victory for the Allies.

Second Battle of the Marne 15 July–4 Aug 1918: this battle formed the final thrust of the ◊German Spring Offensive of 1918. General Erich Ludendorff threw 35 divisions across the Marne, planning to encircle Reims. The French were prepared for the attack, with four armies under good generals, together with a strong US force, and although the Germans initially gained ground they were eventually halted and turned back. The Allied counterattack, beginning 18 July, is sometimes referred to as the *Third Battle* of the Marne and it forced the Germans back to a line running from Reims to Soissons.

Masurian Lakes in World War I, two battles between German and Russian forces between the Masurian Lakes (now the Mazowsze region of Poland) and Königsberg, East Prussia (now Kaliningrad, Russia).

First Battle 5–15 Sept 1914: following the German victory over the Russian general Paul Rennenkampf at the battle of ◊Tannenberg, the German field marshal Paul von Hindenburg attempted to catch and destroy the retreating Russians. Rennenkampf ordered a counterattack to hold the Germans while the remainder of the army made good its escape, avoiding encirclement by the Germans.

Second Battle Feb 1915: the Russians had assembled about 120,000 troops in four corps with the intention of advancing into East Prussia, but Hindenburg brought up reserves until he had a force of over 300,000 troops, divided into two army fronts. As soon as the Russians realised the size of the opposition, they began to withdraw, but the Germans moved quickly and on 7 Feb drove the Russians out of Johannisberg (now Pisz, Poland) and advanced north to capture Lyck (now Elk) and then make a sweeping movement to encircle the Russians. This move was strongly resisted by the Russians, particularly Siberian units, and they were able to fall back behind their defensive lines on the river Niemen, inflicting severe losses on the Germans as they went. On the northern part of the front the Germans were more successful, driving the Russians out of Tilsit (Sovetsk), Pilkallen (Dobrovolsk) and Gumbinnen (Gusev), forcing them to retreat towards Kovna (Kaunas). This rapid retreat exposed the Russian flank, which was promptly attacked by the Germans, and the only thing which saved the Russians from utter destruction was the terrain – swamps and marshes in which organized fighting was impossible and through which small groups of Russians soldiers were able to make their escape. The German offensive ended with their forces established on a line within the Russian frontier.

Messines in World War I, British attack 7–15 June 1917 on German-held Belgian village and ridge in West Flanders, 9.5 km/6 mi south of Ypres. The village was occupied by the Germans Nov 1914, enabling them to hold a dominant position overlooking the British lines. A significant factor in the battle was the unprecedented scale of mining operations by the British; some 20 mines were excavated and charged with 600 tons of explosive, although one was discovered by the Germans before the battle and neutralized. Another innovation in this battle was the use of supply tanks to carry forward ammunition for the infantry and both ammunition and fuel for the 76 tanks which were deployed in the battle itself.

A full-scale battle was sparked by an attempt by the British 2nd Army, under General Hubert Plumer, to take the ridge, held by the 4th German Army under General Sixt von Arnim. The battle began with an exceptionally heavy artillery bombardment, lasting from 28 May to 7 June, which did considerable damage to the German defences. The mines were detonated at 3.10 a.m. 7 June, immediately followed by a joint infantry and tank assault preceded by a creeping barrage. By 10 a.m. the entire German front line was in British hands, and the second line had been secured by 8 p.m. A German counterattack was thrown back and the position was secured. Messines remained in British hands until the ◊German Spring Offensive 1918, but was re-taken, again by General Plumer, Sept 1918.

Metaurus in the Second Punic War, Roman victory over the Carthaginians 207 BC on the Metaurus river (now Metauro) in Italy, about 65 km/40 mi west of Ancona. This proved to be the decisive battle of the war, since it wrecked Hannibal's chances of overthrowing Rome and gave the Romans supremacy over Carthage.

A 40,000-strong Carthaginian army under Hasdrubal was marching inland to reinforce Hannibal. The relief force was attempting to find a ford to cross the river at dawn when they were surprised by a Roman army of about 50,000 troops. The Romans attacked immediately; Hasdrubal's force began to press the Roman right wing back. The Roman commander on the right wing, Nero, was unable to come to grips with the enemy due to the ground in front of his position. He abandoned the right wing, marched his force round the rear of the Roman line, and reinforced the left wing which then totally destroyed the Carthaginian force; Hasdrubal was among the Carthaginians slain.

Metz Prussian victory over the French during the Franco-Prussian War Aug–Oct 1870. Metz was a major fortress in Lorraine, about 280 km/175 mi east of Paris, guarding the approaches from southern Germany. After the battle of ◊Vionville-Mars la Tour, General François Bazaine fell back on Metz and took up a strong position on a ridge to the west of the city. The Prussian army attacked and defeated the French here at the battle of ◊Gravelotte 18 Aug 1870 and Bazaine pulled the remains of his army back into the fortress.

The Prussians besieged Metz the following day. Bazaine attempted to make a sortie from the fortress in order to join up with the rest of the French Army but was easily driven back by the Prussians. He made another half-hearted attempt to break out to the east 7 Oct, which also failed, and on 27 Oct the fortress surrendered, complete with the entire 173,000-strong French Army of the Rhine, who became prisoners of war. Metz, together with the *département* of Lorraine, was ceded to the Prussians as part of the peace settlement when the war ended.

Meuse-Argonne campaign in World War I, US-French offensive against the Germans Sept–Nov 1918. The US 1st Army attacked from the west side of the river Meuse 26 Sept 1918 with complete success, capturing Varennes and Montfaucon, while the French 4th Army attacked in Champagne. The attack was renewed 4 Oct, eventually breaching the Kreimhilde Line and capturing Grandpré. By 1 Nov the US troops had advanced some 6 km/4 mi, taking Buzancy 2 Nov, and the Germans were in rapid retreat. By 7 Nov the Americans held the left bank of the Meuse opposite Sedan, and the bridge at Stenay was taken 10 Nov.

Although the Allied forces did not advance quickly, they achieved vital strategic results; the Montmédy-Sedan and Metz-Mézières railway lines were rendered useless to the Germans, depriving them of a valuable lifeline, and the German left wing was secured while the British advance in Flanders rolled back the right. However, the US forces paid a heavy price for their gains: some 26,227 dead and 96,788 wounded.

Meuse in World War I, battles between French and German forces Aug 1914. After the German invasion of Belgium and northern France, the French 4th Army was ordered to hold the left bank of the river Meuse and maintain contact with the French 5th Army, then in headlong retreat from Charleroi. However, there was a 48 km/30 mi gap between the two armies, into which the 2nd and 3rd German Armies advanced. Troops of the German 4th Army bridged the river Meuse at Remilly, Torcy, and Donchery, establishing a large bridgehead south of Sedan. This was extended by taking other bridges and the Germans advanced along the whole Meuse front.

The 4th German Army was checked by the French at Noyers and demanded assistance from the 3rd Army. However, the 3rd was paralysed by General Helmuth von Moltke's demand to send some of its best troops to the Eastern Front, and had also been told to mount an attack on a fresh objective to the southwest. The 4th German Army was driven back over the Meuse by the French 4th Army, who gained a considerable victory. At this point Marshal Joseph Joffre ordered a general retreat; General Ferdinand de Langle de Cary, the French commander in the field, promptly obeyed, pulling back rapidly and abandoning large areas which could have been used to delay the subsequent German advance.

Midway in World War II, decisive US naval victory over Japan June 1942. The Midway victory was one of the most important battles of the Pacific war, removing Japanese naval air superiority in one day and placing them on the defensive thereafter. Midway island lies northwest of the Hawaiian islands, and in May 1942 the Japanese planned to expand their conquests by landing troops in the Aleutian islands and on Midway.

The Japanese attack involved two task forces; the Aleutian force was to draw the US fleet north, allowing the Midway force a free hand. The Americans deciphered the Japanese naval codes and so were able to deploy their fleet to surprise the Midway force. Both launched aircraft and the Americans sank one Japanese carrier and so damaged another two that they were abandoned. The sole remaining Japanese carrier managed to launch a strike which sank the USS *Yorktown*, but later in the day another US strike damaged it so badly that it had to be scuttled. With no aircraft carriers or aircraft left, the Japanese abandoned their attack and retreated.

Mill Springs (also known as the battle of Fishing Creek) Union victory during the American Civil War 18 Jan 1862 at Mill Springs, a village about 16 km/10 mi west of Somerset, Kentucky; the first significant defeat suffered by the Confederates. The Confederate defensive line, intended to keep out the Union forces, was held at Mill Springs by about 4,500 troops under Maj-Gen Thomas-Crittenden. At the start of the 1862 campaign, Union General George H Thomas advanced on Mill Springs with a force of about 4,000 troops and Crittenden decided to pre-empt matters by attacking first. After fierce fighting, the Confederates were driven back, losing 12 guns and a considerable number of troops, while Union casualties were less than 250.

Milne Bay in World War II, Allied victory over the Japanese Aug 1942, the first time Allied troops defeated a Japanese attack. Milne Bay is on the extreme eastern tip of New Guinea and Japanese intelligence wrongly thought it poorly defended, unaware that it was defended by two Australian infantry brigades, one with experience against the Germans in Africa, and two fighter squadrons of the Royal Australian Air Force (RAAF). A Japanese force landed 26 Aug 1942, expecting to be able to move west easily and take Port Moresby. The Allied strength surprised the Japanese: while the RAAF aircraft attacked the Japanese transports and escorts, the troops resisted the ground attack strongly, and the Japanese withdrew 6 Sept.

Minden during the Seven Years' War, French defeat by a combined British-Hanoverian army 1 Aug 1759 at Minden, 70 km/44 mi west of Hanover, Germany. The Allied army under Prince Frederick of Brunswick, operating on the north German plain, was defeated at Bergen April 1759 and retired before the French, who occupied Minden July. Frederick decided to make a stand here as any further Allied retreat would have given Hanover to the French.

The 60,000-strong French force under Marshal the Marquis de Contades was drawn up in a strong position, with the river Weser on one flank and a marsh on the other. Frederick sent 7,000 of his 52,000 troops to cut the French line of communication to Kassel but the French saw the threat and attacked the main Allied position. Frederick launched a counterattack of six English and three Hanoverian battalions of infantry moving steadily forward in line. They were attacked by the French cavalry which they annihilated with close-range musket fire, and the battle was won. Due to mismanagement of the Allied cavalry, the French were able to withdraw in good order, but at a loss of over 7,000 casualties and 43 guns. Allied losses were some 2,700; over half of these were in the six English battalions, the descendants of which still wear a rose in their caps on the anniversary of the battle.

I have seen what I never thought to be possible – a single line of infantry break through three lines of cavalry ranked in order of battle and tumble them to ruin.

Marshal de Contades on the *Battle of Minden*, quoted in Thomas Carlyle, *History of Frederick II of Prussia*.

The Minden Battalions and their later designation:

12th Foot	(The Suffolk Regiment)
20th Foot	(Lancashire Fusiliers)
23rd Foot	(Royal Welsh Fusiliers)
25th Foot	(King's Own Scottish Borderers)
37th Foot	(The Hampshire Regiment)
51st Foot	(The Yorkshire Light Infantry)

These regiments have been amalgamated and re-organized repeatedly since World War II, but they and their spiritual descendants still wear a rose in their caps on Minden Day, since, according to legend, the soldiers en route to Minden plucked roses from the hedgerows and put them in their caps.

Missolonghi during the Greek War of Independence, Turkish victory over the Greeks 22 April 1826, at the town of Missolonghi about 32 km/20 mi northwest of Patras, Greece. The town had been besieged by the Turks 1821, but after two months the Turks had withdrawn. They returned 1825 and began another siege, but in spite of several months of pressure the town failed to capitulate. Eventually the Turks were reinforced by an Egyptian army under Ibrahim Pasha, adopted son of Mohammed Ali of Egypt, but it was a further three months before they were able to wear down the garrison and take the town by storm. The collapse of the town finally moved Britain, France, and Russia to come to the aid of the Greeks.

Mohács during the Ottoman Wars, Turkish victory over a Hungarian army 29 Aug 1526; the battle marked the end of the Medieval Kingdom of Hungary. Mohács was a Hungarian river port on the Danube, 65 km/40 mi east of Pecs, and the scene of another important battle 1687 (see below). King Louis II of Hungary's 25,000-strong army was attacked by a Turkish army of about 100,000 troops under Suleiman the Magnificent and totally destroyed; 24,000 Hungarians were killed, including Louis. This left the road to Buda open, and the Turks sacked the city 12 Sept 1526.

Mohács during the Ottoman Wars, comprehensive victory of a combined Austrian and Hungarian army under Charles of Lorraine over a Turkish army under Mohammed IV 12 Aug 1687; the battle effectively meant the end of Turkish expansion into Europe. Mohács was the scene of another important battle 1526 (see above). Mohammed's defeat led to his being deposed and replaced by Suleiman III who was far less competent and, unable to withstand western pressure, the Turks were gradually driven out of Christian Europe.

Mons in World War I, German victory over British forces Aug 1914. On 22 Aug the British Expeditionary Force was positioned on a line running from Mons to Condé, two towns in Belgium. The British, in conjunction with French troops on the left and right, were to attack the German forces under General Alexander von Kluck and possibly envelop them.

However, the French force due to operate on the British left did not arrive, leaving the flank open. A German thrust, estimated at some 160,000 troops, broke in between the British right flank and the French 5th Army under General Charles Lanrezac, which broke and began to fall back, leaving the British with both flanks open to encirclement. Assuming that the French would soon return, the British dug in and resisted German attacks; however, by the afternoon of 24 Aug it was obvious that the French would not return and the British would be overwhelmed. They therefore fell back to a prepared defensive position but the German momentum forced them out. They then gradually retreated south in a series of leap-frogging rearguard actions until the Germans overstretched their supply lines and slackened their pursuit. The British formed a fresh line and the retreat was over.

Morhange in World War I, abortive French attack Aug 1914 on German positions around Morhange, a town in Lorraine, southeast of Metz. The French armies in Lorraine opened an offensive 14 Aug, aiming to advance down the valley of the river Sarre to attack Metz. The Germans were expecting such a move and had prepared a deep defensive zone on their side of the border. The French walked into the trap and were torn to pieces by machine gun and heavy artillery fire. The Germans then counterattacked in strength and drove the French some 16 km/10 mi behind their original starting line, capturing Luneville, crossing the Meurthe river, and threatening Nancy. The French reached a suitable defensive line and managed to dig and the front then stabilized.

Mortain in World War II, unsuccessful German counterattack in Normandy Aug 1944, intended to break through invading Allied forces to the sea at Avranches and cut off the US forces to the west. Warned by decrypted Ultra messages, US general Omar Bradley was prepared and repelled the attack, manoeuvring the Germans into a position which led to their defeat at the ◊Falaise Gap.

Moscow in World War II, failed German attack on Moscow, capital city of the USSR Oct 1941–Jan 1942; Moscow was a prime objective of the German invasion plan, Operation ◊Barbarossa, and the failure to capture the city was a severe setback for the German strategy.

After overwhelming a series of hastily assembled defensive lines, the German 2nd Panzer Group approached from the south, while the 3rd Panzer Group and 9th Army outflanked the last defensive line and swung round to the north. The advance was sustained by the rapid movement of German forces and the constant threat that the Soviets would be outflanked; it only slowed mid-Oct due to the onset of winter weather and the stretched German supply lines. By this time most of the city's civilian population had been evacuated, and the remains were formed into citizen's groups, which were armed, hastily trained, and organized into a last-ditch defence line. Meanwhile, limited Soviet counterattacks kept the Germans stalled, until the Germans got their supply system functioning again and mounted a sudden attack 16 Nov 1941. Within a week, they advanced within 24 km/15 mi of the city centre but the bitter cold and a fuel shortage halted them again 5 Dec, with advance patrols actually on the edge of the city suburbs. By this time, Marshal Georgi Zhukov had been appointed commander in chief of the defence of Moscow, and, reinforced with several thousand Siberian troops, he mounted a powerful counterattack 6 Dec. By 15 Jan 1942, the Soviets had pushed the Germans back to a line about 160 km/100 mi west of Moscow and the city was safe.

Mukden Japanese victory over the Russians during the Russo-Japanese War, Feb–March 1905, outside Mukden (now called Shenyang), capital city of Manchuria; this was the last major battle of the war, and the Russian defeat finally persuaded the Tsar to accept the mediation of the USA June 1905, which led to a peace treaty being signed in Sept. After the battle of ◊Liaoyang Sept 1904, the Russians fell back to a defensive line some 80 km/50 mi long on the Sha Ho river, south of Mukden. The Japanese and Russian armies faced each other for some months along this line while the siege of ◊Port Arthur was brought to an end, after which the Japanese began reinforcing their line preparatory to an attack.

In Feb 1905 a fresh Japanese army, the 5th, worked its way through the mountains to the west of Mukden and began attacking the Russian left flank 20 Feb. The main attack against the centre of the Russian line began 27 Feb, and at the same time the Japanese 4th Army, victors of Port Arthur, appeared on the Russian right flank, forcing the two ends of the Russian defensive line to curve backwards. Fighting was bitter, and casualties on both sides high, but it soon became apparent to the Russians that the two Japanese flanking armies would encircle the city. The Russians began a general retreat, in a series of hard-fought rearguard actions, but the continued Japanese successes soon destroyed Russian morale and led to a total collapse; Mukden was evacuated by 10 March and the Russians fell back to the north. Russian casualties were 26,500 killed, about the same number wounded, and 40,000 taken prisoner. The Japanese lost 41,000 killed and wounded.

Murfreesboro (also known as the battle of Stone's River) indecisive battle during the American Civil War 31 Dec 1862–2 Jan 1863, outside the town of Murfreesboro, Tennessee, 51 km/32 mi southeast of Nashville. A Confederate force of about 35,000 under General Braxton Bragg attacked a 45,000-strong Union force led by General William Rosecrans. The Union right wing was driven back, but the centre held and prevented the Union forces being driven from the field, though they lost heavily in prisoners and guns. Rosecrans counterattacked the following day and regained the ground he had lost, so that by the end of the day both armies were back where they had started. However, on 2 Jan Bragg realised that he could not hold off the Union forces and began an orderly retreat. Both sides lost about 12,000 casualties in the action.

Nadzab in World War II, US airborne operation Sept 1943 to capture small Japanese-held town in preparation for a larger assault on the Japanese garrison at Lae, New Guinea; one of the very few airborne operations mounted in the Pacific theatre. A US paratroop regiment and Australian artillery were parachuted into Nadzab Sept 1943. They occupied the town, allowing the 7th Australian Division to be flown in and mount an offensive against Lae itself.

Namur in World War I, German capture Aug 1914 of an important Belgian rail junction and garrison town on the confluence of the Meuse and Sambre rivers. Namur, a Belgian town and capital of the Namur province, 56 km/35 mi southeast of Brussels, was defended by a ring of nine outlying forts. On 19 Aug 1914 the German Army brought up heavy artillery and began bombarding these forts. The Belgian garrison, supported by 3,000 French troops, attempted to attack the German gun positions but were driven back. On 23 Aug the French troops retreated to escape being surrounded and on the following day the Belgian field army also retired for the same reason. What remained of the garrison was overcome by a German attack and the last three forts were silenced 25 Aug. Namur remained in German hands for the remainder of the war.

Narev in World War I, battle between German and Russian forces in Poland July–Aug 1915. Early in July, General Max von Gallwitz decided on an attack across the Narev river and drove the Russian forward troops back to a line on the south side of the river, although the Russians managed to hold a number of bridgeheads on the north side. On the night of 23 July Gallwitz stormed the river, secured a crossing, and managed to get astride the main road and rail lines leading to Warsaw, about 32 km/20 mi away. The Russians succeeded in holding him there, and in spite of receiving reinforcements Gallwitz made no further progress, turning instead to force a crossing of the river Bug.

Naroch, Lake in World War I, failed Russian offensive against German forces March–April 1915. Lake Naroch is in Byelorussia (now Belarus), about 110 km/70 mi east of Vilnius, and in 1914 was in a Russian province. In Feb 1915 the French, hard-pressed at Verdun, asked Russia to launch a diversionary attack. Russia had been contemplating action in the Lake Naroch area anyway and mounted an attack on German positions at the Lake 18 March 1915.

Even though the Germans had spent the winter building strong defences, the attack met with some initial success, capturing parts of the German front line close to the Lake, but the inevitable counterattack followed. The battle moved back and forth for some weeks until the Germans felt they had determined the Russian plans. They then brought in reserves and, in particular, called up more artillery under the command of Col Georg Bruchmüller, which began heavily bombarding the Russians. This barrage, combined with the greater weight of the German attacks, the appalling conditions of the spring thaw, and general weakening of the Russian troops, led to the Germans completely regaining the territory they had lost and the Russians fell back to their original line, having lost about 110,000 troops.

Narva during the Great Northern War, Swedish victory over the Russians 30 Nov 1700 at Narva, a fortified town then in northwest Russia 120 km/ 75 mi west of St Petersburg (now in Estonia). The small Swedish garrison in the town was besieged by a force of about 50,000 Russians. On hearing that Charles XII of Sweden was approaching with an army to relieve the town, the Russians retired to an entrenched camp at Novgorod (now Ivangorod, Russia), a few miles away. Launching his attack in a snowstorm, Charles' force of 8,000 Swedes broke into the entrenchments and after a three-hour hand-to-hand battle, smashed the Russian left wing, defeated their cavalry, and drove the Russians from their position, leaving over 10,000 dead.

Narvik in World War II, unsuccessful Allied attempts April–May 1940 to save town in northern Norway from an invading German force landed by sea 9 April. A British force was landed nearby 15 April but was not trained or equipped to operate in snow; in spite of French reinforcements they were unable to make any progress against German defences until the commander was replaced. They finally captured the town 28 May, but by that time German successes elsewhere in Norway allowed heavy reinforcement of the Narvik area and on 31 May all Allied troops were forced to evacuate the town.

Naseby during the English Civil War, decisive Parliamentarian victory over the Royalists 14 June 1645 at Naseby, 11 km/7 mi from Market Harborough, Leicestershire. King Charles I was retiring toward Leicester with 7,500 troops, pursued by 13,000 Parliamentarians under General Thomas Fairfax and Oliver Cromwell. Charles decided to give battle and fell back on high ground near Naseby.

Both armies drew up in similar formation, infantry in the centre, cavalry on the flanks, and reserves behind. The Royalists opened the battle by dashing downhill, across the intervening valley, and up the facing hill to where the Roundheads were massed. Prince Rupert's cavalry broke the Parliamentary right wing and then recklessly pursued them toward the village of Naseby. On the other wing, however, Cromwell's cavalry routed the force opposing them and then turned inward to take the Royalist infantry in the flank. King Charles ordered his last reserves to charge, but the Earl of Carnwath, seeing this to be a futile move, turned his horse away and led his troops off the field; the Parliamentarians took heart from this, rallied, and completed the victory. Prince Rupert, returning from his chase, found the battle over and could do nothing but follow the king to Leicester. The Royalists lost about 1,000 killed and 5,000 were taken prisoner, together with all their artillery.

Nashville during the American Civil War, Union victory 15–16 Dec 1864 at Nashville, Tennessee. After Atlanta fell to Union troops, a Confederate army of some 55,000 under General John B Hood marched west toward Tennessee. Nashville was held by Union troops under General George H Thomas, with an advance guard at Franklin, about 32 km/20 mi south of the town. Hood fought a fierce battle against the advance guard, losing about 4,500 troops in the process, and the Union troops retired in good order to Nashville. Hood pursued, took up a position on the hills around the town and waited for Thomas to make the next move. The Union commanders felt sure that Hood could not take Nashville, but they were afraid he might side-step it and go on the rampage in Kentucky. Thomas, a painstaking general, took his time organizing his forces, which were largely rejects from other theatres of war, and he was not helped by a sleet-storm of abnormal force which made movement impossible.

By 15 Dec the weather had improved and Thomas unleashed an attack all along the Confederate line. The assault on the right wing was repulsed, and the Confederates appeared to be holding up against the attack, but the Federal 16th Corps pierced the Confederate left just as a regiment of Union cavalry, having made a wide sweep around the left flank, fell on their rear. This broke the Confederates, who fell back across the Tennessee river leaving behind about 2,000 dead and 5,500 prisoners. Thomas pursued Hood out of Tennessee, and Hood's army was never again any threat to the Union.

Navarino during the Greek War of Independence, destruction of a joint Turkish-Egyptian fleet by an Allied naval force 20 Oct 1827, in the Ionian Sea off Navarino (now Pilos) about 220 km/135 mi southwest of Athens. The destruction of their fleet left the Turks highly vulnerable in Greece as they had no protection to their rear and no supply line, and Navarino proved to be the decisive battle of the war.

After the fall of ◊Missolonghi April 1826, Britain, France, and Russia had begun to provide assistance to the Greeks and had assembled a fleet of warships. To face this threat, a combined Egyptian and Turkish fleet had reinforced Navarino, the principal Turkish supply base, with troops from Crete, and shortly after a large Egyptian fleet arrived with more troops. The Allied fleet sailed for Navarino with the intention of negotiating a Turkish withdrawal, but the situation was so tense that as soon as a Turkish ship fired on a British gunboat a general close-quarter battle broke out and within two hours the Turkish-Egyptian fleet had been almost totally destroyed.

Néry in World War I, desperate action to hold off attacking Germans by 'L' Battery of the British Royal Horse Artillery while retreating from ◊Mons Sept 1914. During their heroic stand, 'L' Battery lost 45 officers and troops killed and wounded out of a strength of 170, and won three Victoria Crosses. The battery now carries 'Néry' as its honour title and annually celebrates the battle.

During the retreat from Mons, part of the 1st Cavalry Brigade, including 'L' Battery, were bivouacked in Néry, a French village in the *département* of Oise, near Compiègne. At about 5 a.m. on 1 Sept 1914 the battery, with horse teams hooked to the guns, was waiting to move off in the mist when they were surprised by a German force on nearby hills which poured heavy fire into the area. The guns were immediately unhooked and brought into action under fire in the open. For two hours they kept up a rapid fire against the German positions, losing guns and troops throughout the action, until only one gun remained, served by two wounded men. At 7.15 a.m., reinforcements arrived and were able to drive the German force from its commanding position.

Neuve Chapelle in World War I, inconclusive battle between British and German forces March 1915. Neuve Chapelle, a French village in the *département* of Nord, southwest of Armentières was taken by the Germans Oct 1914.

The British decided to attack Neuve Chapelle to prevent the movement of German troops to the east and to assist the French at ◊Arras. The battle began 12 March with a 40-minute artillery bombardment by 480 guns, followed by a barrage behind the German trench line to prevent the arrival of reinforcements. The infantry assault was a success, carrying four lines of German trenches and taking the village. However, due to failure of communications the reserve troops which should have followed up the attack failed to arrive in time, enabling the Germans to reform their line. The British artillery no longer had sufficient ammunition to produce a superiority of fire, and the battle died away as the British dug in to their new line.

New Britain in World War II, Allied operation 1943 to recapture the main island of the Bismarck Archipelago, northeast of New Guinea. Taken by the Japanese 1941, a major base with five airfields was built at Rabaul at the western end of the island. There was also an excellent harbour and the town held a garrison of about 100,000 troops. The Allies originally planned a direct assault on Rabaul, which could have been very costly; instead they landed on the western end of the island 26 Dec 1943 and established forward airfields to dominate the area, isolating Rabaul for the rest of the war.

New Market during the American Civil War, Union defeat by the Confederates 15 May 1864 at the village of New Market, Virginia. A Union force of about 5,000 troops under General Franz Sigel was moving down the Shenandoah Valley toward Staunton, intending to join forces with a column led by General George Crook which was moving east from West Virginia. Sigel carelessly exposed his flank to a Confederate force under General John C Breckinridge. The Confederates attacked and the Union infantry retreated into a wood, behind their own artillery. A 250-strong company of boys from the nearby Lexington Military School attached to Breckinridge's force charged the Union gun line and routed the gunners, capturing the guns but losing 80 of the boys in the process. The Union troops broke and retreated in disorder for some 40 km/25 mi before pausing to reorganize. Sigel was replaced, and played no further part in the war.

Instead of advancing on Staunton he is already in full retreat on Strasbourg. If you expect anything from him you will be mistaken. He will do nothing but run. He never did anything else.

> telegram from General Henry Halleck to Ulysses S Grant,
> reporting on Sigel's defeat at *New Market*

New Orleans in the War of 1812, inconclusive battle between British and American forces Dec 1814–Jan 1815, at New Orleans; the war was already over by the time the battle was fought – peace had been signed 24 Dec 1814 – but neither of the two forces in the area had received the news.

In late 1814, the city was held by a garrison of about 6,000 troops under General Andrew Jackson. A British fleet overpowered the American warships in the Mississippi river 13 Dec and landed a force of about 6,000 British troops under General Keane. General Sir Edward Pakenham later arrived to take command, and launched a determined attack on the city's defences 1 Jan 1815. The assault failed, largely due to mismanagement and argument between the various commanders; since they were short of supplies and awaiting ships, the British retired. Having restocked with ammunition, they made another attack 8 Jan which also failed, this time because of dispersing their forces across the front rather then concentrating them; the British lost 1,500 troops, among them General Pakenham. The expedition, seeing no further possibility of taking the city, re-embarked and withdrew.

Nile during the Napoleonic Wars, British naval victory over the French 1 Aug 1798 in Aboukir Bay, east of Alexandria, Egypt; their defeat on the Nile put an end to French designs in the Middle East. When the British fleet left the Mediterranean, Napoleon Bonaparte was ordered to seize Egypt, make a channel through the Isthmus of Suez, and secure the Red Sea for

France. Admiral Horatio Nelson was sent back to the Mediterranean with a squadron to ascertain what the French were doing, and 1 Aug discovered their fleet at anchor in Aboukir Bay; it consisted of 13 ships of the line, 4 frigates, and a number of troop transports. Nelson split his force of 14 ships in two and sailed one half into the bay, between the French and the shore, while the other half sailed in line on the seaward side. Caught between two lines of fire, the French fleet was almost entirely destroyed, only two ships escaping capture or destruction.

Nive during the Peninsular War, series of engagements culminating in a French defeat by the British Dec 1813, along the river Nive on the Franco-Spanish border. After Marshal Nicolas Soult's defeat on the Nivelle, he retreated to Bayonne with the Duke of Wellington in pursuit.

Wellington arranged his forces on either side of the river Nive and Soult attacked 10 Dec but was repulsed by the British under General Sir John Hope. Minor engagements took place on the next two days, and Soult launched another powerful attack 13 Dec against the troops under Viscount Hill. Wellington then arrived, took command of the battle, drove the French back and occupied their lines in front of the village of Adour, whereupon Soult retreated into Bayonne. French losses amounted to some 10,000 troops, while British casualties were just over 5,000 killed and wounded.

Nivelle Offensive see ◊Chemin des Dames.

Nördlingen during the Thirty Years' War, two battles between Imperial and Allied armies in the vicinity of Nördlingen, a German town in Bavaria, 80 km/50 mi southwest of Nuremberg.

5–6 Sept 1634 some 40,000 Imperial troops were besieging Nördlingen opposed by a somewhat smaller force of Swedish and German troops who attempted to raise the siege. After a bitter struggle, resulting in heavy losses to both sides, the Swedish-German attack was beaten off. The sole strategic result of this battle was to bring France into the war.

3 Aug 1635 a largely pointless battle which produced no tactical or strategic advantage for the French. An Imperial army under Baron Franz von Mercy was strongly entrenched round a nearby village and was attacked there by the French army under Prince Louis de Condé and Vicomte Henri de Turenne. After a hard struggle, the French succeeded in evicting the Imperial troops and capturing all their artillery; von Mercy was among the dead.

North Cape in World War II, naval battle between British and German squadrons Dec 1943. The German battleship *Scharnhorst* sailed with five destroyers from Norway to attack a British convoy en route to Murmansk. The convoy was escorted by the battleship *Duke of York*, a cruiser and 18 destroyers, with 3 more cruisers close by. One of these detected the *Scharnhorst* by radar and all three opened fire. The Germans turned away but were again found and bombarded by the three cruisers, although one was damaged by the *Scharnhorst*. The German commander sent his destroyers to search for the British convoy; they failed to find it and returned to their base in Norway, leaving the *Scharnhorst* alone. It was discovered by the British convoy escort and the *Duke of York* and a cruiser opened fire, landing thirteen 14-in shells on the *Scharnhorst*, thoroughly wrecking it. After being torpedoed by destroyers and further bombardment from the battleship, the *Scharnhorst* sank with the loss of all but 36 of its 1,839 crew.

Okinawa in World War II, hard-fought US operation 1 April–21 June 1945 to capture the principal island of the Japanese Ryukyu Islands in the west Pacific. During the invasion over 150,000 Okinawans, mainly civilians, died – many were massacred by Japanese forces – and there were 47,000 US military casualties (12,000 dead) and 60,000 Japanese (only a few hundred survived as prisoners).The island was returned to Japan 1972.

Omdurman British victory 2 Sept 1898 over the Sudanese tribesmen (Dervishes) of the Khalifa Abdullah el Taashi. The Khalifa was the successor to the Mahdi Mahomet Ahmed, who had fomented a revolt of Sudanese tribes against Egyptian rule, and had gradually become the unofficial ruler of the southern Sudan; a British force under General Horatio Kitchener was sent to deal with him. The force advanced slowly up the Nile, laying a supply railway to bypass the rapids, and by Sept 1898 there were 8,200 British and 17,000 Egyptian and Sudanese troops positioned in a crescent north of Omdurman, the Khalifa's base (now Umm Durman, about 1,600 km/1,000 mi south of Cairo).

On 2 Sept the British were attacked by about 50,000 Dervishes, few of whom got within 500 yds of the British lines before being shot down, and an estimated 10,000 were killed. Kitchener now considered the battle over and ordered a march on to Omdurman; he did not know that the main Dervish army had not yet moved, and he was about to march straight across its front. As the column moved off a force of 20,000 Dervishes fell upon the rearguard; the rearguard was under the command of General Hector 'Fighting Mac' MacDonald, who wheeled his troops and stopped the Dervishes, killing most and scattering the remainder. When the battle ended it was found that MacDonald's force had an average of two bullets per man left in their pouches. The Khalifa escaped, to be pursued and later brought to battle and killed.

Opequon Creek during the American Civil War, comprehensive Union victory over Confederate forces 19 Sept 1864 in the vicinity of Winchester, Virginia. This battle conclusively removed the Shenandoah Valley from the operational scene for the remainder of the war. A Union force under General Philip Sheridan had been clearing the Shenandoah Valley of Confederates and laying it waste until they were halted by a powerful Confederate force under General Jubal Early. With few good defensive positions in the area, Sheridan retired down the valley to Halltown; Early followed and took up a strong position on the Opequon Creek.

Early initially outnumbered Sheridan, but due to pressures elsewhere a division of Early's troops was removed and Sheridan attacked 19 Sept. As there was only one approach road, the attack moved slowly to begin with, so the first Union troops lacked support and were barely able to sustain their assault. However, as the congestion cleared, Sheridan was able to pour troops in, took personal command at the front, and late in the afternoon drove the Confederates from their line. He pursued the Confederates vigorously, attacked Early again three days later, and drove him well up the valley in disorder.

Orléans during the Hundred Years' War, English defeat by the French Oct 1428–May 1429. The English were rapidly conquering France at this stage of the war until this victory turned the tide of French fortunes; thereafter a string of French successes gradually brought the war to an end.

A force of about 5,000 troops under the Earl of Salisbury attempted to take Orléans 12 Oct 1428. The attempt failed, the Earl was killed, and the English laid siege to the city. They were not present in sufficient strength to seal off the city completely, so that there was no chance of starving out the French, and the siege lingered on until April 1429 when Joan of Arc arrived in Orléans. She took charge of the garrison and led them in a series of attacks on different English positions, taking them one after another until the remaining English, seeing the futility of their enterprise, raised the siege 4 May 1429 and departed.

Ostend in World War I, two British attempts to block the harbour entrance 1918 to deny the Germans use of the harbour and bottle up their vessels. Ostend, a Belgian town in the province of West Flanders, seaport, and fishing harbour, was occupied by the Germans 14 Oct 1914 and remained in their hands for the rest of the war. They developed the port as a U-boat and light destroyer base for the German Navy and it was this that made the port a prime target for the British.

The first attempt was made 23 April but failed when the wind changed and the two blockships destined to be sunk in the harbour mouth drifted away and were blown up outside. In the second attempt 10 May HMS *Vindictive* was run against the eastern pier with the intention of swinging the hull across the entrance and then sinking the vessel. But as *Vindictive* hit the pier, its bridge was struck by a German shell, killing the captain and wrecking the controls so that it proved impossible to swing the ship across. It was blown up and only partially blocked the harbour. The Germans were later able to drag the wreckage aside, leaving them a 9 m/30 ft entrance.

Oudenarde during the War of the Spanish Succession, French defeat by an Allied army of British, Hanoverian, Prussian, and Dutch troops 11 July 1708 near Oudenarde, a Belgian town on the river Scheldt, 16 km/10 mi south of Ghent. A force of about 40,000 French was besieging the small garrison at Oudenarde when they received word of an Allied army of about 30,000 under the Duke of Marlborough marching on the town to raise the siege.

The French moved back and took up a position along the river Norken, a tributary of the Scheldt; Marlborough ordered an attack as soon as his troops had arrived, an advance party went across the Scheldt and the battle began while the rest of the Allied force was still crossing the river. Confined in the angle between the two rivers, the action was almost entirely decided by infantry, and the French found themselves pressed against the rivers with their flanks crumbling. The French left wing was able to rally and stave off the Allied advance while the remainder of the French crossed the river and made off under cover of nightfall. Allied losses amounted to about 3,000 killed and wounded, but the French sustained some 15,000 lost, including prisoners.

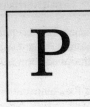

Paardeburg during the South African War, Boer defeat by the British Feb 1900, at Paardeburg Hill, on the Modder river about 95 km/60 mi west of Bloemfontein. The Boer general Piet Cronje was holding an entrenched line at Magersfontein and the British under General Sir John French, with the main army behind him, moved to cut Cronje off from Bloemfontein, his main source of supply. Cronje abandoned his position and marched east along the Modder River toward Bloemfontein. The British scouts found his column near Paardeburg Hill, and while the British main force came up, the Boers were able to dig in and entrench themselves in the dry bed of the river.

The British attacked from both sides 18 Feb but the accurate shooting of the Boers caused heavy casualties and the attack was beaten off. Lord Roberts ordered no further attacks to be made, and the British merely sat and waited for starvation to take effect. The Boers surrendered 27 Feb; Cronje, 4,100 troops, and 4 guns were captured. British casualties numbered 98 officers and 1,437 troops killed or wounded, most of them during the attack on the 18 Feb. The removal of Cronje from the scene allowed Roberts to take Bloemfontein a few days later.

Panipat three battles in the vicinity of this Indian town, about 120 km/75 mi north of Delhi. The first two battles were part of the Moghul struggle for dominance in India, the final battle 1761 was an Afghan victory over the Mahrattas.

27 April 1526 Moghul victory over a large force of Delhi Muslims under Ibrahim. A smaller but highly trained and motivated force of Moghuls under Barbar, later the Moghul Emperor of India, defeated the Muslims. The victory removed the Afghan dynasty from the Delhi throne and opened the way for the Moghul dynasty.

5 Nov 1556 the decisive engagement of the Hindu Revolt. An army of 100,000 Hindus, which had captured Delhi, was met by a Moghul army of about 20,000 troops and totally defeated, restoring Delhi to the Moghuls and confirming Akbar as Emperor.

7 Jan 1761 during the Afghan-Mahratta wars, a Mahratta force of about 80,000 was defeated by an Afghan/Hindu army of similar strength.

Paris, Siege of during the Franco-Prussian War, Prussian siege of the city of Paris Sept 1870–Jan 1871; the war came to an end with the fall of Paris and the city's terms of surrender were incorporated into a general armistice. Having defeated the French armies in the field, Count Helmuth von Moltke invested Paris with 240,000 troops and upwards of 300 siege guns as well as field artillery.

Paris was nominally under the command of General Louis Trochu, with about 400,000 troops of varying quality, but political dissension and sheer incompetence hampered French military efforts. The French made a number of ineffectual sorties but they were all beaten back by the Prussians. Despite this, the actual defence of the city itself was conducted tenaciously, largely in the hope that citizen's armies, raised in the provinces, would be able to come to the aid of the capital. However, these armies were totally untrained and the efforts they made to break through the Prussian lines were in vain. Von Moltke initially expected starvation to cause resistance to collapse quite quickly, but when the siege wore on he massed siege artillery and began bombarding the city. This, combined with shortage of food and a general collapse of morale, led to the city's surrender 28 Jan 1871.

Passchendaele in World War I, successful British operation around a Belgian village in western Flanders, near Ypres, as part of the third battle of ◊Ypres Oct–Nov 1917. The name is often erroneously applied to the whole of the battle of Ypres; Passchendaele was in fact just part of that battle. The nearby Passchendaele Ridge, some 60 m/200 ft high, had been captured and fortified by the Germans Oct 1914. It was a vital strategic gain as it gave them command of the Allied lines. Hence, its capture was an important target of the British strategy during the third battle of Ypres, despite the strong resistance offered by the German defenders. It was re-taken by the Germans March 1918 and recovered again by the Belgians Oct 1918.

Patay during the Hundred Years' War, French victory over the English 19 June 1429 at the village of Patay, 21 km/13 mi northwest of Orléans. Joan of Arc was continuing her determined resistance, forcing the English to send an army to reinforce their siege of ◊Orléans. Led by Sir John Talbot, they reached Patay to discover that the English army mounting the siege had been driven off and their commander, the Earl of Suffolk, taken prisoner. Talbot's force advanced but was accidentally discovered by some French scouts hunting a stag. They called up Joan of Arc and the French fell on the English before they could disperse into a fighting formation. Talbot was taken prisoner and the English advance guard scattered, but the main body were able to make an orderly retreat back toward Paris.

Pearl Harbor in World War II, surprise Japanese air attack on the main US naval base Dec 7 1941; the attack devastated the US Pacific fleet but also brought the USA into the war. The Japanese, angered by US embargoes of oil and other war material and convinced that US entry into the war was inevitable, had opted to strike a major blow in the hope of forcing concessions. Instead, it galvanized US public opinion and raised anti-

Japanese sentiment to a fever pitch, with war declared shortly after. The base itself was situated in an inlet of the Pacific Ocean in Hawaii, on Oahu Island.

The attack, led by Vice Admiral Chuichi Nagumo, took place while Japanese envoys were holding so-called peace talks in Washington and caught the US entirely unawares. The local US commanders, Admiral Husband E Kimmel and Lt-Gen Walter Short, were relieved of their posts and held responsible for the fact that the base, despite warnings, was totally unprepared at the time of the attack. About 3,300 US military personnel were killed, 4 battleships were lost, and a large part of the US Pacific Fleet was destroyed or damaged. The only comfort for the US forces was that their aircraft carriers had been sent on a training exercise and so were saved to form the nucleus of a new fleet.

Petersburg, siege of Union forces' capture of a strategic Confederate city after a prolonged siege June 1864–March 1865; this victory marked the final phase of the American Civil War. Petersburg lay south of Richmond, Virginia, and commanded the main Confederate supply routes. Despite its vital strategic location, in June 1864 it was only garrisoned by a force of about 2,500 largely untrained or over-age soldiers.

The Union general Ulysses S Grant, realising its strategic significance, ordered it to be attacked. However, as was so often the case during this war, the orders were incompetently executed: General William F Smith brought his troops up to the fortifications 15 June, attacked, captured the first line of trenches, and then decided to abandon the assault. He considered a night attack, but abandoned the idea. By the time he began thinking of mounting another attack the following day, the Confederates had rushed in reinforcements from their field armies and the opportunity to end the war immediately was lost. Both sides strengthened their forces and on 17–18 June the Union made a fierce attack which was successfully repulsed, at a cost of over 10,000 Union casualties.

From then on, the siege became a drawn-out affair. A mine charged with four tons of gunpowder was exploded beneath the Confederate line 30 July, leaving an enormous crater and a wide-open avenue for attack, but the attack itself failed. The Union troops congregated in the crater where they were rapidly shot down by Confederates who soon filled the gap and repulsed any further attempt to break through. Eventually, on 29 March 1865, Grant sent General Philip Sheridan with an army around the left flank of the Petersburg position to strike into the country beyond and sever all communications between Petersburg and Richmond. The Confederate commander, Robert E Lee, was forced to abandon Richmond and Petersburg 2 April. He marched to Appomattox, where he surrendered 9 April.

Pharsalus in the Roman Civil War, Julius Caesar's final victory over

Pompey's forces near Pharsalus (now Farsala) in Thessaly 9 Aug 48 BC. After their comprehensive defeat at Pharsalus, the remainder of Pompey's force surrendered, ending all organized resistance to Caesar's rule.

The battle began well for Pompey, who outnumbered Caesar's 22,000 troops two-to-one; his cavalry charged Caesar's cavalry and forced them back. However, this exposed their flank to attack by Caesar's foot soldiers who took full advantage of this weakness, causing the Pompeian cavalry to fall into total disorder and finally ride clear of the battle entirely. The Pompeian foot soldiers heard of their cavalry's panic-stricken flight and themselves turned and ran, pursued by Caesar's troops. The Pompeians were totally routed, losing 8,000 troops compared to only 200 of Caesar's.

Philippine Sea in World War II, decisive US naval victory June 1944; the last of the great carrier battles, it broke the back of the Japanese navy. At various times during the war the Japanese naval staff drew up plans to lure the US fleets into a decisive battle. When US forces landed on Saipan June 1944 orders were given to concentrate the Japanese fleet in the Philippine Sea, east of the islands. The orders were intercepted and the US commander, Vice Admiral Raymond Spruance, was prepared for the Japanese attack. Spruance had 15 carriers with 896 aircraft; the Japanese had only 6 carriers and 430 aircraft, and were relying upon the support of ground-based aircraft from Guam.

Locating the US fleet, the Japanese launched 244 aircraft at 0845 hrs 19 June 1944. A US submarine arrived and torpedoed the Japanese carrier *Taiho*, crippling it. The air action which followed became known as the ◊Great Marianas Turkey Shoot; Japan was short of skilled pilots by this time and the US patrolling carrier aircraft shot them down in droves. A second Japanese attempt at launching an air strike was again foiled when a US submarine torpedoed a carrier, which exploded and sank. The *Taiho*, which had been torpedoed in the morning, had filled up with petrol vapour and now exploded, capsized, and sank. The last Japanese aircraft of the day were now launched with orders to attack the US fleet and fly on to Guam. Half were shot down before they found the fleet, the remainder missed the fleet, flew to Guam, and found the airfield there in ruins and surrounded by US fighters which promptly shot them all down.

The two fleets separated overnight, but the next day the Japanese turned back to find the Americans and resume the battle. A US scout found the Japanese late in the afternoon and despite the risk of launching a strike so late in the day, Spruance decided to gamble on a final blow and launched 77 dive bombers, 54 torpedo-bombers, and 85 fighters. Half an hour later 3 Japanese carriers were dead in the water, 1 sinking; 1 battleship and 1 cruiser were severely damaged; and the Japanese had only 35 aircraft left. The Japanese fleet's refuelling ships had also been found and set on fire and the Japanese commander had no choice but to run for home. The US aircraft returned in the dark: although 80 aircraft landed in the sea, the fleet provided every method of illumination possible and all the crews were rescued.

Piave in World War I, three battles between Austrian and Italian forces 1917–18 on the line of the Piave, a river in northern Italy, rising in the Carnic Alps and flowing 200 km/125 mi to the Adriatic about 32 km/20 mi north of Venice.

After the battle of ◊Caporetto Oct 1917 the Italian army retreated to a defensive line on the Piave. The *first battle* of the Piave took place when the Austrians attacked the Italian line Nov 1917; the Italians managed to hold their line and repel the attackers.

The front then remained quiet until the *second battle* June 1918. The Austrians crossed the river under cover of smoke and gas and managed to establish a bridgehead, but were thrown back by an Italian counterattack 2 July. Close to the sea they managed to pierce the Italian line and advanced about a mile but were again driven back to their starting line. The Piave then flooded suddenly, which put an end to the Austrian assault.

In the *third battle* 23 Oct 1918 (also called the battle of Vittorio Veneto) the Italians, together with British troops, massed on the river and attacked the Austrians. Three Italian armies crossed the river and within two days the Austrians were in general retreat, pursued by the Italians, until the Austrians called for an Armistice 4 Nov 1918.

Plassey British victory over the Nawab of Bengal, Suraja Dowla, 23 June 1757 at the former village of Plassey, about 150 km/95 mi north of Calcutta (the actual battlefield was destroyed by the river Bhagirathi flooding 1801). The Nawab of Bengal had taken Calcutta 1756 and carried out the notorious atrocity of the 'Black Hole of Calcutta', in which 120 British soldiers died.

Troops of the British East India Company led by General Robert Clive were detailed to recover the city and repress the Nawab. Clive's column of about 1,000 European soldiers, 2,100 native troops, and 10 guns marched up the river Hooghli from Chandernagore June 1757. Learning of the Nawab's movements, Clive advanced to Plassey where he met the Bengal army, about 35,000 foot, 18,000 cavalry, and 50 guns – most of the guns were operated by French troops who were encouraging the Nawab against the British. The Nawab hit the British with a violent bombardment from these batteries, which almost emptied his ammunition stocks. Once the bombardment was over, Clive's troops attacked, overcame a stubborn defence by French troops in a fieldwork, and then swept the Nawab's force off the field, losing no more than 72 troops in the process. Clive then installed his agent, Mir Jafir, who had formerly been Suraja Dowla's commander in chief, as the new Nawab. Since Jafir was a figurehead, this effectively gave the East India Company control of Bengal.

Plevna during the Russo-Turkish War, Russian victory over the Turks

July–Dec 1877, at Plevna, (now Pleven) about 130 km/80 mi northwest of Sofia, Bulgaria. Although the Russians technically won, the six-month siege paralysed their armies and was instrumental in turning European opinion against them, modifying their political aspirations and any possible gains they might have made. Plevna was also of considerable importance in demonstrating the power of the defence when armed with rapid-firing, breech-loading weapons, a lesson which was not entirely understood for many years.

The Russians were advancing on two fronts, one south from Romania, the other north from the Balkans, and the obvious strategic move for the Turks was to prevent the two forces meeting. Marshal Osman Pasha occupied Plevna, a small town of no particular importance, with 14,000 soldiers and set them digging fieldworks around the town. He issued each soldier with two rifles: a single shot Martini Peabody and 100 cartridges for long-range fire; and a Winchester repeating carbine and 500 cartridges for short-range fire. The Turkish position threatened the flank of the invading Russian army so they detached a small force to deal with it. This was quickly driven off, and the Russians launched a major attack 30 July; it was met with a storm of bullets which cut down 8,000 troops. They then settled down to a siege, but did not surround the town completely so Osman was still able to receive supplies and reinforcements, bringing his strength up to 30,000. Having achieved little by themselves, the Russians called on the Romanian army to assist and mounted another major assault, this time losing 18,000 casualties. The Russians managed to surround Plevna completely late Oct, isolating Osman, and sent for General Eduard Todleben, a siege expert. Under his guidance the siege was tightened until, after an intrepid but doomed attempt to break out, Osman was forced by starvation to surrender 10 Dec.

Poitiers during the Hundred Years' War, English victory over the French 13 Sept 1356 at Poitiers, a French city 290 km/180 mi southwest of Paris. Prince Edward (the Black Prince) was marching north from Gienne, where he had landed 1355, with an English army of about 8,000 troops when he found his progress barred near Poitiers by 15,000 French troops under King John II of France.

Peace negotiations failed and the battle began with a French attack by dismounted knights which was broken up by English archers. A second attack made slightly better progress but was eventually beaten off. A quarter of the French army fled, but John attacked with the remaining unblooded quarter of his force and pressed the English very hard. The Black Prince sent a small force of English archers around a flank to attack the French from the rear, and this move decided the battle. Although the French fought strongly, by nightfall they had been routed. King John, his son Philip, and 2,000 knights were taken prisoner, while about 3,000 French were killed. English losses were small, and Edward was able to make a gradual retreat to

Bordeaux.

Port Arthur during the Russo-Japanese War, Japanese victory over the Russians after the siege May 1904–Jan 1905 of Port Arthur, Manchuria (now Lushun, Chinese People's Republic). In 1898 Port Arthur was leased to the Russians; it was connected by rail to Mukden and thence to the Trans-Siberian Railway, and gradually converted into a Russian fortress and naval base. However, due to financial restrictions, the full plan for the fortification of the base was never completed, leaving severe deficiencies in its defences.

The Japanese fleet blockaded the harbour from the outset of the war, keeping the Russian Far Eastern Fleet bottled up. The Japanese victory at Nanshan cut off Russian supply lines and the garrison of 47,000 troops under General Anatoly Stössel was besieged from the end of July 1904. Stossel was an incompetent martinet who had actually been relieved of his post by the Tsar, but concealed the order from his staff and continued to exercise command in an ineffectual manner. The Japanese mounted a strong assault on the defensive line 19 Aug, but were beaten off. The Japanese then launched a series of minor attacks periodically to test the Russian defences, until 11-in howitzers, shipped from Japan, were brought into action 1 Oct to batter the Russian defences and also shell the fleet lying in the harbour.

More furious assaults were made 26 Oct–2 Nov without success, until '203-Metre Hill', a pivot of the defensive line, was taken by the Japanese 5 Dec. With this wedge inserted in the Russian line, the Japanese proceeded to deal with individual forts on the northern front, making a huge gap in the line. The garrison's morale began to sink and the death of General Kondratchenko, the moving spirit behind the defence, lowered it even further. Stössel surrendered 2 Dec, with only 24,000 effective troops left and 15,000 wounded. Japanese losses were also heavy: 58,000 killed and wounded plus 34,000 hospitalized with various diseases.

Prague during the Seven Years' War, victory of Frederick the Great and a Prussian army over Charles of Lorraine and an Austrian army 6 May 1757 outside Prague (then in Bohemia, now capital of the Czech Republic). Prague was then held by Charles with 75,000 Austrian troops, and Frederick began his campaign of 1757 by marching on the city with 64,000 troops.

Frederick opened with a strong attack against the Austrian left flank, followed by a general advance. The battle was hotly contested and things were not going well for Frederick until he threw a cavalry attack against each of the Austrian wings. This broke their defence and drove them into a hasty retreat into the fortified city of Prague, losing over 10,000 casualties and 4,300 prisoners. Prussian losses were over 13,000 but they held the field and moved on to lay siege to the city.

Przasnysz in World War I, series of battles between Russian and German forces over an important road junction about 72 km/45 mi north of Warsaw. The most important battle was Feb 1915 when a Russian victory put an end to

Field Marshal Paul von Hindenburg's offensive against the ◊Narev river line.

The Germans initially captured Przasnysz from the Russians Dec 1914 but quickly lost it again. Hindenburg brought up two army corps to recapture it 1915, attacking from three directions. The Russians held the town with a comparatively small force and so evacuated it 25 Feb 1915, but the troops were by then surrounded and had no escape route. They were saved only by the arrival of troops collected from the various Russian border fortresses who deployed west and north of the town and began surrounding the encircling German forces. Battered on both sides by Russians, the Germans fought for two days before disengaging and retiring to their original positions near Mlava, having lost at least 10,000 prisoners to the Russians. The town remained in Russian hands until later in 1915 when a fresh German advance captured it.

Przemysl in World War I, series of engagements Sept 1914–June 1915 between Russian and German forces. Przemysl was an Austro-Hungarian fortress on the Polish border in Galicia, on the river San, 200 km/125 mi east of Cracow. The Russians encircled the fortress in their initial campaign Sept 1914 and settled down to a formal siege. But at about the same time, Austrian resistance in Galicia suddenly stiffened and the German invasion of Poland got under way, both factors which threatened the Russian advance and began to drive it back. By Oct 1914 this movement had opened a route into Przemysl for the Austrian Army to reinforce and attempt to relieve it. After bitter fighting this attempt failed, the Austrians were pushed back, and the siege lines were closed around the fortress once more. The garrison attempted to break out Nov–Dec but was defeated by the besieging force. The shortage of food now began to make itself felt as the Russian pressure tightened and eventually the garrison blew up the major forts and magazines and surrendered the fortress 22 March 1915 along with 9 generals, 2,600 officers, 117,000 troops, and 700 guns.

By May 1915 the tide had turned against the Russians and General August von Mackensen was besieging them; they had not had time to repair the various forts and were unable to withstand the serious attack which took place in the first days of June. By 3 June the fortress was in German hands and remained so for the rest of the war.

Quebec in the Seven Years' War, British victory over the French Sept 1759 at Quebec, Canada. Quebec was a French possession and a British force of 9,000 troops under General James Wolfe set out to capture it 1759. They sailed in a fleet up the St Lawrence river, anchored off the Isle d'Orléans 26 Jun, and set up a camp on the Montmorenci river, with the French offering little opposition.

For some months Wolfe did little but patrol the area, but on 3 Sept the British moved to the south side of the St Lawrence, and a feigned attack was made below the city 12 Sept. While this was in progress, Wolfe secretly took 4,000 troops up the river in boats. They returned after nightfall and landed at a point Wolfe had previously selected, about 2.5 km/1.5 mi above the city. In the early morning of the 13th, the troops made their way up a narrow path to the Heights of Abraham, above the river. The French responded by taking up their battle order on the Heights and the battle began. The British musketry soon broke the French line and they fled into the city, followed by the British, though they were prevented from entering by the French garrison's artillery. Both Wolfe and the French leader Marshal Louis Montcalm were killed in the battle, but the British force remained in position on the Heights and Quebec surrendered 17 Sept.

Quiberon Bay during the Seven Years' War, British naval victory over the French 20 Nov 1759 in Quiberon Bay, off the French coast about 240 km/150 mi southeast of Ushant. The victory wrecked French plans for an invasion of England and reasserted British command of the sea. The French had assembled their invasion force at Quiberon and on 14 Nov Vice-Admiral the Marquis de Conflans left Brest with a French fleet of 21 ships of the line and 3 frigates to safeguard the troops' transport to England. He anchored in Quiberon Bay hoping that a winter gale would force the British fleet under Admiral Edward Hawke to seek shelter in an English port, allowing the French a free run.

Conflans relied on the islands and dangerous rocks which surround the bay for protection, but Hawke knew the bay and took his fleet of 23 ships of the line and 10 frigates through the obstacles in a gale, and sailed down on both sides of the anchored French. Each British ship fired a broadside as it passed the French ships and completely destroyed the French fleet: some ships were sunk, others captured, and some wrecked, including the French flagship which was driven ashore and burned. British losses were comparatively light: two ships were wrecked on the rocks, and one officer and 273 sailors were killed or wounded.

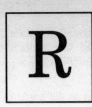

Radom in World War I, Russian victory over Austrian and German forces near Radom, a Polish manufacturing town 112 km/70 mi south of Warsaw. After their defeat at Ivangorod the Austrian army fell back to Radom 24 Oct 1914, closely pursued by the Russians, and a fierce battle developed close to the town. The area was thickly forested so that German and Austrian troops became separated from their parent units and split up into smaller units which the Russians, more experienced in forest fighting, were able to tackle and defeat one at a time. The Russians finally took the town 28 Oct and the Austrians continued their retreat.

Ramillies during the War of the Spanish Succession, English and Dutch victory over the French 23 May 1706, near Ramillies, 19 km/12 mi north of Namur, Belgium. The Duke of Marlborough wished to march his troops into Italy, but was forbidden to do so by his Dutch masters. He therefore turned against the French, who had one army under the Duc de Villeroi close to the Netherlands border and another behind it under Marshal Marsin. They intended to join forces, but before they could do so, Marlborough marched to Ramillies, close to Villeroi's army, and offered battle; Villeroi responded without waiting for Marsin's force.

The French lined up with their centre on Ramillies village, infantry in the centre and cavalry on the wings. The English and Dutch adopted a similar plan, and the battle began by their attacking the French left, the troops having to wade through marshland to reach their targets. Dutch cavalry then attacked in the centre but were thrown back with severe casualties. Next, Marlborough directed the Dutch infantry to attack a small village on the French right flank, and as the French strengthened their flank to meet this threat, threw the English infantry at the centre. They charged, broke through the French line, and entered the village. The Dutch now wheeled and most of the French were caught between the Dutch and the English. The French broke and fled, leaving all their artillery and some 15,000 casualties; English and Dutch losses were fewer than 4,000.

Rapido River in World War II, costly US assault on German lines in Italy based on the Rapido, a river running southwest through ◊Cassino to meet the Garigliano river; it was a major German defensive obstacle in the Gustav Line. The first attempt to cross 20 Jan 1944 was a failure, with over 1,000 killed and 600 wounded; this engagement was known as the ***Battle of***

Bloody River. The second attempt took place 24 Jan north of Cassino where the river was shallower; the US forces took two days to establish a bridgehead, after which reinforcements were put across and the Gustav Line was broken.

Rava Russka (also known as the battle of the Grodek Line) in World War I, battles between Austrian and Russian forces Sept 1914. The Austrians had retreated to a line from Tomasov (now Tomaszow Lubelski, Poland) via Grodek (now Gorodok, Ukraine) to Rava Russka (now Rawa Russkaja, Ukraine). The Austrian line continued further north but with several gaps, and the Russians were able to infiltrate thorough these to make flank attacks. This destabilized the Austrians as parts of their line fell back, while others remained isolated and attempted to make their own way out of the encircling Russians. A series of battles up and down the line ensued, resulting in a general retreat by the Austrians with estimated losses of 250,000 casualties and some 100,000 troops along with 400 guns and quantities of stores captured by the Russians. Rava Russka itself fell 8 Sept 1914.

Reichswald in World War II, hard-fought Allied attack on German defences Feb 1945, part of the general advance into Germany. The Reichswald was a German state forest situated around Cleve, close to the Dutch border, about 25 km/15 mi west of Nijmegen between the Waal and Maas rivers. In the winter of 1945 the Germans released the sluices on these rivers so that the areas north and south of the forest were flooded and impassable. As part of the advance into Germany, the 2nd Canadian Corps and the British 30th Corps were required to advance through this area Feb 1945. Unable to manoeuvre due to the floods, the attack was preceded by an immense artillery barrage, over 6,000 tons of shells being fired on the first day of the attack. In spite of the difficult terrain the attack went well and took the initial objectives, after which German resistance stiffened and it was not until 21 Feb that the entire area was cleared.

There was no room for manoeuvre and no scope for cleverness; I had to blast my way through three defensive systems, the centre of which was the Siegfried Line.

General Sir Brian Horrocks on his tactics in the ***Reichswald***.

Rhine, crossing of the in World War II, Allied operation to cross the river Rhine, the principal obstacle to their advance into Germany 1945. The first crossing was a bridge at Nijmegen in Holland, acquired as a by-product of the ◊Arnhem operation and held by the Canadian Army. The US 3rd Army under General George Patton then crossed near Mainz 21 March 1945. The principal crossings were planned to give access to the Ruhr, so as to threaten the German industrial base. The British crossed at Wesel and the Americans near Rheinberg, both 23 March. Both these crossings were preceded by heavy artillery and air bombardment of the German side, parachute landings to secure bridgeheads, and preliminary attacks by British commando and US Ranger forces.

Riga in World War I, German attacks on Russian forces leading to their capture of Riga, a Baltic seaport and capital of Latvia. It was attacked by the Germans Aug 1915 but successfully defended by Latvian troops of the Russian army. A fresh German offensive Oct 1915 failed to reach the city after severe fighting and the area then fell quiet. A new German offensive began late 1917, in which General Oskar von Hutier and Col Georg Bruchmüller devised a new infiltration tactic. Artillery would fire on specific targets, rather than make a general bombardment, and parties of storm troops would then pass through the defences and take them from the rear or attack headquarters and supply points, thus breaking holes in the defensive line through which the mass of German infantry could pour. This succeeded and the Germans took the city 3 Sept 1917, retaining it for the remainder of the war.

Latvia proclaimed its independence Nov 1918 but Soviet troops captured Riga Jan 1919. They were expelled with the aid of German troops who promptly took the city themselves until the Latvians and Estonians attacked the Germans June 1919. Under the orders of the Allied mission to the Baltic, the Germans evacuated the city later that year.

River Plate World War II naval battle in the South Atlantic between a British cruiser squadron of three ships and the German 'pocket battleship' *Admiral Graf Spee* Dec 1939. Although the British cruisers were no match for the battleship, Admiral Sir Henry Harwood launched an attack. German fire seriously damaged HMS *Exeter*, put half of HMS *Ajax*'s guns out of action, and then damaged HMS *Achilles*, but the cruisers did sufficient damage to the German ship to make its captain break off and run for shelter in Montevideo, Uruguay. The British followed, and waited in international waters outside the neutral port. The Uruguay government ordered the Germans to leave after 72 hours. Hitler, reluctant to risk the *Graf Spee* being sunk by heavier British warships which were sailing for the River Plate, ordered the captain to scuttle the vessel. He did so 17 Dec 1939 and three days later shot himself.

Roanoke Island during the American Civil War, Union defeat of Confederate forces 8 Feb 1862. Roanoke Island, a Confederate stronghold, commanded the entrance to Albemarle Sound on the coast of North Carolina. Union strategy for 1862 included a landing on the Sound and an advance inland which would cut the Richmond-Wilmington railroad and also threaten the Confederate naval base of Norfolk, Virginia, from the south.

A previous attempt 29 Sept 1861 had failed due to gross mismanagement; this second attempt was better organized, using three Union brigades under General Ambrose Burnside and 20 gunboats under Flag Officer Louis Goldsborough. Aided by a naval bombardment, the infantry were put ashore and soon overpowered the garrison and took the island. Unfortunately, the naval bombardment of Roanoke Island and of the nearby Confederate Fort Barrow used up all the navy ammunition, and further advances had to wait until the navy had re-stocked. By that time, the Confederates had been able to develop further lines of defence in and around the Sound, and Burnside's expedition found it difficult to advance. Then the Union strategy changed again; the overland expedition was cancelled and the troops withdrawn, but the island remained garrisoned by Union forces, giving them naval control of the area for the rest of the war.

Rocroi during the Thirty Years' War, French victory over the Spanish 19 May 1643 at Rocroi; this battle marked the beginning of the decline of Spanish military power in the war. An army of 27,000 Spanish troops was besieging Rocroi, a French fortified town 24 km/15 mi northwest of Mézières and 3 km/2 mi from the Belgian frontier. A French force of 22,000 troops under the Duc d'Enghien (later known as the Great Condé) marched to relieve the town and gave battle to the Spanish. The French left wing and centre fared badly, but the Spanish failed to follow up their advantage. French cavalry on the right wing routed their opponents, rode round the Spanish centre to the opposite wing, and then charged the Spanish infantry. After four assaults they broke the Spanish line and routed them, the Spanish leaving 8,000 dead and 6,000 prisoners. French losses were about 2,000 killed and 2,000 wounded.

Rolica during the Peninsular War, French defeat by the Duke of Wellington 17 Aug 1808 at Rolica, a village 65 km/40 mi north of Lisbon, Portugal. A relatively small action in itself, it is worthy of note for two reasons: it was the first British engagement of the Peninsular War; and it was the first time that Col Henry Shrapnel's Spherical Case Shot – later to be more widely known as the Shrapnel shell – was used in action.

About 3,000 French troops under Marshal Delaborde had taken up a position in the village, barring the British route to Lisbon. Wellington attacked with 4,000 troops and drove the French out of the village, costing them 500 casualties.

Rorke's Drift during the Zulu War, British victory over a Zulu army 22 Jan 1879 at Rorke's Drift, a farm about 170 km/105 mi north of Durban, Natal. After the disaster at ◊Isandhlwana a party of some 4,000 Zulus descended on the farm which was operating as a British field hospital and supply depot. It contained 36 troops in the hospital itself, 84 troops of the 24th Regiment, a company of native infantry, a chaplain, a surgeon, Lt Gomville Bromhead of the 24th Regiment, and Lt John Chard of the Royal Engineers.

A handful of survivors from Isandhlwana arrived, most continuing their flight, and Chard set his fit troops to making what defences they could from wagons, sacks of flour, and other available items. The native contingent fled, together with their officers and NCOs, leaving Chard with 140 troops to protect a 300-metre perimeter.

The Zulus arrived late in the afternoon of 22 Jan. The soldiers took up position on the barricades and began shooting, but the waves of Zulus came faster than the troops could shoot, and hand-to-hand fighting broke out. The Zulus broke into the hospital, resulting in savage fighting even involving the sick and wounded soldiers; the hospital caught fire, the sick were dragged out, and the battle went on. It was 4 a.m. before the Zulus ceased their attacks, though even then they threw spears into the compound. At dawn, 80 troops were still fit to fight, and the Zulus had vanished. The troops had breakfast, and at 7.30 a.m. the Zulus re-appeared. Chard's troops took up the barricades once more, but the Zulus simply sat down on a nearby hill and watched for about an hour before they stood, turned about, and went. They too had had enough.

Eleven Victoria Crosses were awarded to the defenders, the most ever given for a single battle, and nine Distinguished Conduct Medals. British casualties were 17 killed and 10 wounded while the Zulus left 400 dead on the field.

Rossbach during the Seven Years' War, Prussian victory over a French-Austrian coalition 5 Nov 1757 at Rossbach, a small village in what was then Prussian Saxony, now Germany, about 37 km/23 mi southwest of Leipzig. The coalition troops were intent upon attacking Leipzig and had crossed the river Saale to confront the Prussians who, under Frederick the Great, held the high ground around Rossbach. The French general, the Prince de Soubise, commanding the coalition, decided to outflank Frederick. Frederick drew his wing in, making a feint retreat, lured the coalition troops out of their strong position, and, once they were well spread out in what they assumed to be a pursuit, launched the Prussian cavalry, under General von Seidlitz, against the Austrian infantry, throwing them into total disarray. This was followed by a Prussian infantry charge which added to the confusion and utterly routed the rest of the coalition army which lost about 3,000 killed and wounded, 5,000 prisoners, and 63 guns. Survivors of the coalition force retreated in disorder into Bavaria, while Frederick marched off to Silesia to inflict another defeat on the Austrians at ⟡Leuthen the following month.

Rostov in World War II, German defeat Nov 1941 by Soviet forces in fighting for Rostov, a city on the river Don in the southern USSR close to the Sea of Azov; the first military setback in the German invasion of the Soviet Union. In late 1941 Rostov was defended by the Soviet 9th Army against an attack by the German 1st Panzer Army under General Ewald von

Kleist but after a hard battle the city was captured 21 Nov 1941. The River Don was frozen hard, and the Soviets were able to cross the ice and establish two bridgeheads to begin a counterattack, while other Soviet units moved to the flanks and began threatening the German supply lines. Field Marshal Gerd von Rundstedt, Kleist's superior, ordered the city be abandoned 29 Nov and Kleist fell back to a better defensive position. Hitler ordered Rundstedt to cancel his orders to retire and stand firm, whereupon he resigned; his loss was a serious blow to the army.

St Mihiel salient in World War I, US operation to remove a German salient in northern France Sept 1918; French attempts to drive the Germans back from 1915 onward had met with heavy losses and no success. The salient was a triangular protrusion of the German front line, with its tip at St Mihiel on the river Meuse and its base stretching 48 km/30 mi from Fresnes to Pont-à-Mousson.

On 11 Sept 1918 seven US divisions lay on the north side and two US divisions plus the French 15th Colonial Corps lay on the south, while the French 2nd Colonial Corps fronted the tip and two US divisions lay in support. The plan was a simultaneous attack on both sides of the base to cut off the salient while the French launched a frontal holding attack. Assisted by tanks and ground attack aircraft, the US assault went forward on schedule, leading to hard fighting. On the morning of 13 Sept the 1st and 26th Divisions (coming from the south and north respectively) met at Vigneulles, neatly cutting off much of the German forces, although the Germans were, by this time, already in retreat. General John Pershing's troops took over 13,000 prisoners and 200 guns, the salient was flattened out, and the US forces went on to drive the Germans from the heights of the Meuse.

St Quentin during the Franco-Spanish war, Spanish victory over the French 10 Aug 1557 at St Quentin. A Spanish force, estimated at 5,000 cavalry and 3,000 foot under Duke Philibert of Savoy was threatening St Quentin, a French town 150 km/95 mi northwest of Paris, and the Constable of France, the Duc de Montmorency, set out to relieve it with a 20,000-strong army of mainly French troops, but including some German mercenaries. Their route lay through a narrow valley, at which the Spanish set up an ambush. This proved so effective that Montmorency lost some 15,000 troops and all but two of his guns were captured. The Spanish lost only 50 troops and were able to deal with St Quentin at their leisure.

St Quentin during the Franco-Prussian War, French defeat by the Prussian Army 19 Jan 1871. The French Army of the North (see ◊Hallue River) under General Louis Faidherbe had, after the Hallue River stand-off, retired into bivouacs in the region of the Somme and gradually recovered its morale. By the beginning of 1871 the French position in the siege of ◊Paris was becoming desperate; the Provisional Government demanded that

Faidherbe take his army and make a demonstration of some sort to draw the Prussians away from Paris in order to allow the mass of troops in Paris to make a sortie through the Prussian lines.

Faidherbe considered his options and felt that a thrust to the east, toward St Quentin and the Oise valley, would cause the maximum commotion and threaten the German lines of communication, and that with some luck he might well make a round tour and return to his stronghold without actually having to fight. There were difficulties: the Prussians occupied strategic points, so that his only available route was a tortuous way round through confined country lanes; he had to march straight across the front of the Prussian occupation army, a desperate enough manoeuvre with experienced troops but near-suicidal with barely trained militia; the weather was bad; and the Prussians facing him had a new commander, General August von Goeben, a clear-headed and highly skilled professional. Von Goeben's cavalry informed him as soon as the French began to move, his infantry raced ahead of the French and stopped them at the Oise river, though without a serious battle, and Faidherbe realised his only course was to fall back on St Quentin and make a stand.

The French far outnumbered the Prussians, but their morale was poor after a week of trudging through the rain and mud; orders went astray and the deployment was not what Faidherbe planned; on top of all this, desertion was weakening his army by the hour. Nevertheless, the first Prussian attack was held off by the French 22nd Corps which had taken up a sound defensive position on a hill. On the other flank, though, the 23rd Corps collapsed rapidly, and by sending Prussian reserves to the aid of the wing that had been held off, Goeben was able to push the 22nd Corps out of its position so that by the afternoon all resistance had gone and the French were streaming back through St Quentin. Faidherbe bowed to fate and ordered a retreat, the remains of his force pulling clear under cover of night; fortunately the Prussians had become disorganized and were in no condition to pursue. Leaving behind 3,000 killed and wounded and some 11,000 prisoners and deserters, Faidherbe got his troops clear but knew that they were no longer an army; he distributed them through the remaining French fortresses in the North, and organized resistance to the Prussians in western France ended.

St Vincent during the French Revolutionary War, British defeat of a Spanish fleet 14 Feb 1797 off Cape St Vincent on the Portuguese coast; the British victory wrecked French plans to invade England. A Spanish fleet of 27 ships was en route to join with the French fleet at Brest, to protect the invasion force, when it encountered a British fleet of 15 ships under Sir John Jervis. The British were in tight line formation, whereas the Spanish were in two loose groups. Jervis headed for the gap between the two groups, intending to get to the windward side of one group and attack it, which would give him freedom of manoeuvre but would prevent the leeward

Spanish group from coming close. Commodore Horatio Nelson, at the rear of the British line, saw that the leeward French could, in fact, circle around and come on Jervis from the rear, and in total disobedience of his orders, sailed on his own to attack the Spanish line which was already showing signs of the movement Nelson had foreseen. He engaged them single-handed for some time before other ships from Jervis' command, seeing the threat, came to support him. A fierce fight ensued, and four Spanish ships and 3,000 prisoners were taken. The remainder of the Spanish fleet turned back to Cadiz, but Jervis did not pursue. Jervis became Lord St Vincent and Nelson gained his knighthood.

Saints, The during the American War of Independence, British naval victory over the French 12 April 1782, off the islands of Les Saintes in the channel separating Dominica from Guadeloupe in the Windward Islands. The British achieved their short-term aim of preventing a French convoy from sailing, but more importantly this battle also had the effect of reasserting British naval supremacy in the western hemisphere.

A British fleet of 36 ships under Admiral Sir George Rodney was in the area watching a French convoy and a fleet of 33 ships which was being assembled by Admiral François de Grasse to protect the convoy. As the convoy was being escorted to Guadeloupe, Rodney fell on the rearmost ships, forcing the French fleet to turn about and come to their rescue. The two fleets approached each other in parallel lines but the French formation was ragged and a gap opened. Rodney took his squadron through the gap, breaking the French line, and he captured or destroyed five French ships and took two others a few days later. French losses numbered some 3,000 casualties and 8,000 prisoners, while British losses were 261 killed and 837 wounded.

Saipan in World War II, US capture 1944 of Japanese-held island of the Marianas group about 1,900 km/1,200 mi north of New Guinea. The operation was mainly notable for the mass suicide of the Japanese civil population, several hundred of whom threw themselves over a cliff rather than be captured.

Saipan was invaded by US forces 17 June 1944, before the Japanese had completed their planned fortifications. An airfield was captured on the first day, allowing US fighters to provide instant air support, but clearing the island was a slow and hard fight which lasted until 17 July. Even then numbers of Japanese troops hid in the more remote areas until the war ended.

Salamanca during the Peninsular War, British victory over the French 22 July 1812 south of Salamanca. After taking ◊Badajoz and Cuidad Rodrigo 1812, Wellington entered Spain with 42,000 troops and took up a position south of Salamanca, 170 km/105 mi northwest of Madrid, which protected his supply route back to Portugal. The 46,000 French troops occupying Salamanca moved out to oust the British and capture the road. Wellington forestalled their plans by moving his force to the intervening North Arapiles Hill, and sending General Sir Edward Pakenham with a force of infantry to make a head-on attack on the advancing French army. Once this battle was under way, he then sent the rest of his infantry to attack the French flank. A severe battle ensued, and Wellington then directed Sir Stapleton Cotton against the other flank of the French column with his cavalry. This attack scattered the French and totally ended their resistance. Marshal Auguste Marmont was able to collect his forces and made a fighting retreat to Valladolid, while the British entered Salamanca. French casualties came to 15,000, and Marmont himself was forced to return to France to recover from a wound sustained in the operation; British losses were 6,000.

Salamaua in World War II, Australian capture of Japanese supply base Sept 1943. The Japanese launched their attack on Port Moresby over the Kokoda Trail from Salamaua, a seaport on the north coast of New Guinea, and when the attack failed, turned the port into a major supply base. It was eventually attacked by Australian troops flown into Wau, about 40 km/25 mi away. Japanese reinforcements failed to arrive and the town was taken 11 Sept 1943.

Salamis in the Persian Wars, Greek naval victory over the Persians 480 BC in the Strait of Salamis southwest of Athens. Despite being heavily outnumbered, the Greeks inflicted a crushing defeat on the invading Persians which effectively destroyed their fleet.

After the sack of Athens by the Persians, the commanders of some 370 Greek war galleys then lying off the island of Salamis debated what action they could take; their debate was ended by the appearance of the Persian fleet in the Bay of Phalerum. Themistocles, the Athenian commander of the Greek fleet, sent a fake message, ostensibly from a spy, to the Persians warning that the Greek fleet was about to withdraw and that the Persians should blockade the entrance to the Bay of Eleusis. The Persians fell for the ruse and spread their 1,000 ships thinly across the bay. The Persians were so confident they could deal with a mere 370 vessels that they had a throne prepared for their king, Xerxes, on nearby Mount Aegaleus so that he would have a grandstand view from which to watch the anticipated crushing of the Greek fleet.

Unfortunately, the Greeks came out into the bay at full speed, broke the Persian line, and then sowed mayhem in all directions, sinking over 500 Persian ships for the loss of only about 40 of their own. Xerxes, disgusted at this humiliation, returned to Asia, leaving a subordinate, Mardonius, to continue the land campaign.

Sambre in World War I, Allied victory over the Germans Nov 1918; the final part of the British advance across Flanders. The British 1st, 3rd, and 4th Armies were pitched against the 2nd and 18th German Armies along the line of the Sambre, a French river which rises in the *département* of the

Aisne, flows northeast, and joins the Meuse at Namur. The battle began by the British and Canadians taking the town of Valenciennes 1 Nov, then advancing through Le Quesnoy to attack the main German defensive line, known as the Hermann Line, which ran along the Sambre. By 8 Nov this line had been broken and the town of Landrécies taken; German troops began destroying stores dumps and burning equipment, and Canadian troops entered Maubeuge 9 Nov with no German resistance. On the night of 10 Nov the Canadians entered Mons, drove out the German occupants and pressed their advance until three minutes before 11 a.m. on 11 Nov, when the Armistice took effect.

San in World War I, series of engagements between Russian and Austrian forces 1914–1915 on a line along the San, a Polish river rising in the Carpathian mountains and flowing northwest to join the Vistula near Sandomierz, a length of about 420 km/260 mi.

Oct–Nov 1914 the advancing Austrians met the Russian defensive line on the river and were beaten off, allowing the Russians to begin advancing toward Cracow.

May–June 1915 after the Russians had been defeated on the ◊Dunajetz, they retired to the San line. Once again they beat off several Austrian attacks, but a German army under General August von Mackensen then crossed the river and began advancing toward ◊Przemysl. The Russians counterattacked but were unable to cross the San again; Mackensen made another determined attack, the Austrians did likewise, and the Russians were driven back on the fortress of Przemysl. A flanking movement by Mackensen threatened the Russians' supply lines and they abandoned the fortress and fell back to the east.

Sangro River in World War II, successful British attack Nov–Dec 1943 on a German defensive line. German troops set up a defensive line on the Sangro, an Italian river rising in the Apennines and flowing northeast to the Adriatic near Ortona, Nov 1943 which was then attacked by the British 8th Army. Severe rains led to flooding which made the river almost impassable and the British had to wait three weeks before being able to establish a bridgehead. By the end of Nov tanks were across the river and the British advanced on Ortona, which they took 27 Dec 1943.

Santa Cruz World War II naval engagement between US and Japanese fleets north of the Solomon Islands Oct 1942; it left the US Navy without an operational aircraft carrier in the Pacific area. A Japanese force waiting for the recapture of the airbase at Henderson Field and a US force intent on preventing Japan reinforcing ◊Guadalcanal found each other and flew off air strikes against each other almost simultaneously. The aircraft met and fought, and the survivors continued on to attack the enemy fleets. The USS *Hornet* was struck by two torpedoes, six bombs, and two suicide aircraft, and was abandoned on fire and later sunk by the Japanese. The

USS *Enterprise* was also hit, while two Japanese carriers were severely damaged.

Saratoga during the American War of Independence, British defeat by the Americans Sept 1777 near Saratoga Springs, about 240 km/150 mi north of New York. General John Burgoyne was marching a British column of about 4,000 troops from Canada to join General Sir William Howe who was based lower down the Hudson River. They met a 3,000-strong American force under Benedict Arnold near Saratoga 19 Sept. After two hours of hard fighting, the result was inconclusive, though both sides suffered severe casualties and eventually withdrew. Burgoyne launched another attack 7 Oct, but the Americans were prepared for it and met him with a spoiling attack, forcing the British to retreat 19 km/12 mi from Saratoga and entrench. On 17 Oct Burgoyne surrendered to the American commander General Horatio Gates, who by now had some 5,000 troops.

Under the terms of the surrender, known as the Convention of Saratoga, the British were to be allowed to march to Boston and there embark for England, but Congress refused to ratify it and Burgoyne and his force became prisoners of war until peace was signed.

Sarikamish World War I battle between Russian and Turkish forces, Dec 1914–Jan 1915 which led to the collapse of the Turkish offensive in the Caucasus. This was a bold scheme to advance from Erzerum via Sarikamish to Kars over a 3,000-m/10,000-ft mountain range in the depths of winter. Although by Dec 1914 they had reached Sarikamish, their progress was slow and they had been unable to bring up heavy artillery. This allowed the Russians to bring up reinforcements and guns, and they were attacked by the Turks 25 Dec, who took the town the following day. The Russians fell back, regrouped, and then counterattacked, regaining the town. They pursued the Turks back on their tracks and the Turkish offensive collapsed.

Savo Island World War II naval battle between a Japanese cruiser force and a US-Australian force protecting US transports reinforcing ◊Guadalcanal 8–9 Aug 1942. The Japanese achieved complete surprise, and in two engagements sank three US and one Australian cruiser and damaged two others. The Japanese commander, fearful of air strikes as dawn broke, then withdrew without attacking the transports which were at his mercy. He was reprimanded for his temerity.

Scarpe (also known as the fifth battle of ◊Arras) World War I battle between British and German forces Aug 1918; the Scarpe is a French river rising near St Pol, and flowing east past Arras and Douai to join the Scheldt near the Belgian frontier.

The British, under General Henry Horne, were attempting to prepare the ground for a general advance by driving the Germans out of a subsection of the Hindenburg Line. They attacked along both sides of the river, taking several villages and completing the operation with the capture of Bullecourt

31 Aug. The battle then died down into a series of local skirmishes until the opening of the final battle for ◊Arras 2 Sept.

Sedan during the Franco-Prussian War, disastrous French defeat by the Prussians 2 Sept 1870 at Sedan, a fortified town in northern France, close to the Belgian border and about 195 km/120 mi northeast of Paris. Emperor Napoleon III was captured and, on a broader scale, the defeat was a disaster for the French who no longer had any effective regular army – in the future, war would have to be carried on by mostly citizen armies – and now only Paris held out; once the siege was over, the Prussians were to win the war. So severe was the defeat that the French decided to return to Republican government.

The Prussian advance from the east had forced the principal French armies, under General Marie MacMahon, to encamp at Châlons, where MacMahon reorganized them into a 150,000-strong army. The other main French army was besieged in the fortress of Metz, which MacMahon was ordered to relieve 21 Aug. To avoid the Prussians, he took a circuitous northward route via Reims (in order to resupply his force there) and then intended to march east via Verdun to Metz. However, Prussian cavalry patrols discovered his route and he was gradually forced further north, fighting rearguard actions, until the army arrived in Sedan in a disorganized state 30 Aug.

Nous sommes dans un pot de chambre, et nous y serons emmerdés.

General Auguste Alexandre Ducrot, on the night before the *Battle of Sedan*.

The town was surrounded by three Prussian armies with a ring of troops and artillery. The Prussians attacked 2 Sept, pouring concentrated artillery fire into the exposed French troops who held a stretch of country north of the town. MacMahon was wounded and the command fell to General Auguste Alexandre Ducrot, who ordered a retreat, though in truth there was little chance of breaking out of the Prussian encirclement. However, General Emmanuel Wimpffen, who had arrived from Paris just before the Prussians sealed the town off, produced orders from the Government appointing him to succeed MacMahon, and he cancelled the order to retreat, electing instead to fight where they stood. Meanwhile the Prussians tightened their grip, and by evening the Emperor Napoleon III ordered the French to surrender. The victory cost the Prussians about 9,000 casualties, but the French lost 17,000 killed and wounded, and 104,000 troops were taken as prisoners of war including the Emperor himself.

Selle in World War I, successful Allied operation in northern France 17–25 Oct 1918. The 2nd and 18th German Armies were encamped in positions on the line of the river Selle in front of ◊Cambrai. The British 4th Army with two attached US divisions attacked this position from a line from Le Cateau to Bohain; the French 1st Army mounted a similar attack on their right. Tanks, specially waterproofed and adapted for crossing the river, led the attack and drove the Germans back across the canal forming their second line obstacle. The attack was then extended northward and eventually the German line was pushed back to Valenciennes and Landrécies and the Scheldt river. The Allies captured 475 guns and 20,000 troops.

Sevastopol during the Crimean War, British and French victory over Russia Oct 1854–Sept 1855, at Sevastopol, a fortified town in southeast Russia on the Black Sea. The harbour at Sevastopol was the base of the Russian fleet, so the town was the prime objective of the main Allied attack in the Crimea. After the battle of the ◊Alma Sept 1854 the Allies closed up on Sevastopol and entrenched around it, commencing the siege 17 Oct. The lines did not extend completely round the town so it was possible for the Russians to reinforce and move supplies in; they also brought in General Eduard Todleben, their principal engineer, to strengthen the fortifications.

Little progress was made until June 1855; on 7 June the French took the Mamelon fortress which protected the Malakoff line, the principal defensive line for the town. The British attack on the Redan, another defensive complex, a few days later was a failure. A regular bombardment of the town began early Aug and the French victory at ◊Tchernaya signalled the end of effective Russian resistance. After a final assault by the Allies 5 Sept, Sevastopol was evacuated and the Russians retreated inland, leaving their wounded behind.

Sevastopol World War II German victory over Soviet forces 1942. The German advance into the Crimea Nov 1941 isolated it and the Germans left it to concentrate on ◊Moscow and ◊Leningrad. In May 1942 they began a siege, bringing up super-heavy artillery including the 800 mm Gustav gun, and 540 mm and 600 mm self-propelled howitzers. Air strikes and a naval blockade added to the pressure and infantry and tanks made the initial assault 7 June. After bitter house-to-house fighting, the Soviets ordered their troops to fall back into the inner city 23 June. By now the defenders were short of food and ammunition, and the Germans broke into the city 30 June, at which the Soviets authorized evacuation and were able to get most of their troops away by small boats before the Germans completed the occupation 3 July. It remained in German hands until recaptured by the Soviet Army April 1944.

Seven Days during the American Civil War, series of engagements June–July 1862, resulting in a general Confederate victory over Union forces. A Union Army of about 100,000 troops under General George McClellan had landed at Fort Monroe on the Virginia Peninsula intending to attack Richmond from the flank, but an attempt to outflank Confederate defences had ground to a halt in marshy ground. At the same time a second

Union Army under General Irwin McDowell began moving south from Alexandria, aiming at Richmond and a junction with McClellan's force. With these two threats in view, the Confederate general Joseph E Johnston decided to abandon his defensive line at Yorktown and retire toward Richmond; this movement was slowly followed up by McClellan's advancing force.

General Robert E Lee, then merely an adviser to Confederate President Jefferson Davis, had directed General Thomas 'Stonewall' Jackson to start some activity in the Shenandoah valley; this caused the Union to hold McDowell in place and remove some of his troops to counter Jackson. Lee went out to the Peninsula to find that McClellan's army was split in two by the flood-swollen Chickahominy river, and directed Johnston to attack the force lying south of the river. This became known as the *Battle of Seven Pines*, a confused and bloody affair in which Johnston was severely wounded.

Lee was given command of the army and, knowing McClellan to be a slow mover, began shuffling troops around in front of the Union Army so that McClellan was finally convinced that there was an enormous force in front of him. Lee then moved across the river and attacked the Union forces there; these fell back so that Lee could attack the southern half on its flank, and this, in turn, fell back. Lee continued in this manner, pushing one flank and then the other, McClellan backing away before him, and only the relative inexperience of Lee's staff and army allowed McClellan to escape without total loss. Fighting a series of sound rearguard actions through Mechanicsville, Cold Harbor, Savage's Station, White Oak Swamp, and finally Malvern Hill, McClellan managed to extricate most of his army and concentrate it on the James River, protected by his artillery and the Union navy. By that time the incessant rain had turned all the roads to mud and Lee's troops were exhausted with pursuit and fighting, so the Seven Days campaign came to an end.

Shiloh during the American Civil War, Confederate defeat by Union forces 6–7 Apr 1862 near Shiloh Church, about 150 km/95 mi east of Memphis, Tennessee. A Confederate force of 40,000 under General Albert Sidney Johnston which was concentrated in this area was approached by a Union Army of 42,000 under General Ulysses S Grant. The Confederates attacked the Union right flank 6 April, a division commanded by General William T Sherman, and in a few hours threw back the entire Union line toward the river behind them; during this phase of the battle Johnston was killed and replaced by General Pierre Beauregard.

The fighting died away at nightfall, as both sides were exhausted, but General Grant reinforced his left with three fresh divisions during the night and threw in an attack at 6 a.m. next morning. By this time the Confederates had lost more than a quarter of their original force and in spite of tenacious fighting were slowly forced back some 8 km/5 mi before the battle again died down and Beauregard was able to disengage and make his escape. Confederate losses were 10,690 killed and wounded and 960 prisoners; Union losses 10,150 killed and wounded and 4,045 prisoners. The failure of the Confederates to stop Grant's army led to the Union gaining control of the Mississippi valley.

Sidi Barrani during World War II, British victory over Italian forces 1940 at an Egyptian village close to the Libyan border. In Sept 1940 Italian forces crossed the border and set up a fortified camp with five infantry divisions, artillery, and tanks. On 8 Dec the British 4th Indian and 7th Armoured divisions, under General Sir Richard O'Connor, launched an attack. The Indian division made a frontal assault while the armour swung round and set up a road block. Between them they captured 38,000 prisoners, 237 guns, and 73 tanks.

Sidi Rezegh in World War II, series of engagements Nov 1941 between Allied and German forces near a village in Cyrenaica southeast of Tobruk, with a small airfield. Taken by the British 19 Nov 1941 during Operation ◊Crusader, it was fiercely attacked by the 15th and 21st Panzer Divisions 22 Nov and almost recaptured, but the Germans were forced to withdraw as they were running short of ammunition and fuel. A second battle took place on 27 Nov when 15th Panzer Division was halted by dug-in tanks and artillery and then driven off by 4th Armoured Division.

Silistria in the Russo-Turkish war, unsuccessful Russian siege of a Turkish fortress Dec 1853–March 1854 at Silistria, Bulgaria, about 110 km/70 mi northwest of Varna; the incident provided the spark for the Crimean War. Following the defeat of the Turks at ◊Sinope Nov 1853, a Russian army crossed the Danube from Romania and laid siege to the fortress. The garrison put up a strong resistance to the Russian attacks, though the Turks made no attempt to relieve the place.

Britain and France intervened and demanded that Russia evacuate the area. The Russians ignored this demand, but by March had given up hope of taking Silistria and raised the siege and moved off 20 March. France declared war on Russia 27 March and Britain followed suit next day, thus turning what had been a Russo-Turkish conflict into the Crimean War.

Singapore World War II Japanese victory over the British as part of their general advance through Southeast Asia 1942. Singapore was a British naval base at the tip of the Malayan peninsula. The base had been slowly constructed during the 1930s and was never fully completed. It was well protected against sea attack by coastal artillery, but had no landward defences (although the coast guns could, and did, fire inland). When ◊Malaya fell, the collapse of Singapore was inevitable and it surrendered 15 Feb 1942. Some 16,000 British, 14,000 Australian, and 32,000 Indian troops were taken prisoner.

Sinope in the Russo-Turkish war, Russian naval victory over the Turks 30 Nov 1853 off Sinope (now Sinop), a Turkish town on the southern shore of the Black Sea, about 320 km/200 mi northwest of Ankara. The Turks had declared war on the Russians 4 Oct after a Russian invasion of what is now Romania, but was then part of the Turkish Empire, and had won a minor battle there.

The Tsar ordered the Black Sea Fleet to bombard Sinope in retaliation. Approaching Sinope, they found a Turkish squadron anchored in the harbour, and in the course of bombarding the town sank nine Turkish ships, wrecked most of the harbour installation, and killed about 4,000 people. This caused the British and French governments to order their own fleets into the Black Sea in order to protect Turkish shipping, and began the series of events which was eventually to lead to the Crimean War (see also ◊Silistria).

Smolensk in World War II, German capture of a Soviet city and rail junction 400 km/250 mi west of Moscow, an objective of German Army Group Centre during Operation Barbarossa, the German invasion of the USSR, 1941. Aided by an encircling movement of Army Group North, the Germans captured 310,000 troops, 3,200 tanks, and 3,000 guns. However, this delayed the forward thrust of Army Group Centre, allowing the Soviets to organize the defence of Moscow. Smolensk remained in German hands until retaken by Soviet troops 25 Sept 1943.

Soissons in World War I, series of battles between Allied and German forces over a French town on the river Aisne, 105 km/65 mi northeast of Paris and one of the oldest in France. Fortified as a barrier against invasion from the north, it has always been among the first to suffer in war. It was taken by the Germans early in the war but recaptured 12 Sept 1914, after which they bombarded the town and caused great destruction. In Jan 1915 a French attack drove the German line back a few miles, but a German counterattack 10 days later drove the French back to their original line, with considerable losses on both sides. The line then stabilized until the German advance of May 1918 captured the town again, and they were finally driven out by the French 2 Aug 1918.

Solma-Ri in the Korean War, defeat of United Nations forces by North Korean and Chinese Communist forces 22–25 April 1951 on the Imjin River, South Korea, about 50 km/30 mi north of Seoul. After the intervention of the Chinese late 1950, the United Nations forces had established a line on the Imjin River and the British 29th Infantry Brigade was protecting a crossing over this river which controlled the route to Seoul.

On 22 April British patrols on the north side of the river were driven in by an entire Chinese Army and by nightfall the British positions, notably that held by the Gloucestershire Regiment, were almost surrounded. During the next day some of the defenders were able to extricate themselves, but by the end of the day the Chinese had completely enclosed the British positions;

nevertheless, they continued to fight, supported by a mortar battery of the Royal Artillery, until they were completely overwhelmed. On the morning of 25 April, with scarcely any ammunition, Lt-Col James Carne, commanding officer of the Gloucesters, ordered his troops to break out independently as best they could; only 39 troops reached the safety of their own lines, the remainder being either dead or prisoners. Although a tactical defeat, Solma-Ri was a strategic victory, since the stubborn defence put up by the British force had imposed sufficient delay upon the Chinese to allow other UN forces to establish a new defensive line on the Han river to protect Seoul, and the Chinese offensive was halted there and eventually thrown back north of the Imjin.

Somme, Battle of the in World War I, major Allied offensive July–Nov 1916 at Beaumont-Hamel-Chaulnes, on the river Somme in northern France, during which severe losses were suffered by both sides. It was planned jointly by Marshal Joseph Joffre and General Douglas Haig. The German offensive around ◊St Quentin March–April 1918 is sometimes called the Second Battle of the Somme. In 1916, the Allies decided to launch a coordinated offensive on the Western, Eastern, and Italian Fronts in the summer. In the event, the Germans pre-empted the Allied strategy with an attack on ◊Verdun Feb 1916; by the summer it had become obvious that the French were occupied fighting off this attack and any offensive on the Somme would have to be primarily a British effort.

The *First Battle* of the Somme was launched 1 July by the British 4th Army, supported by the 3rd and the French 8th Army Group, in an attack on the 2nd German Army which was well-protected by deep dug-outs. The British had made obvious preparations for the assault, including a week-long artillery bombardment of the well-entrenched German positions which had little effect other than to serve as a warning of an impending action. Consequently, the Germans were able to stiffen their defences prior to the arrival of the infantry assault, so that the British suffered the heaviest casualties in their history; 19,000 troops were killed on the first day. In spite of this, the attack continued and several small gains were made – the German line was almost breached 14 July. After a lull, the battle started again 15 Sept when tanks were used for the first time; some 47 tanks were available to the Allies of which most broke down. This attack made some progress but when the battle finally died away mid-Nov the total Allied gain was about 13 km/8 mi at a cost of 615,000 Allied and about 500,000 German casualties.

The *Second Battle* of the Somme 21 March 1918 was the first act of the ◊German Spring Offensive; it was intended to capture Amiens and split the French and British armies. The attack forced the British 5th Army under General Sir Hubert Gough to fall back, which in turn forced the flanking British 3rd and French 3rd Armies to retreat. The Germans advanced as far as Montdidier and were within a few miles of Arras before they were finally held.

Spanish Armada during the Anglo-Spanish War, English naval victory over the Spanish, 21–30 July 1588 in the waters around England. The Armada was a disaster for the Spanish and wrecked their plans for an invasion of England; more importantly, it marked a change in English sea tactics and the birth of English naval supremacy. Hitherto, sea battles had been fought by ships that were simply floating castles full of soldiers which came alongside each other and engaged in hand-to-hand fighting. Sir Francis Drake, and his successor John Hawkins, showed how to use ships with guns as weapons, relying upon seamanship and gunnery to cripple enemy vessels, and not grappling until the cannon had done their work.

King Philip II of Spain resolved to mount an invasion of England in response to the English army supporting the Netherlands in their revolt against Spain. A fleet assembled at Cadiz for this purpose was largely destroyed by Sir Francis Drake's raid April 1587. The Spanish assembled another fleet, the Great Armada, late in the year, which the Admiral Santa Cruz refused to risk in the winter gales of the Bay of Biscay. By spring 1588 Santa Cruz had died and command was given to the Duke of Medina Sidonia, who set sail 12 July with 130 ships carrying 20,000 soldiers.

The English fleet, consisting of 34 Queen's ships and 163 mainly small privateers had been ready since Feb. Sidonia's orders were to sail up the English Channel to the Netherlands and there embark more troops from the Spanish army operating in the Low Countries; the English fleet's objective was to break up the Armada before it reached the Netherlands. As the Spanish came up the Channel, the English sailed out parallel to them, delivering heavy cannon fire whenever opportunity offered. Twice the English attempted to force the Spanish to give battle but they refused and sailed on. Shortage of ammunition, and the skilful handling of their vessels by Spanish captains, meant that little damage was caused to the ships of either side in this phase of the battle.

On the night of 27 July the Spanish anchored in Calais, where, during the night, English fire-ships drifted down into their midst, creating panic and forcing them to cut free their anchors and sail northeast in confusion. The English fleet fell upon their rear off Gravelines and sank or burned several more ships, only ceasing their destruction because they ran out of ammunition. The English ships turned back to port to replenish, while the reduced Armada continued sailing north, only to run into a fierce gale. This broke up what formations remained and the individual ships attempted to sail around the north of Scotland and west of Ireland to return to Spain, with 28 ships being wrecked in the process. Fewer than half the Spanish ships managed to get back to Spain.

Spicheren during the Franco-Prussian War, Prussian victory over the French 6 Aug 1870 at Spicheren, a French village 3 km/2 mi from Saarbrücken. At the start of the Franco-Prussian War the French had occupied Saarbrücken and then planned an advance into Germany; the plan was abandoned due to logistic problems, and the French then settled on a defensive stance and withdrew behind Saarbrücken. A German cavalry patrol discovered the town empty, pressed on, and saw French troops moving away around Spicheren; they reported back that the French were in retreat. Count Helmuth von Moltke had drawn up a careful Prussian invasion plan, but when this report reached the commanders of the Prussian 1st and 2nd armies they ignored these plans and set out to pursue the French.

The French, under General Charles Frossard, were not in fact retreating but instead were moving into an excellent defensive position on a ridge overlooking Spicheren. Hence, as a result of the cavalry's erroneous report, the Prussian 14th Division blundered into two well-sited French corps. They should have been annihilated, but due to French incompetence in command, the Prussian attack was considered a probable feint and neighbouring commanders sent no assistance to Frossard. In contrast, every Prussian unit which heard gunfire marched toward the sound and soon the 14th Division was reinforced by General von Zastrow and the remainder of the 2nd Army.

General Frossard, undefeated, thought he had been defeated, and so he was. General von Zastrow was half-defeated but refused to be and so was not. That is the secret of the Prussian victory.

Bonnal on the **Battle of Spicheren**, La Manoeuvre de St Privat

---

Prussian artillery silenced the French guns and pushed the French infantry away from their commanding positions, allowing the Prussian infantry to clamber up the hillsides and gain the plateau at the summit. Nevertheless, French troops held their positions and inflicted severe casualties on the Prussians, and when night fell their commander pulled them into a tighter perimeter and prepared to fight on. However, no reinforcements came for the French, their last reserves had been put into battle, and as more Prussians appeared and began outflanking the position, Frossard realised he had to retire. He pulled out all his troops during the night to move south and take up a new defensive line. French losses were about 2,000 casualties and 2,000 prisoners, while the Prussians lost some 4,500 casualties.

Spion Kop during the South African War, Boer victory over the British 24 Jan 1900 at Spion Kop, a small hill a few miles southwest of Ladysmith, Natal. As part of General Sir Redvers Buller's plan to relieve Ladysmith by outflanking the Boers on the Tugela River, a column under General Sir Charles Warren crossed the river upstream and then moved down to attack the Boer position on Spion Kop, the centre of their right flank. British troops made a surprise attack on the night of 23–24 Jan and captured the hilltop, but were unable to get artillery up to the top due to the steep incline of the hill.

Morning revealed that their position was very exposed to Boer fire, and Brig-Gen E R P Woodgate, who had commanded the attack, was mortally wounded; command devolved on Col Thorneycroft, who stubbornly defended the position for the rest of the day. By nightfall he regarded the position as being untenable, and ordered a withdrawal. At the same time, the Boers had decided that they were unlikely to drive the British off and were withdrawing their artillery from nearby positions; they sent a final 'forlorn hope' of 2–300 troops to try and retake the hill, and, to their surprise, found it unoccupied except for about 300 British dead. Buller recrossed the Tugela river and ended his second attempt to relieve Ladysmith.

Spotsylvania during the American Civil War, indecisive engagement 7–12 May 1864 at Spotsylvania Court House about 80 km/50 mi northwest of Richmond, Virginia. After the Battle of the ◊Wilderness, the Confederate army under General Robert E Lee entrenched themselves 7 May around Spotsylvania Court House, an important road junction blocking the Union commander Ulysses S Grant's route to Richmond.

Grant was slower to react than Lee, and by the time he had issued his orders and got the army moving, he discovered Lee had beaten him to the junction and was standing in his way. Seeing that Lee was strong in the east, Grant attempted to outflank him in the west, sending General Winfield S Hancock with three divisions. However, by the time Hancock had got his troops into place night had fallen, and Lee was able to rush reinforcements in during the night so that when dawn came on 11 May Hancock realised he had no hope of success. Grant assumed that Lee must have weakened his centre, and ordered an attack there. It met well-constructed fieldworks backed by intense rifle fire and was thrown back; Hancock attacked on the flank with no better result. The Confederates remained unshaken and the Union had lost about 3,000 troops.

The Union forces then tried an attack with a brigade under Col Emory Upton, who had new ideas about attacking fieldworks. His solution was to charge in a tight column, without pausing to fire, swamp the first line with bayonets, spread out, and take the second line of defences, so punching a hole through which reinforcements could flow to continue the advance. His brigade did their work but the reinforcements failed to appear in time, and were stopped by Confederate fire when they finally did appear. Upton's troops had to scramble out of it as best they could, leaving 1,000 dead behind them.

Hancock launched another attack 12 May, this time against the tip of a Confederate salient thrusting into the Union lines, with another corps under

General Ambrose Burnside attacking the eastern face. This attack was successful, taking over 3,000 prisoners and 20 guns, but a fierce Confederate counterattack forced the Union troops into the tip of the Salient, and then degenerated into a face-to-face struggle known ever after as the 'Bloody Angle'. Attacks on the flanks of the salient by Burnside did little good; the Confederates held out all day, but after dark Lee drew his troops back and straightened his line, abandoning the salient. With that the battle more or less ended and both sides began edging eastwards, Grant to seek a way to Richmond, Lee to forestall him.

Stalingrad in World War II, heavy fighting between German and Soviet forces Aug 1942–Jan 1943. The siege of Stalingrad was a horrific campaign, with both sides sustaining heavy casualties and enormous suffering on the part of the citizens of Stalingrad who nonetheless fought bravely to defend their city.

Stalingrad was a Soviet city on the river Volga (now Volgograd), a major industrial centre and the objective of German Army Group B during the 1942 campaign to occupy the Caucasus region. The city was reinforced by the Soviets, and General Friedrich von Paulus, the commander of the German 6th Army, began attacking with units as and when they arrived instead of waiting until all his army had reached the area. As a result the Soviets were able to concentrate and destroy them one by one, whereas they might not have resisted a massed attack. Von Paulus halted his piecemeal attacks, waited for reinforcement by 4th Panzer Army, and launched the first major assault 19 Aug 1942. The initial advance through the suburbs was relatively smooth, but once into the built-up areas it became a house-to-house battle which went on for two months without either side gaining any advantage.

While staving off the Germans the Soviets were preparing a massive counterattack with 1 million troops, 13,500 guns, and 894 tanks commanded by Marshal Georgi Zhukov. This was launched 19 Nov and swept around the flanks of the 6th Army and encircled it. Fending off German attempts to relieve von Paulus, the Soviets then set about destroying the 6th Army until it surrendered 31 Jan 1943 with the loss of 1.5 million troops, 3,500 tanks, 12,000 guns and mortars, 75,000 vehicles, and 3,000 aircraft.

Stamford Bridge English victory over a Norse army 25 Sept 1066 during the Norse invasion of Britain, at Stamford Bridge 14 km/9 mi northeast of York. The Norse, under Harald Hardraada and the English king's brother Tostig Godwinson, had invaded England, landing east of York. King Harold II of England was in the south with an army he had collected to meet the anticipated invasion by the Normans, and upon news of the Norse invasion immediately marched north.

Harold confronted the Norse army at Stamford Bridge and offered Harald generous compensation if he retired or seven feet of earth for a grave if he stayed. Harald elected for the latter and a fierce battle ensued, in the course of which both Harald and Tostig were killed and the Norse army driven back to their ships, to flee to Norway. A few days later, news came that William the Conqueror had landing at Hastings; Harold marched south and with a weary army fought the Battle of ◊Hastings.

Stangebrö alternative name for the battle of ◊Linköping.

Styr in World War I, series of engagements between Russian and Austro-German forces 1915–16 along the line of a Polish river rising in Galicia and flowing north past Leuck to join the Pripet near Pinsk.

The first battle followed the withdrawal of the Russians from Leuck 28 Sept 1915 and was a fluctuating struggle in which the Russians gained ground to the north of the sector and the Austro-Germans to the south. The lines then remained relatively stable until the second battle June 1916 when Russian forces attacked a prominent Austro-German salient at Czartoryszk, cut it off, crossed the river, and advanced on the Stokhod.

Talavera during the Peninsular War, British victory over the French 27–28 July 1809 near Talavera, a Spanish town 110 km/70 mi southwest of Madrid. Advancing into Spain from Portugal, a British army of 20,000 troops under the Duke of Wellington reached the river Tagus and took up positions on the hills north and west of the town. A Spanish army held the town itself, which was under threat from a French army numbering about 50,000 under Marshal Nicolas Soult.

The French attacked the British force in an attempt to drive it off, and succeeded in pushing the British line back for some distance. The British finally held their position, which was subjected to a fierce bombardment by French artillery and then another assault which threatened to overwhelm the British. Just as the British position looked untenable, reinforcements under Viscount Hill appeared and with their aid the lost ground was recovered.

The battle died down at nightfall but was renewed by a French assault at dawn the following day. More severe fighting broke out but the French were held off by heavy fire from the British infantry and the intensity of British cavalry charges. Wellington counterattacked and the French retired toward Madrid. The British were so weakened by the battle they were unable to pursue Soult, and Wellington fell back into Portugal. The British lost some 6,200 killed and wounded; the French about 7,400 killed and wounded.

Tannenberg victory of a combined Polish and Lithuanian army over the Knights of the Teutonic Order 1410, at Tannenberg, a village in East Prussia (now Grünwald, Poland). The Teutonic Knights were originally formed during the Crusades, and later undertook the conversion and conquest of Old Prussia (approximately modern Poland). Eventually the Teutonic Knights took control of Poland, responsible to nobody other than the Pope, but their rule was oppressive and in 1410 the population, led by King Wladislas II, Grand Duke of Lithuania and nominal King of Poland, rose against them. Wladislas lead an army of 20,000 to meet some 15,000 Knights near Tannenberg and completely defeated them, slaughtering several thousand Knights. The Order lost its hold over Old Prussia; their defeat led to the Treaty of Thorn and to an independent Polish state.

Tannenberg in World War I, German victory over Russian forces Aug 1914 at a village in East Prussia (now Grünwald, Poland) 145 km/90 mi northeast of Warsaw. General Alexander Samsonov attacked East Prussia Aug 1914, defeating the Germans at Frankenau. Field Marshal Paul von Hindenburg concentrated a force of about 100,000 German troops around Gumbinnen against both the immediate threat posed by Samsonov and that of General Paul Rennenkampf's army which he knew was approaching from the north.

Hindenburg was waiting for Samsonov's attack, resisted it, turned the Russian left flank, and drove him back to Hohenstein. The Russians attempted to make a stand there but were driven into retreat. Hindenburg now extended his left flank through Allenstein, with the intention of encircling Samsonov and driving a wedge between him and Rennenkampf. He surrounded Samsonov on three sides at Tannenberg, the fourth being swamps and lakes, and tore his army to shreds; only about 60,000 troops managed to escape back to Russia. The Germans took 90,000 prisoners and several hundred guns. Hindenburg then struck north against Rennenkampf but he, having seen what had happened to Samsonov, retreated to his base on the Niemen river line.

Tarawa in World War II, costly US attack Nov 1943 on Japanese-held atoll in the Gilbert islands, consisting of a number of small islands bound by a coral reef. Attacked by US 2nd Marine division and US Army 27th Division 20 Nov, the landing used amphibious tractors to ferry the men ashore. Due to tidal changes the second wave beached on the reef and the troops had to wade ashore, leading to excessive casualties. The pre-landing air and naval gunfire support was badly coordinated and the Japanese defence formidable and it took three days of hard fighting to capture the island. The US forces suffered over 1,000 killed and 2,100 wounded.

Tarnopol in World War I, Austro-German victory over the Russians July 1917 at a town in Polish Galicia (now Ternopol, Ukraine) about 110 km/70 mi southeast of Lemberg (Lvov); one of the first instances of the more general collapse of the Russian armies following the Russian Revolution 1917.

The Russian offensive had been halted by July 1917 and the Austro-German forces began a counterattack 19 July. At first they made little progress, until the 6th Grenadier Division of the Russian 11th Army deserted en masse due to Bolshevik agitation, leaving a gap in the Russian line some 40 km/25 mi wide. Panic spread through the rest of the 11th Army and many more troops absconded. General Alexei Brusilov was in Tarnopol and had just ordered a change of command, so there was no senior officer at the front capable of repairing the damage caused by the desertions. The Austro-Germans attacked 20 July and were able to go straight through the gap, as the Russian troops on their route showed no inclination to obey their commanders or make any defence. In spite of a last-minute stand by some loyal Russian regiments, there was little they could do to stop the advance and Tarnopol fell to the Germans 22 July. Within two days the whole Russian front was beginning to crumble. The Austro-German forces kept up their advance until they reached the Russian frontier at Husiatyn (now

Gus'atyn), where they halted and awaited the outcome of the dramatic events overwhelming Russia.

Tchernaya during the Crimean War, Russian defeat by a combined French and Piedmontese force 16 Aug 1855 on the Tchernaya river to the northeast of ◊Sevastopol. In an endeavour to break the Allied siege lines and relieve Sevastopol, a force of three divisions under General Prince Gortschakov launched an attack against three French and one Piedmontese division holding the river line. The Allied force was able to resist the attack with artillery support; the Russians sustained some 5,000 casualties, while Allied losses were about 1,200. This was the final Russian attempt to raise the siege; the following day, the Allies opened a bombardment which led to the final assaults and surrender of the fortress.

Tel-el-Kebir British victory over Egyptian rebels 13 Sept 1882 at Tel-el-Kebir, a stretch of desert some 65 km/40 mi northeast of Cairo, Egypt. In 1876 Egypt went bankrupt and its creditors prevailed upon the Sultan of Turkey to depose the spendthrift Khedive Ismail and replace him with his son Tewfik. He, in turn, agreed to British and French administrators running his country and putting its finances in order. But a revolt led by Col Ahmed Arabi 1879 threatened to overthrow the Khedive and evict all foreigners. After a massacre of Europeans at Alexandria 1882, the port was bombarded by British and French fleets and a British expeditionary force under General Sir Garnet Wolseley was sent to deal with the rebellion. Wolseley set some of his staff on making plans to invade from Aboukir Bay near Alexandria, and these plans were soon known throughout Egypt. Meanwhile, he quietly sailed off with his army and captured Port Said, Ismailia, and the Suez Canal. He then marched west across the desert toward Cairo, and Arabi's forces prepared a defensive line at Tel-el-Kebir, a move Wolseley had foreseen.

Arabi had some 25,000 troops and 70 guns in well-prepared field fortifications which, after a night march, Wolseley attacked at dawn, with 17,400 troops and 61 guns. The initial assault was by the Highland division, who unfortunately struck against a sector held by very tough Sudanese troops, and the line could not be broken until a second, reinforced, assault was made. A cavalry brigade began sweeping in on the right, and on the left an Indian infantry brigade also met with success, just as the initial assault broke through the first lines; the Egyptian force immediately began to crumble. Within two hours of starting, the battle was over, with the British losing 57 killed and 382 wounded. Egyptian losses have never been accurately calculated, but they were exceedingly heavy. Wolseley entered Cairo two days later and joint British-French control was ended, the British assuming full responsibility for Egypt thereafter.

Telissu during the Russo-Japanese War, Russian defeat by the Japanese 15 June 1904, close to Telissu (now Songshu) about 120 km/75 mi northwest of Port Arthur (Lushun) Manchuria; the only Russian attempt to relieve

◊Port Arthur which they gave up after this defeat. At the start of the war the Japanese had crossed the ◊Yalu river, the border with Korea, and sent one army north to meet the Russians at ◊Liaoyang, another to besiege Port Arthur, and a third, under General Oku, was positioned on the approaches to Port Arthur to frustrate any attempt to relieve the garrison there.

The Russians made this attempt with a force of about 35,000 under General Baron Stackelberg who advanced down the north coast of the Port Arthur peninsula to find Japanese cavalry patrols on his front. Under orders not to provoke a battle with superior forces, he took up a defensive position near Telissu in the valley of the Fuchou river. The Japanese attacked 15 June, crushing the Russian right flank, and forcing Stackelberg to retreat, leaving 3,500 casualties and several guns in Japanese hands; Japanese losses came to less than 1,200.

Tet Offensive in the Vietnam War, North Vietnamese army and Vietcong guerrilla operations against US and South Vietnamese forces Jan 1968; the operation was a tactical defeat for the Vietcong but a political victory. Although the Vietcong attacks were all eventually beaten off, with an estimated loss of some 30,000 communist casualties, the political gain was considerable, and the Tet Offensive might be considered the watershed of the Vietnam War.

By 1967, it had become apparent to the Vietcong leaders that American popular support for the war in Vietnam was faltering, and they therefore planned a web of offensive operations against major cities, towns, and districts throughout southern Vietnam early 1968. The offensive was preceded by the operation at ◊Khe Sanh, and the operation launched simultaneous attacks 31 Jan on 150 different targets, from Saigon to small villages. US and ARVN reaction was swift and ruthless and the offensive was repulsed. However, subsequent television reports of death and destruction made a considerable impact upon the US public, especially since a Presidential election was in the offing. Questions were asked about the worth of US involvement in Vietnam, political debate on the subject increased, and the search began for a negotiated settlement.

Texel during the Anglo-Dutch Wars, decisive English victory over the Dutch fleet 31 July 1653 in the North Sea off Texel, the most westerly of the Frisian Islands; the Dutch defeat was severe and led to peace early 1654. The English fleet, under General George Monck, encountered the Dutch admiral Maarten van Tromp 30 July and fought an indecisive action. During the night the English were reinforced by another 18 ships under Admiral Robert Blake. This newly strengthened force renewed the battle 31 July and completely defeated the Dutch, who lost 11 ships and 1,300 prisoners; Admiral van Tromp was killed in the action. The English lost 20 ships and over 300 killed and wounded.

Tiberias Moslem defeat of Crusaders 1187; see ◊Hattin.

Tinchbrai during the Norman War, English victory over the French 28 Sept 1106, near Tinchbrai (now Tinchbray) about 50 km/30 mi southwest of Caen, Normandy. King Henry I of England had invaded Normandy and met an army under his brother Robert, Duke of Normandy, outside Tinchbrai. Henry dismounted his knights and formed them into a solid phalanx which first beat off an attack by Norman cavalry and then moved forward and completely shattered the French foot soldiers. Robert was taken prisoner, and remained in captivity for the rest of his life, while Henry annexed Normandy to the English crown.

Tinian in World War II, US Marines operation July 1944 to capture Japanese-held island in the Marianas group. It was a difficult target, unusual among Pacific islands in having a cliff-bound coastline with only a few small beaches. It was attacked 24 July by US Marines who made a mock attack against the main beach and settlement while actually landing on small beaches no more than 45 m/50 yds wide several miles away. Over 15,000 troops got ashore against light resistance and by nightfall had secured a beachhead at a cost of only 15 killed and 225 wounded. The Japanese launched a counterattack during the night but suffered severe loses and the island was completely secured by 1 Aug.

Tobruk in World War II, series of engagements between British and Axis forces over a Libyan port 96 km/60 mi west of Bardia. Occupied by Italy 1911, Tobruk was taken by Britain in Operation ◊Battleaxe 1941, and unsuccessfully besieged by Axis forces April–Dec 1941. It was captured by Field Marshal Erwin Rommel June 1942 after the retreat of the main British force to Egypt, and this precipitated General Sir Claude Auchinleck's replacement by General Bernard Montgomery as British commander. Montogomery recovered it after the second Battle of El ◊Alamein and it remained in British hands for the rest of the war.

Torgau during the Seven Years' War, Austrian defeat by Prussians under Frederick the Great 3 Nov 1760, outside Torgau, a German town on the banks of the Elbe river about 50 km/30 mi northeast of Leipzig; the victory gave Frederick command of the state of Saxony. The Austrians, about 64,000 troops with 400 guns commanded by Count Leopold von Daun, had set up an entrenched camp outside Torgau. Frederick arrived with 45,000 Prussians and, splitting his army in two, directed one half under General Hans von Zieten to make a frontal attack while he took the rest and made an attack on the rear of the position. He was beaten off in both attempts, and withdrew his force to rejoin Zieten toward evening.

As night fell, Zieten's scouts found that one section of the Austrian defences was thinly guarded, and a sudden assault was able to break through and capture several batteries of artillery. This was followed up by a general advance, and the Austrians broke and began to retreat. The

Austrians lost about 5,000 killed and wounded and 700 prisoners; Prussian losses were 13,100 killed and wounded.

Almost 200 years later, Torgau was the meeting place of the US 1st Army and the Soviet 5th Guards Army, the first contact between the Western and Eastern Fronts in World War II.

Toulon during the War of the Austrian Succession, British naval defeat at the hands of a combined French and Spanish fleet 21 Feb 1744 off Toulon, a French port in the Mediterranean, 68 km/42 mi east of Marseilles. The British fleet, 27 ships of the line and 8 frigates, was commanded by Admiral Thomas Mathews, described as 'dull and clumsy'; he mounted an inept attack against the 28-ship French fleet, a move with which his second-in-command Vice-Admiral Richard Lestock disagreed and hence refused to cooperate. Capts James Cornwall and Edward Hawke, by independent action, managed to prevent the affair being a total disaster. Mathews, Lestock, and three other captains were court-martialled and dismissed the service.

Toulon during the French Revolutionary Wars, British defeat at the hands of the French revolutionary army under General Jacques Dugomier Aug 1793. The city authorities were monarchists and had welcomed a small British military force to assist in defending Toulon against the revolutionaries. It was then besieged by about 11,500 troops, ably supported by Napoleon Bonaparte in his role as artillery commander. Heavy and accurate bombardments breached the defences and allowed most of the outworks to be taken, after which the town was indefensible. The British commander Lord Mulgrave called up elements of the fleet and was able to evacuate his force by sea.

Trafalgar during the Napoleonic Wars, British naval victory over a combined French and Spanish fleet 21 Oct 1805, off Cape Trafalgar on the southwest coast of Spain. The British fleet, commanded by Lord Nelson, consisted of 27 ships of the line mounting 2,138 guns; the Franco-Spanish fleet consisted of 33 ships with 2,640 guns under Admiral Pierre de Villeneuve.

The French were sailing in a loose line formation and Nelson divided his force into two parts which he intended to drive through the French line at different points. The manoeuvre was successful, Nelson's flagship *Victory* passing the stern of the French flagship *Bucentaure* and discharging its broadside at 10 yds range, causing 400 casualties, and other British ships used similar tactics of close-quarter gunnery. The battle commenced at about 12 noon, and at 1.30 p.m. Nelson was mortally wounded by a musket-shot. By 3 p.m. the battle was over, and the surviving French and Spanish ships were concentrating on escape. Of their number, 15 had been sunk and of the 18 which escaped 2 were wrecked 24 Oct and 4 taken by a British squadron 3 Nov. The British lost no ships and sustained casualties of 449 killed and 1,242 wounded; French and Spanish casualties amounted to about 14,000.

Trentino, Campaigns in in World War I, operations between Austrian and Italian troops 1915–18. Trentino was a district of the southern Tyrol in Austria during the war, now a province of Italy; broadly, the area between Lake Garda and the Brenner Pass. This area was the Italian Army's first objective after declaring war on Austria and they began their advance 24 May 1915. By the end of the year they held a line a few miles past the north end of Lake Garda.

In May 1916 the Austrians assembled a force of about 350,000 and swept down between Trento and Roverino, destroying the Italians' line and driving them back to a line in the mountains southwest of Roverino. The Austrian offensive then slackened and stopped. The Italians counterattacked June 1916 and regained much of what they had previously held. More fighting in the summer of 1918 was inconclusive; the severe nature of the mountainous country and supply difficulties often cancelled out purely military considerations, and the struggle continued until the Austrian armistice 3 Nov 1918.

Tsingtao in World War I, Japanese seizure 1914 of a German colony in China (now Qing Dao). Germany had been given the lease of Tsingtao for 99 years from 1898 in recompense for the murder of two German missionaries and they fortified the area and constructed a port and naval base. In 1914 the Japanese declared war on Germany and demanded the surrender of Tsingtao. The Germans refused and a Japanese force of 23,000 troops and 142 guns besieged the colony 2 Sept 1914. The Japanese were joined 23 Sept by a combined British and Indian force of about 1,500 troops. The siege was conducted in the traditional manner by trenching and mining, until the final assault was prepared 6 Nov. The fortress surrendered the following day and was handed over to the Japanese 10 Nov, whereupon the British withdrew.

By an agreement of 25 May 1915 the Japanese undertook to hand the area back to the Chinese 'under certain conditions', most of which were the 'Twenty-One Demands' which were aimed at obtaining full control of Chinese economic and political affairs. China agreed to most of the demands, but Anglo-American objections to this self-aggrandizement led to the fall of the Japanese government.

Tsushima during the Russo-Japanese War, Japanese naval victory over the Russians 27–28 May 1905, in the Strait of Tsushima between Japan and Korea; the only engagement between Dreadnought-type battleships and probably one of the greatest naval battles ever fought. The Russian Far Eastern fleet had been badly damaged by Japanese action and the remainder was bottled up in ◊Port Arthur. The Home Fleet, under Admiral Zinovi Rozhdestvensky, sailed from the Baltic Oct 1904 but due to difficulties in arranging coal supplies, poorly trained crews, and mechanical problems, took seven months to reach the theatre of war. The Russian fleet, consisting of 46 ships, of which 7 were Dreadnought-type battleships and 6 cruisers, was met by a Japanese fleet under Admiral Count Heihachiro Togo of similar size and composition but capable of greater speed and with better-trained sailors.

The main action was fought in the afternoon of 27 May, and the Japanese rapidly sank 4 Russian battleships without any loss themselves. Other Russian ships were severely damaged by accurate gunfire, and the Russian fleet broke up as individual ships attempted to run for safety in the harbour of Vladivostok. This allowed Japanese destroyers to engage with torpedoes, sinking another 3 Russian ships during the night. The Japanese main fleet took up the battle on the following morning, and the remaining Russian division of battleships was forced to surrender. All but 12 minor ships of the Russian fleet were sunk, captured, or driven aground, while the Japanese lost only 3 torpedo-boats.

U

Ulm series of actions during the Napoleonic Wars, generally known as the Campaign of Ulm, in which the French, under Napoleon Bonaparte, defeated the Austrians Sept 1805, in the area of Ulm, about 70 km/45 mi southeast of Stuttgart, Germany. The Austrians joined the alliance of Britain and Russia against France Aug 1805, and invaded Bavaria (an ally of France) without waiting for Russian troops to join them.

In my youth we used to march and countermarch all summer without gaining or losing a square league, and then we went into winter quarters. But now comes an ignorant, hot-headed young man who flies from Boulogne to Ulm, and from Ulm to the middle of Moravia, and fights battles in December. The whole system of his tactics is monstrously incorrect.

Anonymous Prussian officer expressing
exasperation at Napoleon's *Ulm* campaign

Baron Karl Mack, the Austrian commander, advanced with 72,000 troops to a position between Ulm and Memmingen. Napoleon saw his chance to cut off the Austrians while the Russians were still marching through Poland; he had an army of 180,000 troops at Boulogne, waiting to invade England, and he marched this force south through Hanover and the smaller German states to come up behind the Austrian position and take them by surprise. Mack reversed his troops but the French moved around his flank; an attempted breakout across the Danube met the French 6th Corps head-on and was rapidly driven back into Ulm. By 16 Oct Napoleon had completely surrounded the Austrians and three days later Baron Mack surrendered with about 30,000 troops. Of the remainder, 20,000 managed to escape, 10,000 had become casualties in the various skirmishes and actions during the envelopment, and the rest were prisoners. Baron Mack was court-martialled and given 20 years imprisonment, although he only served a few months.

Ushant see ◊Glorious First of June.

Valmy during the French Revolutionary Wars, French victory over the Prussians 20 Sept 1792, near Valmy, a French village about 55 km/35 mi southwest of Reims. After the French Revolution, Prussia, among other countries, saw the opportunity to profit from the disorder in France and 34,000 Prussians under the Duke of Brunswick marched into France. A French army under Charles Dumouriez halted them and his force was then reinforced by more troops under Marshal François Kellermann; the total French strength was about 50,000 and they were particularly strong in artillery. The Prussians attacked Kellerman's force and the French used their artillery to break up the attack. They then counterattacked, and as night fell the Prussians began to retire, finally marching back across their own border two days later. This forthright defeat of a powerful army by the previously despised revolutionary forces set the seal upon the authority of the revolutionary French government.

Vardar two battles in World War I between Serbian forces backed by Allied troops and the Bulgarians, both part of the larger Allied operation surrounding Salonika. The Vardar is a Balkan river, rising in Serbia, flowing northwest then southeast and emptying into the Gulf of Salonika.

Oct 1915 a joint French and British force moved up the Vardar valley from Salonika to assist the Serbs against the Bulgarians. Outnumbered about four to one by the Bulgarians, the Allied forces fell back and retired into Greece 12 Dec.

Sept 1918 the battle opened with a strong offensive by the Serbs and French southeast of Monastir while British forces were attacking on the ◊Doiran-Struma Front. The French and Serbs drove the Bulgarians up the valley until the Bulgarians signed an Armistice 20 Sept.

Vaux-Fossoy in World War I, US operation against German forces on the Western Front July 1918. Vaux and Fossoy are villages close to ◊Château-Thierry and in July 1918 were held by the US 3rd Division. A German attack against Vaux 15 July was held and then driven back by US troops, who succeeded in following up and taking several German positions. Later in the day another German force crossed the river Marne and took Fossoy, but again the US troops counterattacked and drove the Germans back across the river.

Verdun in World War I, series of bitterly fought actions between French and German forces around a French fortress town in the *département* of the

Meuse, 280 km/174 mi east of Paris. Verdun became a first-class fortress after the experience of the Franco-Prussian war 1870, its ring of modern forts being one of the principal French frontier defences. In 1916 the Germans attacked it in great strength; it had great psychological value to the French and the Germans assumed that they would throw large masses of troops into battle rather than lose it. The German plan was not necessarily to capture Verdun but to decimate the French army by constant bombardment and attack. The battle continued for the rest of the year, both sides moving back and forth capturing and re-capturing forts and ground, until the fighting finally died away early Dec 1916. The French lost an estimated 348,300 men, but the German losses were 328,500.

The front then remained relatively stable until the French launched an offensive to regain some of their lost territory Aug 1917. They succeeded in regaining the Mort Homme area by 12 Sept and captured about 10,000 prisoners and 100 guns. Although an attack launched north from Verdun would have liberated useful territory and threatened the German lines of communication throughout the war, German defences in this sector were extremely strong and it was not until Sept 1918, after the reduction of the ◊St Mihiel salient, that a successful attack was launched as part of the general Allied offensive.

Vicksburg during the American Civil War, Union victory over Confederate forces May–July 1863, at Vicksburg, Mississippi, 380 km/235 mi north of New Orleans. Vicksburg was a well-fortified communications hub of great importance on the Mississippi and the Union capture of the town virtually split the Confederacy in two, and also brought Grant into the public eye, so that he was eventually given command of all Union forces. The first Union attempt to take it June 1862 was made by a small force of no more than 5,000 with a fleet of gunboats; they were unable to make any impression on the defences and withdrew.

Two Union corps under General John A McClernand, an incompetent political appointee, laid siege to the place Jan 1863. They had some initial success against an outpost fort, but none against the town, and General Ulysses S Grant brought up three more corps to strengthen the siege. McClernand demanded that he be given the chance to assault Vicksburg, and failed spectacularly 22 May, after which he was relieved by Grant, who took personal command of the siege. He pressed the town hard and Lt-Gen John C Pemberton, the Confederate commander, surrendered 4 July with 25,000 troops and 90 guns.

Vienna during the Ottoman Wars, unsuccessful siege of Vienna Sept–Oct 1529 by the Turks, commanded by Suleiman the Magnificent. Vienna was held by a garrison of about 16,000 soldiers when an army of 120,000 Turks besieged it. Several desperate assaults were made and repulsed, and Turkish artillery bombarded the walls and eventually breached them. A final attempt by the Turks to storm this breach and enter the city was beaten off with heavy casualties among the Turks. Suleiman therefore raised the siege and retired east; Vienna marked the farthest westward point of the Ottoman invasion.

Vienna in a continuance of the Ottoman Wars, defeat of the Turks at the hands of a Christian army 12 Sept 1683. The Turks had launched a fresh invasion of the west and they were once again around the walls of Vienna with about 138,000 troops under Mustapha Pasha, besieging a force of about 40,000 in the city. King John Sobieski of Poland assembled a relief army of 30,000 of various nationalities and came up in the rear of the Turkish lines. This, together with a sortie from the city, brought the Turks under pressure from two directions, and after a day of severe fighting the Turks were routed, with enormous losses, and again retired to the east.

Vimiero during the Peninsular War, British defeat of the French 21 Aug 1808 near Vimiero, a Portuguese village 50 km/31 mi northwest of Lisbon. After the battle at ◊Rolica, the Duke of Wellington pushed closer to Lisbon with a force of about 17,000 troops and was attacked by some 13,000 French under Marshal Andoche Junot at Vimiero. Wellington held a strong position, and although the French attack was pushed hard, it was beaten off and the French fell back in disorder. Wellington wanted to pursue, but General Sir Henry Burrard, who was in overall command of the expeditionary force, refused permission and the French escaped and were allowed to leave Portugal in English ships under the terms of the Convention of Cintra. As a result, the Peninsular War was to drag on for several more years.

Well gentlemen, since there is no fighting to be done, we may as well go and shoot red-legged snipe.

> The Duke of Wellington, in disgust at being refused permission to pursue the defeated French force after the *Battle of Vimiero*.

Vionville Mars-la-Tour during the Franco-Prussian War, Prussian victory over the French 18 Aug 1870, in the area of the French villages of Vionville and Mars-la-Tour about 24 km/15 mi west of Metz. The French army under Marshal François Bazaine was retiring from Metz to Verdun, with the entire force of 140,000 troops, their transport, and artillery all compressed on to one road. At the same time the Prussian Army extending westward to the south of the French, was ordered by Count Helmuth von Moltke to press north and force Bazaine either to fight for his route or be pushed away from Paris. In the event the Prussian left went far ahead of the other Germans in the army before moving north, leaving the right wing to encounter the French and commence the battle.

Battle was eventually joined in the evening; the Prussian attack the following morning, by General Rheinbaben, was not pressed with much vigour and was therefore beaten off by the French. It served only to alert the French to the danger, so that when a second Prussian force, under General Constantin von Alvensleben, appeared it fared badly. In fact, the Prussians thought they had caught up with the French rearguard, but they had actually marched straight into the middle of the entire army. Reinforcements were on their way to the Prussians, but the situation was grave, and as a last resort von Alvensleben called on his cavalry to charge the French artillery, the principal threat to the Prussians.

Two divisions of cavalry led by Baron von Bredow were able to approach to within 600 m of the French under cover of a ravine, from which they launched a charge that was to became known as 'Von Bredow's Death Ride'. They succeeded in scattering the French guns and gunners, but at the cost of 380 of the 800 troops who set out; it was the last successful cavalry charge ever seen in Europe. This bought sufficient time to allow Prussian reserves to arrive and strengthen the battle line, while at the same time the extended left flank turned north and curled round the front of the French to cut their escape route. After further severe fighting the French began to retreat in disorder, falling back towards Metz and the battle died away. Prussian losses came to 15,780; the French lost 13,761 troops.

Vitoria during the Peninsular War, British victory over the French 21 June 1813, near Vitoria, a north Spanish town 80 km/50 mi south of Bilbao; this battle effectively ended French influence in Spain, and after clearing out French stragglers from the border area, the British were able to march into France to continue their campaign. The Duke of Wellington had re-entered Spain after wintering in Portugal and marched across northern Spain to outflank the French, manoeuvring them out of their positions by threatening to cut their communication with France.

With a combined British-Portuguese-Spanish force of about 75,000 troops and 90 guns, he attacked the French close to Vitoria. After a hard fight, General Sir Thomas Picton's division broke the French centre, causing the French to collapse. Wellington's force now gained the Vitoria–Bayonne road, preventing the French regaining their own country, and the demoralized French retired toward Pamplona, having lost 8,000 casualties, 2,000 prisoners, and 152 guns; Wellington lost 4,500 killed and wounded.

Vittorio Veneto in World War I, official Italian name for their victory over the Austrians, Oct–Nov 1918, which heralded Austria's final defeat. Also called the third battle of the ◊Piave.

Wagram during the Napoleonic Wars, French victory over the Austrians 6 July 1809 near Wagram, an Austrian village 18 km/11 mi northeast of Vienna. The Austrians, 158,000 strong under the Archduke Charles, had taken up a defensive position at Wagram; Napoleon Bonaparte advanced from Vienna with 154,000 troops and crossed the Danube during the night of 4–5 July.

Napoleon launched an attack in the afternoon of 5 July which was driven back by the Austrians, and on the following morning the Austrians launched a counterattack, which managed to drive the French line back for some distance. Napoleon now deployed his reserve and brought up the Guard artillery, which checked the Austrian advance. At the same time Marshal Louis Davout moved to the right and outflanked the Austrian positions, causing them to fall back. This movement of their flank was felt by the centre, which also began to give way, and by mid-afternoon the Austrians were routed and in full retreat, leaving 30,000 casualties and 9,000 prisoners on the field. The French lost about 32,000 casualties, but the Austrians were now out of the war for all practical purposes.

Wake Island in World War II, costly Japanese victory Dec 1941 over US forces; the casualties did not reflect a Japanese victory: while there were 120 US dead, the Japanese lost 2 warships, 21 aircraft, and 820 dead. Wake island was a small island 3,200 km/2,000 mi west of Hawaii and in 1941 it had a radio station, a small airstrip with 12 fighters, and a garrison of 525 US Marines.

A Japanese air raid 8 Dec destroyed eight of the aircraft and on 11 Dec a Japanese force of two cruisers, four destroyers, and four troop transports arrived. The Marines opened fire with 5-in coastal defence guns and severely damaged a cruiser, blew up a destroyer, set one transport on fire, and damaged all the others. The Japanese withdrew, pursued by the four remaining US fighters, one of which landed a bomb on the stern of a destroyer, detonating its load of depth charges and blowing off its stern. This spirited defence gave US morale a much-needed boost after the fiasco of ◊Pearl Harbor. The Japanese reappeared in much greater strength 25 Dec; the defences were swamped with troops and the US force was obliged to surrender.

Walcheren in World War II, hard-fought battle as part of the Allied operation to clear German defences around the Scheldt estuary Nov 1944.

Walcheren was an island on the north side of the Scheldt estuary, Holland, mostly below sea level and occupied by strong German coast defences. When the Allies began the clearance of the Scheldt, this strongpoint was the most difficult target.

In order to isolate the defences the RAF bombed the dykes, breached them, and allowed the sea to flood into the centre of the island. They also dropped 9,000 tons of bombs on the German gun batteries and flew 250 fighter-bomber sorties. A landing was then made by commandos to establish a small beachhead, through which infantry and pack artillery was landed. A further landing was made on the western shore, supported by naval gunfire, in which amphibious carriers, tanks, and rocket launchers were landed. After a six-day battle the island was finally secured 8 Nov 1944.

Warsaw in World War I, German operation to capture the capital city of Poland, on the river Vistula, Sept 1914–Aug 1915. The Germans attacked Warsaw Sept 1914 in order to relieve Russian pressure on the Austrians in Galicia, and hoping to take the city and conquer Poland up to the line of the Vistula. Five armies, totalling 1.5 million troops, advanced under Field Marshal Paul von Hindenburg, four against Warsaw and one against Ivangorod (now Pulavy). By 17 Oct the Germans were outside Warsaw but a powerful Russian force from the Niemen swung across the Vistula north of Warsaw and struck the German flank and rear, compelling them to withdraw.

The Germans made a second attempt to take the city to parry a Russian thrust against Cracow Nov 1914. Hindenburg set out again, this time with 2 million men, striking south from Thorn in East Prussia (now Torun, Poland). The attack was diverted from Warsaw by the need to deal with various Russian manoeuvres. A third attempt on the city was made Jan 1915. This was foiled by the Russians holding off the Germans at the battle of ◊Bolimov. Eventually the Russians decided that holding on to Russian Poland was too expensive and they conducted a skilled fighting retreat, holding the Germans on a line east of Warsaw for long enough to allow the city to be cleared of all military stores and personnel. The Vistula bridges were then blown and the city abandoned; the Germans finally captured it 5 Aug 1915.

Waterloo final battle of the Napoleonic Wars; defeat of the French by a British-Prussian-Dutch coalition 18 June 1815 at Waterloo, a Belgian village about 16 km/10 mi south of Brussels. Napoleon Bonaparte had an army of about 120,000 on the French-Belgian frontier 12 June; the Duke of Wellington, at Brussels, had about 90,000 troops of whom 30,000 were British, and was expecting Napoleon to march on Brussels to attack him. However, on their way to attack Wellington the French fought the Prussians at ◊Ligny, and also fought a combined Dutch-Belgian army at Quatre Bras, all of which delayed Napoleon and enabled Wellington to concentrate his forces at Waterloo, in anticipation of the arrival of Marshal Gebbard von Blücher with the Prussian army.

Napoleon despatched the Marquis de Grouchy with 33,000 troops to block the road upon which the Prussians were expected to arrive and took the rest of his army to face the Allies. The forces actually facing each other on the field were 67,000 Allies and 74,000 French, the latter being stronger in artillery and cavalry. The French opened the battle at 11.30 a.m. 18 June, and a fierce struggle developed for Hougoumont Farm. On the left, a long bombardment by French artillery, followed by an infantry assault, forced the Dutch and Belgians to give way, but the situation was saved by a charge of British cavalry under General Sir Thomas Picton. In the centre, the action revolved around the farmhouse of La Haye Sainte, where the British stubbornly beat off the French until about 6 p.m., when the French managed to seize the farmhouse, although they were evicted from it shortly afterwards. The French cavalry, meanwhile, was expending its energy against the British squares of infantry without breaking them, though causing heavy casualties. Also in the afternoon, the first elements of Blücher's Prussians arrived, but Grouchy managed to push them back. Napoleon then made his last attempt, ordering the Guard, under Marshal Michel Ney, to advance against the British Guards division. These stood firm until the French were very close, then at Wellington's orders fired a devastating volley, followed by a bayonet charge. The French attack was thrown into confusion, and at this moment Blücher's main force thrust Grouchy aside and came on to the field. British cavalry charged forward, the French broke, and were pursued off the field by the Prussians. Allied casualties came to about 37,000; the French lost about the same.

Wilderness, The during the American Civil War, an indecisive battle between Union and Confederate forces 4–8 May 1864 in the wooded area known as 'The Wilderness' about 24 km/15 mi west of Fredericksburg, Virginia. At the start of the 1864 campaigning season, General Robert E Lee, holding a position behind the Rapidan river in the Wilderness area, was confronted by General Ulysses S Grant who had been given command of the Union armies. Lee assumed Grant's objective was Richmond, and spread his force across the various roads in the Wilderness in order to confront him. However, Grant's objective was simply to destroy Lee's army and he ordered that 'if any opportunity presents itself for pitching into a part of Lee's army, do so without giving them time for disposition'. Lee sent a division forward under General Richard Ewell, with orders not to bring on any general battle until General James Longstreet's corps, following Lee, had arrived. But as soon as Ewell's advanced guard met Union troops they were brought under attack and the battle began.

Initial Union success was soon stopped by Confederate reinforcements aided by the close nature of the country and the thick undergrowth which allowed them to conceal their positions, and soon the Confederates had routed a Union corps. Due to poor communications, Lee was unaware of this and missed the chance to split the Union force in two. Before the Confederates could take advantage of the situation, Grant brought up reinforcements, and when the Confederates finally tried to advance they were soon stopped. Nightfall came and both sides rested where they lay.

Lee assumed Grant, like previous Union generals, would lick his wounds and stop to make up his mind, and so he allowed his soldiers to rest all night without making any fresh dispositions. Grant attacked at dawn, broke through the Confederate lines, and was only stopped by a concentration of artillery. His troops spread out to outflank this, but the delay was sufficient to allow Longstreet to arrive and push the Union troops back. Lee now tried an outflanking movement, but Longstreet was wounded during this move and the resulting delay was enough to allow the Union troops on the flank to throw up breastworks and dig in, repulsing the attack when it finally came. The day ended with Lee pressing hard and Grant only just hanging on. However, Grant did not resume the fight the next day; he slipped his army sideways in order to cross the Rapidan near Spotsylvania. Lee, though, had foreseen this and moved quickly enough to forestall him. As the battle for the Wilderness ended, so the opening shots of the battle for ◊Spotsylvania were being fired.

Wörth first major battle of the Franco-Prussian War 6 Aug 1870; see ◊Froeschwiller.

Yalu River during the Sino-Japanese War, Chinese naval defeat by a Japanese fleet 17 Sept 1894 at the mouth of the Yalu River, the border between Korea and Manchuria. This was the first large-scale naval action in which breech-loading guns, quick-firing guns, and torpedoes were used, though the Chinese were handicapped by a shortage of ammunition. The Chinese had two battleships and eight cruisers, while the Japanese had ten cruisers and two gunboats. The battle lasted for over four hours, at the end of which three of the Chinese ships had been sunk and a fourth run aground. The Japanese then retired, leaving the Chinese to limp into Port Arthur. Japanese losses were 96 killed and 208 wounded; Chinese losses were never known.

Yalu River during the Russo-Japanese War, Russian defeat by the Japanese 1 May 1904 in the vicinity of Antung (now Dandong), Manchuria. The Yalu River formed the border with Korea, and a 40,000-strong Japanese army under Marshal Count Tamesada Kuroki forced a crossing against light opposition; the following day, they launched an attack at the Russian garrison near Antung, a force of about 30,000. The attack was carried through very quickly and the garrison driven out, leaving some 3,000 casualties, 500 prisoners, and 48 guns. The Russians retired north, while the Japanese secured their crossing and began to move off in two directions: north after the Russian field armies and to the west in order to besiege ◊Port Arthur.

Yorktown during the American War of Independence, decisive British defeat by American forces Sept–Oct 1781 at Yorktown, Virginia, 105 km/65 mi southeast of Richmond. The British commander Lord Cornwallis had withdrawn his entire force of about 6,500 into the town and entrenched it, awaiting reinforcements to arrive by sea. However, the Royal Navy had lost command of the sea, and so these reinforcements did not arrive; Cornwallis was besieged by 7,000 French and 8,850 American troops from Sept. The British held out until 19 Oct when, with no reinforcements or supplies forthcoming, they were forced to surrender, effectively ending the war.

Ypres in World War I, three major battles 1914–17 between German and Allied forces near Ypres, a Belgian town in west Flanders, 40 km/25 mi south of Ostend.

Oct–Nov 1914 a British offensive aimed at securing the Channel ports of Dunkirk and Ostend clashed with a German offensive aimed at taking those ports. The subsequent fighting was extremely heavy and ended with the Germans gaining the ◊Messines Ridge and other commanding ground but with the British and French holding a salient around Ypres extending into the German line. German losses were estimated at 150,000 troops, British and French at about the same number.

April–May 1915 the battle opened with a German chlorine gas attack; this made a huge gap in the Allied lines but the Germans were unprepared for this success and were unable to exploit it before the Allies rushed in reserves. More gas attacks followed, and the British were driven to shorten their line, so making the Ypres salient a smaller incursion into the German line.

July–Nov 1917 (also known as Passchendaele) an Allied offensive, including British, Canadian, and Australian troops, was launched under British commander in chief Sir Douglas Haig, in an attempt to capture ports on the Belgian coast held by Germans. The long and bitter battle, fought in appalling conditions of driving rain and waterlogged ground, achieved an advance of only 8 km/5 mi of territory that was of no strategic significance, but the Allies alone lost more than 300,000 casualties.

Yser World War I battle between Allied and German forces 15–31 Oct 1914; the final engagement of the Allied 'race to the sea'. This battle saw the successful defence of the river Yser from Nieuport to Dixmude by a mixed Belgian and French force against the 4th German Army.

Allied troops took up positions on a railway embankment and, with support from British monitor ships shelling German positions from the sea, managed to stave off successive German attacks. The Germans brought up heavy artillery and the Belgians, running short of ammunition, decided to open the sluices at Nieuport and let the sea flood the area in front of their position, which lay below sea level. Several hundred German troops were drowned, but the Germans managed to capture Dixmude, though without penetrating the rest of the line, which stayed more or less firm for the remainder of the war.

Zama during the Second Punic War, decisive Roman victory over the Carthaginians 202 BC near Zama, a city in the Roman province of Numidia (now El Kef, Tunisia) about 160 km/100 mi southwest of Tunis. This battle marked the end of the Second Punic War: not only were the Carthaginians forced to give up Spain but they were also subject to harsh peace terms.

The Carthaginians, commanded by Hannibal, had 80 elephants as their shock arm, but these got out of control, some turning back and throwing their own cavalry into disorder. The Romans, under the younger Scipio, simply parted their ranks to allow the elephants to dash past, then closed up and attacked the Carthaginians, killing 20,000 according to legend, although Hannibal himself escaped.

Zenta during the Ottoman Wars, Austrian victory over the Turks 11 Sept 1679, near Zenta, Hungary (now Senta, Yugoslavia) 215 km/135 mi southeast of Budapest. The Austrians, under Prince Eugène Maurice of Savoy, caught up with the Turkish Army as it was crossing the river Theiss by means of a temporary bridge. Eugène waited until the Turkish cavalry had reached the far side, then cut the bridge, isolating the Turkish infantry. His army then set about destroying the infantry, safe from interference by the Turkish horse. Turkish losses are said to have been about 30,000, while the Austrians lost only about 500.

Zeebrugge in World War I, daring British raid on German naval base April 1918. Zeebrugge, a Belgian coastal town in the province of West Flanders, was occupied by the Germans 1914 and developed as a major U-boat and torpedo-boat base. It was frequently bombarded by British warships and bombed from the air but the Germans built large concrete shelters, which were impervious to the bombs of the time, for their U-boats.

It was finally put out of action by a British attack 23 April 1918. A party of Royal Marines was landed from HMS *Vindictive* on the 'mole' or breakwater, to cause what damage they could, while a submarine packed with explosives went beneath the bridge connecting the mole with the shore and exploded, cutting off the defenders on the mole from any reinforcement. All this was a diversion to attract the attention of the German defences, and while they were diverted, three blockships, obsolete cruisers filled with concrete, were sailed into the harbour and sunk in the channel so as to prevent any German vessels entering or leaving. The *Vindictive* then recovered the landing parties and sailed back to Britain, leaving Zeebrugge sealed up for the rest of the war.

Zorndorf during the Seven Years' War, Prussian victory over the Russians 25 Aug 1758 at Zorndorf, a Prussian village (now Debno, Poland) about 8 km/5 mi northwest of Kostrzyn, the bloodiest battle of the Seven Years' War. The Russians were besieging Kostrzyn (then known as Kustrin) with an army of 40,000 when Frederick the Great brought up an army of 25,000 to raise the siege. Frederick attacked the Russian lines and after a day-long battle drove them out and into retreat, leaving some 10,000 casualties; Prussian casualties were about the same.

Zurich during the French Revolutionary Wars, defeat of two Russian armies by the French June 1799 in the mountains near Zurich, Switzerland, which caused the Tsar to withdraw from the coalition against the French. The French had invaded Switzerland and created the Helvetian Republic 1798, in response to which the Archduke Charles Louis of the Holy Roman Empire led a coalition army into Switzerland and defeated the French under Marshal André Masséna. Shortly after, the Archduke became ill and the Russian General Alexander Korsakov entered Switzerland with 30,000 Russian troops to take over command of the coalition troops there.

At the same time the Russian Marshal Alexei Suvarov, based in northern Italy, set out across the St Gotthard Pass to join Korsakov, bringing another 40,000 troops. Masséna sent a corps of troops to harass Suvarov in the mountains, then turned his main strength on Korsakov, defeating him and scattering his army. He then turned and attacked Suvarov, who retreated, harassed by French ambushes and short of supplies. Suvarov returned to Italy leaving about 14,000 casualties behind him.

Battle Plans

The five battle plans which follow are selected because each shows either a particularly clear and typical battle of its period or a particulary telling example of the succession of one type of warfare over another on the battlefield. Taken together, in chronological order, the plans and their captions provide a brief overview of the changing nature of battle throughout history.

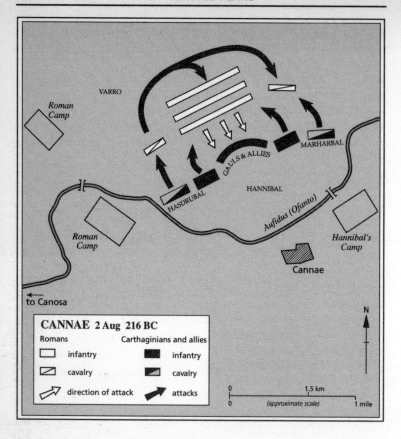

CANNAE 2 Aug 216 BC

Romans   Carthaginians and allies

▢ infantry   ▰ infantry

▱ cavalry   ▰ cavalry

⟱ direction of attack   ➤ attacks

0 _____ 1.5 km
0 (approximate scale) 1 mile

Cannae 2 Aug 216 BC A dramatic victory of the Carthaginians under Hannibal over the Romans during the Second Punic War; one of the most celebrated battles of the ancient world. Hannibal invaded Italy via the Alps with an army of Carthaginians, Gauls, Spaniards, Numidians, and other allies 218 BC. Initial Roman defeats were followed by a defensive strategy of avoiding pitched battle, until Hannibal's descent on the town of Cannae in Apulia offered the Roman consuls Varro and Paulus the opportunity to trap the Carthaginian army against the river Aufidus (Ofanto) with a Roman force almost twice as large. Hannibal allowed Varro's 80,000 infantry to push back the Gauls and Spaniards in his centre, while his superior cavalry attacked the Roman cavalry on both flanks. The Spanish under Hasdrubal, on the left, drove their opponents from the field, then rode around the Roman centre to assist Marhabal's Numidians. As his centre gave ground to the advancing Roman infantry, Hannibal launched his heavy Carthaginian troops against the flanks of the Roman formation, and his cavalry regrouped to attack the Romans from the rear. Some 50,000 Romans were killed, and Hannibal's flawless execution of a double-envelopment attack against a numerically superior opponent was adopted as a military lesson at least until the twentieth century.

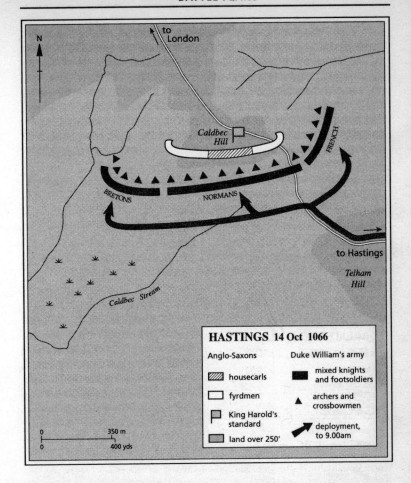

HASTINGS 14 Oct 1066

Anglo-Saxons

▨ housecarls

☐ fyrdmen

🚩 King Harold's standard

☐ land over 250'

Duke William's army

■ mixed knights and footsoldiers

▲ archers and crossbowmen

➤ deployment, to 9.00am

0 ___ 350 m

0 ___ 400 yds

Hastings 14 Oct 1066 The victory of William, Duke of Normandy, over the last Anglo-Saxon king, Harold II, was a turning-point in English history; it is also a uniquely clear example of conflict between the major military systems of the early Middle Ages. Harold's housecarls, armed with a heavy two-handed axe adopted from the Vikings, were the most formidable infantrymen in Western Europe. In William's army, they and their supporting fyrdmen (levies) faced warriors at the forefront of an emerging new form of warfare, the shock charge by mounted knights with lances held firm so as to focus the whole weight of man and horse at the point of the lance. The axemen resisted repeated attacks, but the steady attrition of Harold's army through archery and combined attacks by infantry and cavalry finally told, after fighting which lasted all day. The shock charge became the characteristic feature of European warfare until the development of effective firepower tactics in the sixteenth century.

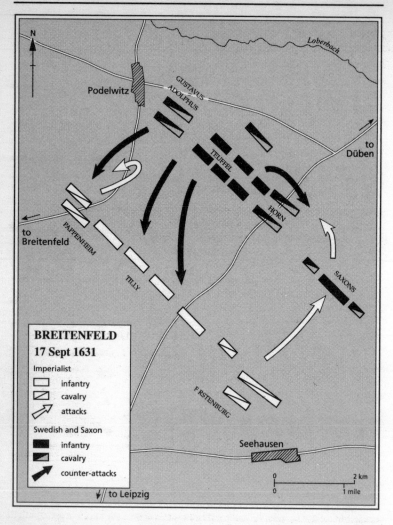

Breitenfeld 17 Sept 1631 The advent of Gustavus Adolphus, King of Sweden, as military champion of the hard-pressed Protestant cause during the Thirty Years' War brought new military thought to the fore in seventeenth-century Europe. At Breitenfeld, the Imperialist cavalry under Fürstenburg routed the Saxons, but the Swedish centre, in smaller and more mobile units than their opponents, reformed to hold him off, while Gustavus' cavalry overcame the Imperialist left and the cumbersome *tercio* formations of pikemen and musketeers in the Imperialist centre. Swedish tactics emphasized infantry firepower, leading to the development of line formations which dominated European warfare until the French Revolutionary Wars.

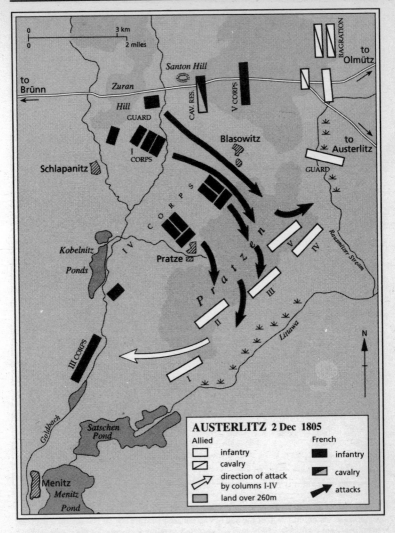

AUSTERLITZ 2 Dec 1805

Allied

☐ infantry

▨ cavalry

⇨ direction of attack by columns I-IV

▧ land over 260m

French

◼ infantry

◣ cavalry

➤ attacks

Austerlitz 2 Dec 1805 Regarded by many as Napoleon's greatest victory, Austerlitz exemplifies the new flexibility and mobility which the mass French armies brought to European warfare after the eighteenth century. After outmanoeuvring substantial Austrian armies at Ulm Nov 1804, Napoleon concentrated his widely-dispersed corps against powerful Russian and Austrian forces near Olmütz. He feigned withdrawal towards Brünn and invited an allied attack on his exposed right wing. As the heavy allied columns swung south from Austerlitz to outflank his position, I and IV Corps struck the allied centre. The Russian columns under Buxhowden were driven into the Satschen Pond with casualties of nearly 27,000 compared with 8,500 French losses.

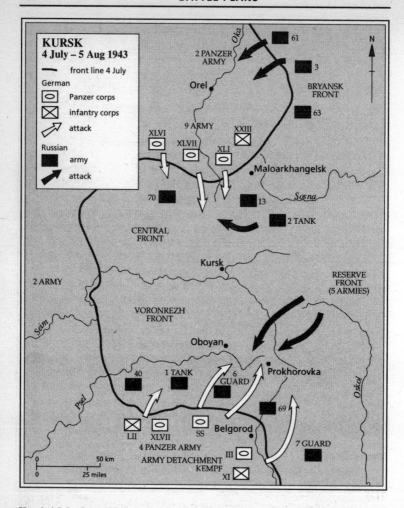

Kursk 4 July–5 Aug 1943 Perhaps the largest tank battle of all time, Kursk may be regarded as the culmination of the age of mechanized warfare which had resulted from the twentieth-century addition of motorized transport to the mass armies of the nineteenth century. Soviet advances after Stalingrad created a huge salient between Belgorod and Orel, against which the German high command launched Model's 9th Army and Hoth's 4th Panzer Army in a pincer attack. Soviet defences were well-prepared; Model's advance made little progress, and Hoth's was finally halted by Soviet armoured reserves in a huge tank battle at Prokhorovka. Kempf's attempted intervention in this struggle was called off as massive Soviet strategic offensives opened north and south of the battle and Allied troops landed in Italy.

Weapons Development Chronology

1000 BC	Clubs, hammers, axes daggers, spears, swords, slings, and bows are all common weapons by this time. Armour is also in use for personal protection.
700 BC	The Assyrians develop the ram for battering down walls.
500 BC	The crossbow appears in China.
600 AD	The stirrup, introduced into Europe from the East, gives riders better control and allows the more effective use of lances and swords from the saddle.
668	First reported use of 'Greek Fire', an incendiary compound.
1232	First reliable report of the use of rockets by the Chinese.
1242	First written record of gunpowder.
1326	First mention of firearms, in England and Italy, in the form of small cannon.
1378	Cannon mounted in warships by the Venetians.
1400	Hand firearms – 'hand-gonnes'– appear in Europe.
1411	First mention of the matchlock to ignite hand weapons.
1421	First record of gunpowder-filled explosive shells fired from cannon.
1450	Casting of cannon becomes common.
1451	Mortars, fired at a high angle to drop projectiles on to the enemy, are developed by the Turks.
1500	The arquebus and hackbut, the first shoulder-fired arms.
1530	The wheel lock appears, allowing guns to be carried ready for firing, leading to the development of the pistol, a single-handed weapon.
1547	Earliest flintlocks developed in Spain.
1570	Rifled firearms developed in Germany.
1579	First use of red-hot shot from cannon.
1596	Introduction of a wooden, gunpowder-filled fuse to ignite explosive shells so as to burst them in the air over the target.
1625	Introduction of wheeled carriages for field artillery.
1635	The perfected French flintlock mechanism, which becomes the standard ignition method in universal use by 1660.
1647	The French introduce the bayonet.
1750	Introduction of horse artillery, in which the gunners are mounted, giving greater mobility than ordinary horse-drawn artillery where the gunners march alongside their guns.
1776	British adopt the Ferguson breech-loading rifle for use during the American War of Independence.
1778	The Carronade, a light, short-range gun developed for naval use.
1787	Lt Shrapnel begins development of the 'spherical case shot' which eventually becomes the 'shrapnel' shell.
1792	The Indians under Tipu use rockets against the British at Seringapatam.
1806	British use the Congreve rocket against Boulogne.
1807	Rev. Forsyth patents the percussion principle for ignition of firearms.
1812	Self-contained cartridges for small arms.
1813	British artillery first fires over the heads of assaulting infantry in order to suppress enemy fire until the infantry are close enough to charge.

Weapons *continued*

1814	Development of the percussion cap.
1818	Collier and Wheeler develop a hand-rotated flintlock revolver.
1836	Samuel Colt patents his percussion revolver.
1841	The 'Needle Gun', first bolt-action breech-loading rifle with self-contained cartridge, adopted by Prussia.
1846	Invention of guncotton, the first 'modern' explosive, by Schonbein.
1849	Beginning of a move to convert muzzle-loading muskets into breech-loaders.
1855	Rifled muzzle-loading cannon adopted in France.
1857	Smith and Wesson patent the first metallic rim-fire cartridge revolver.
1859	Britain adopts Armstrong's rifled breech-loading cannon.
1858	French introduce ironclad warships.
1861	The Gatling gun, first successful mechanical machine gun.
1862	American Civil War introduces breech-loading small arms into military use.
1862	First battle between ironclad warships (*Monitor* and *Merrimac*) and first use in combat of a gun turret on a warship (*Monitor*).
1864	The British revert to rifled muzzle-loading cannon in order to produce guns of sufficient power to attack ironclad ships.
1865	Invention of smokeless powder by Schultz.
1866	Whitehead's self-propelled naval torpedo.
1866	Nobel invents dynamite.
1868	General adoption of electrically-fired sea mines for harbour protection.
1870	German development of an anti-aircraft gun to shoot at balloons escaping from besieged Paris.
1880	General adoption of breech-loading artillery.
1880	TNT (high explosive) perfected.
1884	Hiram Maxim develops the first automatic machine gun.
1885	The Brennan wire-guided torpedo adopted in Britain for coastal defence.
1886	France adopts the Lebel rifle, the first bolt-action, magazine repeater of small calibre.
1888	First use of the Maxim machine gun in war.
1890	Bolt action magazine rifles such as the Mauser, Lee-Enfield, Mannlicher, and Krag-Jorgensen models become the universal infantry weapon.
1890	General adoption of cast picric acid as a high explosive filling for artillery shells under various names such as 'Lyddite', 'Schneiderite'.
1893	The Borchardt, first practical automatic pistol.
1897	The French introduce the 75 mm quick-firing gun, the first field artillery piece to have on-carriage recoil control, self-contained ammunition, and a shield to protect the gunners.
1898	Development of the Madsen light machine gun, the first single operator magazine-fed machine gun.
1898	First practical submarine.
1904	Russo-Japanese war sees the revival of the hand grenade.
1906	First successful flight of a Zeppelin airship.
1909	Self-propelled anti-aircraft guns developed in Germany.
1912	TNT adopted as a filling for artillery shells in place of picric acid.
1911	Aircraft are used for scouting, observation and bomb-dropping, in the Italian-Turkish War.
1914	Development of rifle-propelled grenades.
1914	First use of firearms from aircraft.
1914	Armoured cars in use in Belgium.

Weapons *continued*

1915	First use of chemical gas in war: the Germans use tear-gas shells against the Russians at Bolimov.
1915	Introduction of synchronised machine guns capable of firing through a spinning propeller without hitting the blades.
1315	First use of cloud poison gas in war by the Germans against the British at Ypres.
1915	German introduction of the flamethrower.
1915	Stokes' trench mortar is developed; it is the precursor of all mortars since then.
1916	Introduction of the first sub-machine gun.
1916	Introduction of the tank.
1917	First recoilless gun, the Davis cannon, used from aircraft against submarines.
1925	The Oerlikon aircraft cannon.
1931	Germany begins development of rockets for air defence and long-range bombardment.
1932	First studies in biological warfare – the use of disease germs – in Europe, the USA, and Japan.
1936	US Army adopt the Garand automatic rifle, the first such weapon to become standard infantry issue.
1936	Discovery of nerve gases in Germany.
1938	British defensive radar system goes into operation.
1940	First use of the shaped-charge principle, in demolition charges against Eben Emael fort in Belgium.
1940	The British use a shaped-charge rifle grenade.
1940	The British introduce air defence rockets.
1940	The Germans introduce lightweight recoilless guns for field use.
1942	The Germans develop the 'assault rifle'.
1942	US development of the shoulder-fired 'Bazooka' anti-tank rocket.
1942	Germany introduces rocket-boosted artillery shells.
1943	First use of proximity fuse against aircraft by US Navy.
1943	First guided aircraft bombs.
1944	Germany introduces pilotless flying bombs ('V1').
1944	Germany introduces ballistic missile (the 'V2' rocket).
1944	First air-defence guided missiles developed in Germany.
1944	First wire-guided anti-tank missile developed in Germany.
1945	The atomic bomb is dropped on Japan.
1950	First military use of helicopters, for casualty evacuation (Korea).
1955	First strategic guided missiles (Soviet SS-3) enter service.
1965	First anti-missile missile (the US 'Sprint').
1982	Anti-ship missiles are first used in the Falklands War.
1992	'Smart munitions' are used in the Gulf War.

Notable Military Commanders

Setting aside the well-known requirement, laid down by several authorities, that a good general must be a lucky general, there are, broadly speaking, three basic requirements for a commander to be considered among the greats. He must win consistently; he must be capable of waging different types of warfare – attacks, defences, retreats, and sieges – with equal facility; and he must exercise his command in battle. Unfortunately, all three – plus luck – are rarely present together.

The US general George Marshall, for all that he was a brilliant administrator, never commanded in battle and so cannot be ranked among the great commanders (though he perhaps deserves to be for his humility in knowing that he was the best man in the best place and staying there). General George Patton, on the other hand, is ranked among the greats for his handling of armour in attack, but he was far from competent in a set-piece battle. Among British commanders, Field Marshal Montgomery, for all his brilliance, made sure he had marked all the cards in the deck before he sat down to play. Further back in time, the Confederate general Robert E Lee was a brilliant strategist and tactician but had no control over his subordinates, who lost him more battles than he ever won.

To add to these difficulties in assessing individual commanders, there is the problem of comparing commanders of one era with those of another: could Montgomery have stood on the bridge, or Horatio have commanded the Eighth Army? Could Nimitz have fought Trafalgar and would Nelson have shown any talent with carriers? We shall never know, and speculation is pointless. The following list is therefore very much a subjective choice of some of the commanders whose battles feature in the dictionary, with brief remarks upon their careers.

Alexander the Great 356–323 BC King of Macedonia Alexander first showed signs of his tactical abilities leading a Macedonian army at the age of sixteen in the battle of ◊Chaeronea. He succeeded his father, King Philip I, as king of Macedonia at the age of twenty and followed his success at Chaeronea with a series of lightning campaigns in which he crushed the rising of the northern Macedonian tribes and a revolt against Macedonian rule in Greece.

He then led an army across the Hellespont (the Dardanelles) 334 BC to carry out his father's plan of conquering the Persian Empire. By the summer of 333 BC he was in complete control of Asia Minor, and destroyed the army of Darius, King of Persia, on the river ◊Issus. After this he swept through Syria and Phoenicia, and entered Egypt where he was hailed as Pharaoh as the country, formerly a Persian province, surrendered without waiting to be conquered. Alexander advanced on Babylon 331 BC, defeating Darius again at ◊Gaugamela and pursuing him to his death. By the age of 26 was undisputed master of the known world east of the Adriatic.

He conducted various campaigns to subjugate the various barbarian tribes as far as the border of India 330–27 BC, founding colonies in Afghanistan reaching Sogdiana 328 BC, where he married Roxana, daughter of King Oxyartes. He advanced from Afghanistan into India itself 326 BC and defeated a number of Indian princes but his army finally refused to go any further when they reached the river Hyphasis (now Beas), the farther boundary of the Punjab. He consolidated his gains and returned to Macedonia, rested for two years, and set out once more 323 BC on a campaign to conquer Arabia. He was on the point of starting this expedition when he was stricken with fever and died. After his death, his empire was divided between his generals, the Seleucids, who struggled for ascendancy in a series of actions over subsequent years known as the Syrian Wars.

Alexander, General Sir Harold Rupert Leofric George, 1st Earl Alexander of Tunis 1891–1969 British Army
The third son of the 4th earl of Caledon, Alexander was commissioned in the Irish Guards, and had a lively career from 1914 onward, first in France and then on the Northwest frontier of India, becoming the army's youngest general 1937.

In World War II, he led the 1st Division to France 1939 and was the last British soldier to leave from Dunkirk 1940. He was then general officer commander in chief, Southern Command, until he became general officer commander in chief in Burma (now Myanmar) March 1942 where he commanded British forces during the retreat from Rangoon. He replaced General Sir Claude Auchinleck as commander in chief in the Middle East Aug 1942, directing the campaigns of ◊Montgomery's 8th Army in North Africa, and became deputy to Eisenhower in charge of the Allied forces in Tunisia 1943. After the Axis forces in North Africa surrendered, Alexander commanded the British forces in Sicily and Italy 1944, where his best endeavours were hampered by the greater priority accorded to the preparations for ◊D-Day. He was promoted to field marshal and then appointed Supreme Commander in the Mediterranean Dec 1944.

Following the end of the war, he was appointed governor general of Canada 1946–52 and UK minister of defence 1952–54. An outstanding tactician and popular commander, he was rarely downcast by misfortune.

Bradley, General Omar Nelson 1893–1981 US Army
A West Point instructor between the wars, Bradley commanded an infantry division 1942 and was sent to North Africa 1943 to reorganize the US II Corps, leading it for the rest of the Tunisian and Sicily campaigns. He then commanded US 1st Army in the ◊D-Day landings June 1944, a post he handled with considerable efficiency. After breaking out from the bridgehead at Normandy, he was given command of 12th Army Group which grew to 1.3 million troops, the largest US force ever assembled. He led this force into

Germany 1945, and thereafter commanded the entire US campaign until the war ended. A sound tactician, his great strength was his imperturbable demeanour and quiet confidence under pressure.

Brusilov, General Alexei Alexeievich 1853–1926 Russian Army Brusilov entered the Russian Army as a dragoon and served in the Russo-Turkish war of 1877–78, and then became commander of the Guards Cavalry Division 1906. At the outbreak of World War I 1914, he was general commanding the 8th Russian Army and played a distinguished part in the conquest of Galicia. In 1916 he was appointed commander of all Russian armies between the Pripet and Pruth rivers (the central front) and was responsible for the ◊Brusilov offensive June 1916, conquering a considerable area of Galicia and the whole of Bukovina.

He replaced General Mikhail Alexeyev as commander in chief of the Russian Army June 1917 but his politics were deemed to be suspect and he was replaced three months later. After the Bolsheviks took power Nov 1917, he was arrested, but by 1920 was commander of the Red Army which drove the Poles to within a few miles of Warsaw before being repulsed by them. His subsequent career is not accurately known.

Brusilov was one of the few competent generals produced by the Tsar's army, and bearing in mind the quality of the troops and the paucity of supply and other services, his victories were quite a remarkable testimony to his skill.

Collins, General J Lawton ('Lightnin' Joe') 1886–1963 US Army A good example of the talent which emerged in the US Army during World War II, Collins first came to notice when he led the 25th Infantry Division on ◊Guadalcanal 1942, and, relieving the US Marines who had made the initial landings, completed the capture of the island. He then commanded a corps in New Guinea, took command of VII Corps late 1943, and led them in the ◊D-Day invasion of France 6 June 1944. His forces captured Cherbourg, closed the ◊Falaise Gap, liberated large areas of Belgium and led the counterattack in the Battle of the ◊Bulge Jan 1945. He then crossed the Rhine at Remagen, fought in the Ruhr, and his army made the first US contact with Soviet forces at ◊Torgau 1945. A sound tactician and good handler of troops, his rapid responses and quick manoeuvres earned him his nickname.

Dönitz, Admiral Karl 1891–1980 German Navy Commissioned in 1910, Dönitz commanded the Navy's U-boat force 1939–43 and devised the 'wolf-pack' technique of submarine warfare, which sank 15 million tonnes of Allied shipping during the course of the war. His brilliant handling of the U-boats placed a stranglehold on Britain's supply lines which was only gradually overcome.

He succeeded Admiral Erich Raeder as commander in chief of the Navy Jan 1943 and devoted himself to trying to overcome Allied naval superiority, with some degree of success. He retained Hitler's trust after

Army and Luftwaffe commanders had fallen from grace and was nominated as his successor May 1945. His sole deed as leader of the Reich was to negotiate its surrender. He was arrested 23 May, tried at Nuremberg 1946, and was sentenced to 10 years' imprisonment.

Eugène, Prince of Savoy 1663–1736 Italian prince and Austrian soldier The son of Prince Eugène Maurice of Savoy-Carignano, he was born in Paris and educated in France. When Louis XIV refused him a commission he entered the Austrian army, and was thereafter fiercely anti-French He served against the Turks at the defence of Vienna 1683, and against the French on the Rhine; he did well and advanced rapidly in rank.

He held a command in Italy 1691 and gained several victories over the French; he returned to deal with the Turks again 1697. When the War of the Spanish Succession 1701–14 broke out, he went back to Italy and defeated the French in several more engagements. In 1704 he began his association with Marlborough at ◊Blenheim, made a quick trip to Italy to capture Turin, then returned for the battle of ◊Oudenarde.

After a short peaceful interlude he took the field once more against the Turks 1716 and captured Belgrade. He served as governor of the Netherlands until 1734 when he led the Austrians in the War of the Polish Succession 1734–35, dying in Vienna 1736. A superb tactician, he had an innate sense of risk-taking, winning many victories over greatly superior forces by his skill in manoeuvre.

Frederick (II) the Great 1712–1786 King of Prussia Frederick began his military career campaigning on the Rhine with Prince Eugène of Savoy 1734. He succeeded his father Frederick William I to the throne 1740, just as Maria Theresa took the throne of Austria and refused to recognise Prussia's claim to Silesia. Frederick waged a successful war against Austria to pursue his claim in the War of the Austrian Succession, after which he was joined by France, Bavaria, and Saxony to put Austria in its place. The Austrians returned 1742 and Frederick took to the field again, throwing the Austrians back at ◊Hohenfriedburg. This was followed by a series of battles, after which the Austrians finally agreed that Silesia was Prussian in the peace of 1745. The struggle was renewed in the Seven Years' War 1756–63, after which he had several years of peace in which to perfect his autocratic rule in Prussia and acquired West Prussia in the first partition of Poland 1772. He embarked on his final campaign 1779, once again to assert his claim to Silesia against Austria. This time the Austrians had made better preparations and Frederick was unable to make any impression before peace was mediated by Catherine of Russia. Frederick's principal contribution to military science was the perfection of horse artillery in which all the gunners were mounted, rather than walking alongside horse-drawn guns; this made his artillery considerably more mobile which gave them much more influence upon the course of a battle.

Grant, General Ulysses S(impson) 1822–1885 US Army Grant graduated from West Point 1843 and fought in the Mexican War of 1845–48, resigning from the army in 1854 to become a somewhat unsuccessful businessman. He returned to the army by way of a state commission on the outbreak of civil war 1861 in command of a militia regiment and shortly afterward became brigadier-general. He was given command of a corps in the Mississippi valley campaign and came to prominence by his capture of Fort Donelson 1862. His military career nearly ended in failure when Confederate forces surprised him at the Battle of ◊Shiloh 1862, but Abraham Lincoln's support was unwavering and Grant quickly redeemed himself, showing an aggressive fighting spirit and he was given the 13th Army. He embarked on a successful campaign which resulted in the capture of ◊Vicksburg July 1863 and brought the whole Mississippi front under Union control. Promoted to major-general, he gained another resounding victory at ◊Chattanooga, and was made lieutenant-general .

He was called to Washington 1864 and given command of the entire Union Army; he established his headquarters with General George Meade's Army of the Potomac and conducted a savage campaign against the Confederates under Robert E ◊Lee, fighting the battles of the ◊Wilderness, ◊Spotsylvania, ◊Cold Harbor, and ◊Petersburg before finally accepting Lee's surrender at Appomattox 1865. He was elected president 1868 and re-elected 1872.

Grant might be considered the first of the 'modern' generals: he scorned pomp and showy manoeuvres but had an uncommon appreciation for the logistics of a widespread war, and he also saw, as did few others of the time, that his primary object was not Lee's capital city but Lee's army; destroy that and the rest would follow. His losses were somewhat greater than those of Lee, but he could replace them whereas Lee could not.

Guderian, General Heinz 1888–1954 German Army After serving in World War I he became a transport specialist and in particular an enthusiast for mechanization, leading to an interest in tanks and their employment. He effectively created the Panzer (German 'armour') divisions that formed the ground spearhead of Hitler's *Blitzkrieg* attack strategy and commanded armoured columns in the occupation of Czechoslovakia and Austria 1938, and 19 Panzer Corps in the invasions of Poland and France 1939. In both campaigns he demonstrated the shattering effect that rapidly moving armoured formations could have on a static enemy: his operations terrified his own commanders, but he proved the truth of his pre-war theories. During the invasion of the Soviet Union 1941 he commanded 2 Panzer Group and tore holes though the Russian defences, taking prisoners by the hundreds of thousands. However, he made a tactical withdrawal which incurred Hitler's wrath and he was retired 1942. He was reinstated as inspector general of armoured troops 1943, responsible for provision of equipment and training, but at this point in the war there was little he could do, dogged by ill-health and political interference. After the July Plot against Hitler 1944, he became Chief of Staff but following another disagreement with Hitler he was finally retired March 1945. He was, without doubt, the finest exponent of armoured warfare the century has produced.

Haig, Field Marshal Sir Douglas 1861–1928 British Army Haig served in the Omdurman and South African campaigns, and in World War I commanded the 1st Army Corps 1914–15 and the 1st Army 1915 before succeeding Sir John French as commander in chief 1915. His Somme offensive in France in the summer of 1916 made considerable advances only at enormous cost to human life, and his Passchendaele offensive in Belgium from July to Nov 1917 achieved little at a similar loss. He loyally supported the French marshal Ferdinand Foch in his appointment as supreme commander of the Allied armies and in his victorious 1918 offensive, and it was Haig's foresight that persuaded Foch to extend his attack north, so breaking the Hindenburg Line. He has been stringently criticized by some modern historians for the appalling losses on the ◊Somme and at ◊Passchendaele and for his so-called 'lack of imagination', but in this respect he was no worse than his contemporaries and somewhat better than many. He commanded the largest British army in history and led it with great success in the summer of 1918 to tear the heart out of the German Army.

Hannibal 247–182 BC Carthaginian general As a child, Hannibal's father Hamilcar Barca took him to Spain 237 BC where he made him swear an oath to devote his life to the overthrow of Rome. He served in Spain under Hamilcar and after Hamilcar's death under his brother-in-law Hasdrubal. When Hasdrubal was assassinated 221 BC, Hannibal succeeded to the command of the Carthaginian army at the age of 25. Two years later he engineered a war with Rome with the siege of Saguntum (now Sagunto, near Valencia) which precipitated the Second Punic War. He marched from Spain (his base) through southern France and over the Alps to attack northern Italy 218 BC and defeated the Romans at Trasimene 217 BC. He then advanced south, defeated more Roman forces, by-passed Rome, and descended upon another Roman army at ◊Cannae which he annihilated.

By now, however, he was in some difficulty: he was unable to replace his casualties while his enemies had no such problem, and for the next few years his actions were circumscribed by this so he never had the strength to lay siege to Rome. In 207 BC another Carthaginian Army, under another Hasdrubal, Hannibal's brother, entered northern Italy – had this force been able to fight its way south and join Hannibal, things might have been different – but it was met by the Romans at ◊Metaurus and totally destroyed. After various defensive actions, Hannibal was recalled to Carthage 203 BC, as the Romans had now mounted a major offensive against Carthaginian bases in Spain and Sicily and an army under Scipio was threatening Carthage itself. Hannibal was given poor quality troops and subjected to political interference, and so was less successful in this campaign and was ultimately defeated at ◊Zama 202 BC. The Romans demanded his surrender, but he fled from Carthage and ended up in Bithynia where he took poison 182 BC when the Romans put pressure on the Bithynians to extradite him.

Hindenburg, Field Marshal Paul Ludwig Hans von Beneckendorf und von 1847–1934 German Army

Born in Posen of a Prussian Junker (aristocratic landowner) family, Hindenburg was commissioned 1866, served in the Austro-Prussian and Franco-German wars, and retired 1911. During World War I he was supreme commander and, with Ludendorff, practically directed Germany's policy until the end of the war.

He was given the command in East Prussia Aug 1914 and received the credit for the defeat of the Russians at Tannenberg and was promoted to supreme commander and field marshal. After the war, he used his position as a national hero to launch a career in right-wing politics, becoming president of the Weimar Republic 1925–31. Re-elected president 1932, he was compelled to invite Hitler to assume the chancellorship Jan 1933.

Hutier, General Oskar von 1857–1934 German Army

Von Hutier joined the German army 1875 and by 1912 was a lieutenant-general commanding the 1st Guard Division in Berlin. Thereafter, he held various minor commands but first came to prominence in the summer of 1917, when commanding the 8th German Army, by capturing ◊Riga 3 Sept. During the capture of Riga Sept 1917, he developed the tactic of using small armed parties of well-trained infantry to infiltrate the enemy positions, outflank and turn them, and thus force gaps for larger parties to follow up; this was assisted by well-planned artillery support devised by his artillery commander Col Bruchmüller. Known at the time as 'Ludendorff tactics', since the idea was believed to have come from General Ludendorff, it was not until some time later that von Hutier's part was appreciated. The tactic was refined and used later with considerable effect in the ◊German Spring Offensive 1918.

Kesselring, Field Marshal Albert 1885–1960 German Army

A staff officer in World War I, he transferred to the air force and became Chief of Air Staff 1936, commanding part of the Luftwaffe 1939–40 during the invasions of Poland and the Low Countries and the early stages of the Battle of Britain. He then commanded air forces on the Russian and Italian fronts, and became German commander in chief in Italy 1942. Here he fought a brilliant defensive campaign, holding the combined Allied forces at bay throughout 1943. In March 1945 he was moved to Germany to become commander in chief on the western front, but there was little he could achieve by this time, and upon the death of Hitler he surrendered his forces. His death sentence for war crimes at the Nuremberg trials 1947 was commuted to life imprisonment, but he was released 1952.

Lee, General Robert Edward 1807–1870 Confederate States Army
Lee graduated from West Point as a military engineer and distinguished himself in the Mexican War 1846–48, becoming a colonel. In 1859 he suppressed John Brown's raid on Harper's Ferry. Lee had freed his own slaves long before the war began, and he was opposed to secession, however his devotion to his native Virginia led him to join the Confederacy. At the outbreak of the civil war 1861, he resigned his commission in the US Army, resolving to stay in Virginia, his home state, and 'only draw his sword in her defence'. But he was persuaded to take command of the Virginian militia and became military adviser to Jefferson Davis, president of the Confederacy. In 1862, when Maj-Gen George McClellan was threatening Richmond, he began to take a more active role and after J E Johnston was wounded in May, took over command of the Army of Northern Virginia.

He then manoeuvred McClellan out of the district in the ◊Seven Days battles, defeated Pope at ◊Bull Run, invaded Maryland, fought an indecisive battle against McClellan at ◊Antietam, gained a notable victory at ◊Chancellorsville, advanced into Pennsylvania where he encountered General George Meade and was repulsed at ◊Gettysburg. He then retired to Virginia and fought a series of defensive battles against Ulysses S Grant, culminating in the siege of ◊Petersburg June 1864–April 1865. He was manoeuvred out of his position and was driven to surrender at Appomattox Court House 9 April 1865. Lee was a most able tactician and a good strategist, but he was badly served by his subordinates who frequently ignored or disobeyed his instructions; his fault was that he gave suggestions rather than firm orders. From 1864 onwards his task was made impossible by the gradual attrition of his forces and his inability to replace casualties.

Lettow-Vorbeck, Paul Emil von 1870–1946 German Army He entered the German artillery 1890 and served in the Boxer Rebellion in China 1900 and then in German Southwest Africa. In 1914 he was military commander in German Southeast Africa (Now Tanzania) where he displayed tactical brilliance. With a force numbering about 3,000 German and 11,000 native troops and with virtually no support from Germany, he kept the 130,000 strong Allied force under General Jan Smuts constantly at bay until he finally retired over the border into Portuguese East Africa 1917. From there he continued to wage a guerrilla campaign against the Allies for the remainder of the war. He was never seriously defeated in the field, and did not surrender until two weeks after the Armistice. Promoted to general 1917, although his operations never affected the major course of the war he nevertheless kept a considerable Allied force tied down in Africa and effectively out of the rest of the war. He returned to Germany to wide public acclaim and retired 1920.

Ludendorff, General Erich 1865–1937 German Army Ludendorff joined the army 1882 and the General Staff 1898 where, among other things, he perfected the details of the Schlieffen Plan for the invasion of Belgium in 1914. He served in the field during 1914 and took the surrender of Liège, after which he went to the Russian front as Hindenburg's Chief of Staff and planned and executed the defeat of the Russians at the Battle of ◊Tannenberg. He then undertook a major reorganization of the German army and planned the strategy which allowed them to paralyse Romania while holding the French and British in check. On the Russian front, in conjunction with von Hutier, he developed new tactics involving 'storm troops' and skilful artillery concentrations, which were used at ◊Riga and ◊Caporetto.

He planned the ◊German Spring Offensive of 1918 which came close to breaking through the Allied defences, but from July of 1918 he suffered a series of defeats, and was unable to replenish his army as fast as the Allies could. The collapse of the Hindenburg Line under British attack in Sept and the collapse of Bulgaria shortly after caused him to lose confidence and he called for peace negotiations. When talks were opened he changed his mind, refused to cooperate, and was dismissed by the Kaiser 26 Oct 1918. A bold and enterprising strategist, he was, however, careless of the welfare of his troops and had little political sense.

Marlborough, John Churchill, 1st Duke of Marlborough 1650–1722 English soldier Churchill entered the army as an Ensign of the Guards and was in action at Tangier at the age of 16. He then fought under Turenne in the Netherlands and was made a colonel in his mid-20s. He was given command in the army under James II, but in 1688 he deserted his patron for William of Orange, for whom he fought at the ◊Boyne, but in 1692 fell into disfavour for Jacobite intrigue and again tended to favour the exiled James II.

On the accession of Queen Anne 1702 he was made a duke and given command of the British and Dutch armies. He was hampered by the requirement that all his moves had to be approved by the Dutch, but he nevertheless manoeuvred the French out of one position after another before winning the battle of ◊Blenheim 1704. Finally freed of Dutch supervision two years later, he achieved victory in Belgium at the battle of ◊Ramillies 1706 and cleared the French entirely from Flanders. He then turned to diplomacy, averting the possible intervention of Sweden into the war, then returned to the Low Countries to win the battle of ◊Oudenaarde 1708. France refused the peace terms which were offered, and Marlborough defeated them again at ◊Malplaquet 1709, but after this political interference tied his hands and he faced a charge of misappropriation of public money. The affair blew over, but he suffered a stroke 1716 and thereafter played no part in public affairs. Marlborough is remembered with respect not only for his tactical, strategic and diplomatic skills, but also for his insistence upon decent pay and conditions for his soldiers, a rare commodity in those days.

Moltke, Helmuth Carl Bernhard, Count von 1800–1891 Prussian Army

Moltke (the Elder) began his career as a lieutenant in the Danish Army 1819; he resigned three years later to join the Prussian Army and by 1832 was on the General Staff. He served as military adviser to the Turkish Army 1835–40 and was made Chief of General Staff 1858 when he had been planning retirement.

In this role he planned and executed the lightning war against Denmark 1863–64, then developed tactics suited to the employment of breech loading weapons and proceeded to plan and win the Austro-Prussian War 1866. This campaign revealed several shortcomings in the organization and operations of the Prussian Army which Moltke set about correcting, in time for the Franco-Prussian War 1870–71. He directed three armies across the French frontier, intending to make a converging attack on Marshal Bazaine's front and flanks. The impetuous attack of General Steinmetz, one of his Corps commanders, ruined this plan, allowing Bazaine to escape into Metz. After this Moltke directed the war from day to day as opportunities presented themselves and conducted a skilful campaign which effectively removed the entire French regular army from the war within a month.

After the war, he continued as Chief of Staff until 1888. His skill rested on a solid foundation of the study of military history and a readiness to introduce new ideas. He virtually invented the principle of command by devolution, giving great freedom and responsibility to his subordinate commanders – who sometimes failed to meet his standards. For energy, boldness and determination he is scarcely matched by any commander in history.

Montgomery Field Marshal Bernard Law, 1st Viscount Montgomery of Alamein 1887–1976 British Army

After fighting throughout World War I, Montgomery built up a reputation as a meticulous trainer of troops. He commanded part of the British Expeditionary Force in France 1939–40 and took part in the subsequent evacuation from ◊Dunkirk. In Aug 1942 he took command of the 8th Army, then barring the German advance on Cairo; his victory at El ◊Alamein in Oct turned the tide in N Africa and was followed by the expulsion of Rommel from Egypt and rapid Allied advance into Tunisia. In Feb 1943 Montgomery's forces came under US general Eisenhower's command, and they took part in the conquest of Tunisia and Sicily and the invasion of Italy.

Montgomery was promoted to field marshal 1944 and commanded the

Allied armies during the opening ◊D-Day operation June 1944, and from Aug the British and imperial troops that liberated the Netherlands, overran N Germany, and entered Denmark. He received the German surrender 3 May 1945 at his 21st Army Group headquarters on Lüneberg Heath. He was in command of the British occupation force in Germany until Feb 1946, when he was appointed Chief of the Imperial General Staff. Created 1st Viscount Montgomery of Alamein 1946. A forthright and abrasive man, he planned carefully and was a master of the set-piece battle, though his views on how the war should be conducted cost him several friends, particularly among the Americans.

Napoleon Bonaparte 1769–1821 Emperor of France Born in Corsica, he was commissioned into a French artillery regiment as a second lieutenant 1785. When the French Revolution took place he was on leave in Corsica, but immediately rejoined the army and his handling of artillery at the siege of ◊Toulon brought him to notice. He was imprisoned for a short time, but after the fall of Robespierre returned to the army. He campaigned in Italy and crushed a serious Royalist rising in Paris 1795. He then set out on his Italian campaign, forcing Sardinia to surrender and defeating a succession of Austrian armies, over-ran Tuscany, made the Pope and the King of Naples negotiate for peace, pushed back the Austrians once more, and crushed Venice. An unknown general when he started, by the time this campaign was over he had the complete trust of the French army.

His next move was to conquer the East by seizing Malta, taking Alexandria, and overthrowing the Mamluks at the battle of the Pyramids. He then occupied Cairo and set about reorganizing Egypt. He received his first setback when Nelson defeated his fleet on the ◊Nile, but Napoleon was able to extricate his troops and get back to France. Here he found the Austrians causing discontent in the Directory, so with a few companions he overthrew the government and set himself up as 'First Consul'. He made some much-needed changes in government and administration, then set out across the Alps to defeat Italy at ◊Marengo, and agreed a peace with Britain at Amiens 1803. In 1804 he became emperor of the French, and 1805 he embarked on the series of campaigns which came to be called the Napoleonic Wars, starting with ◊Ulm and culminating at ◊Waterloo. After his defeat at Waterloo, he was banished to St Helena where he died 1821.

Napoleon was undoubtedly a great figure in European history, political and military, but he had many sides to him. He was undoubtedly a skilful tactician, a master strategist, a military opportunist of the first order, and a competent diplomat; against this, he was an autocrat with a great sense of his own self-importance and a profound contempt for ordinary citizens, which led him to squander lives in battle.

Nelson, Admiral Viscount Horatio 1758–1805 British Navy Nelson joined the Navy as a 'captain's servant' 1770 and became a captain himself by 1779. He served in the East and West Indies and the Arctic, joined Lord Hood's fleet at New York 1782 and returned to the West Indies 1784. In 1793 he was in the Mediterranean, under Hood, and was largely responsible for the capture of Basti and Calvi in Corsica, where he lost an eye. He fought the French fleet, blockaded the French coast, and disobeyed orders at the battle of ◊St Vincent which saved the day, as a result of which he was knighted.

He destroyed the French fleet in Aboukir Bay 1798 (at the battle of the ◊Nile) and received a peerage. He was at Copenhagen 1801 where, under Admiral Sir Hyde Parker, he engaged the Danish forts and fleet. When Parker sent out a recall, Nelson famously put his telescope to his blind eye and fought on, successfully, which earned him his viscountcy. Upon the outbreak of war with France 1803 he set out in his flagship *Victory* for the Mediterranean, then pursued the French fleet for two years before finally meeting and destroying them at Trafalgar 1805, where he met his death. His genius as an admiral was due to a combination of great daring with energy, knowledge, and judgement. He made his tactical plans with care and explained then in detail to his officers, so that in battle they invariably performed as he required, with energy and without hesitation.

Ney, Marshal Michel 1769–1815 French Army Ney enlisted in the ranks 1788 and rose rapidly during the French Revolutionary Wars to the rank of brigadier-general by 1796. He displayed great skill in fighting the Austrians and further distinguished himself at ◊Jena, ◊Friedland, and ◊Eylau. He was sent to fight in the Peninsula 1808, but returned 1812 having quarrelled with Masséna, his superior, over French tactics in Portugal.

His victory at Borodino, during Napoleon Bonaparte's Russian campaign, earned him the title of Prince of Muscovy, and it is due to his exertions that much of the French army managed to survive the disastrous retreat. In 1813 he fought at ◊Lutzen, ◊Bautzen, and ◊Leipzig and after the overthrow of Napoleon made his peace with the Bourbons. When Napoleon returned from Elba, Ney was sent to oppose him, but, faithful to his old master, deserted with his army and commanded Napoleon's centre at Waterloo. After the battle he was tried for desertion, sentenced to death and shot.

Ney was practically Napoleon's right hand through most of the latter's campaigning, a subordinate commander who could be relied upon to do what he was told and do it efficiently. Nevertheless, he was a sound tactician and field commander in his own right, as he showed after the fall of Napoleon; and he can hardly be faulted for carrying his loyalty to extremes.

Nimitz, Admiral Chester W 1885–1966 US Navy Nimitz joined the US Navy 1905 and by 1941 was Chief of the Bureau of Navigation. After Pearl Harbor he became commander in chief of the US Pacific Fleet and held this post until the war ended. He defeated the Japanese navy at ◊Midway, headed the invasion of ◊Guadalcanal, then 'island-hopped' toward Japan by way of Makin, Tarawa, the Marshalls and the Marianas. He then combined with General MacArthur's forces to liberate the Philippines, followed by ◊Iwo Jima and ◊Okinawa. The Japanese surrender was signed aboard his flagship USS *Missouri* in Tokyo Bay 2 Sept 1945. One of the greatest naval strategists of the war, he was a quiet and self-effacing man with a well-deserved faith in his own ability.

Plumer, General Hubert Charles Onslow, 1st Baron 1857–1932

British Army Plumer entered the York and Lancaster Regiment 1876, served in the Sudan, raised a mounted force in the Matabele Uprising of 1896, and served in the South African War 1899–1902, at the end of which he was made major-general. Knighted 1906 he held various commands in Britain, became quartermaster-general and served on the Army Council.

He spent most of World War I on the Western Front around the Ypres area, scene of much heavy fighting, and took command of the 5th Army Corps Jan 1915 and the 2nd Army May 1915. He was responsible for the planning and execution of the attack on ◊Messines 1917, generally considered to be one of the best organized British operations of the war. He commanded the British forces in Italy Nov 1917- -March 1918, then returned to the 2nd Army in France. After the Armistice he marched his army to the Rhine as part of the forces of occupation. He was made a field-marshal and created a baron 1919, and was appointed governor of Malta.

Plumer was highly popular with his troops (who referred to him as 'Daddy') since he never wasted their lives in profitless attacks but planned carefully, organised meticulously and executed his plans generally at far less cost in lives than any of his contemporaries could have managed.

Rommel, Field Marshal Erwin 1891–1944 German Army

A veteran of World War I, during World War II he played an important part in the invasions of central Europe and France but really achieved fame as the commander of the German Afrika Korps, operating against the British in North Africa. Quick to see an advantage and profit from it, he ran rings round the British for almost two years before being stopped by General Claude Auchinleck at El ◊Alamein and then driven out of Africa by Field Marshal Montgomery. He was assigned to the defence of N Italy 1944 and then moved to France as commander of Army Group B, strengthening coastal defences prior to the ◊D-Day landings June 1944. Had his defensive theories been listened to, he could have made life very difficult for the invading Allies. Unfortunately he was implicated in the July Bomb Plot against Hitler 1944 and, offered the choice of a court-martial and reprisals against his family or suicide, he chose the latter.

Slim, Field Marshal Sir William Joseph, 1st Viscount 1891–1970

British Army He served in France and Gallipoli during World War I, and in World War II was wounded in the Sudan 1941 and then led the 10th Indian Division in operations in the Middle East 1940–42. He commanded the 1st

Burma Corps 1942–45, in time to conduct the difficult retreat from Rangoon to India. In 1943 he was given command of the 14th Army and in 1944 defeated the Japanese offensive against ◊Imphal and ◊Kohima. He followed this up by driving the Japanese back across the Chindwin river and, in 1945, destroyed the Japanese armies in Burma in a series of well-planned manoeuvres. An outstanding soldier, he restored the Burma army's morale, and was a pioneer in the use of behind-the-lines penetration groups and air-supply.

Soult, Marshal Nicolas Jean de Dieu 1769–1851 French Army After enlisting in the ranks 1785, he was a brigadier-general by 1794 and served under Masséna in Switzerland and Italy with distinction. He was made a Marshal 1804, and fought at ◊Eylau, ◊Austerlitz, and other battles against the Austrians and Prussians, receiving the title Duke of Dalmatia 1808. He was sent to Spain the same year and forced the British to evacuate Portugal; he settled his headquarters in Oporto, but was later evicted by Wellington.

Given the chief command in Spain 1809, he fought with varying success until he was decisively beaten by Wellington at ◊Albuera, while his deputy Marmont was similarly worsted at ◊Salamanca. After a dispute with Joseph Bonaparte he left Spain to take command in Germany, but after Wellington's victory at ◊Vitoria he was hurriedly sent back to Spain to prevent Wellington invading France. In spite of good planning and generalship his half-trained troops were no match for Wellington's veterans and he was defeated at Toulouse. Like Ney, Soult made his peace with the Bourbons and took command in the new royal army, but on the return of Napoleon he joined him and then went into exile after Waterloo. Soult had good tactical sense, was skilled at manoeuvre, and was well capable of exercising independent command, as he showed in Spain. Unfortunately, in the end he found he did not have the luck a general needs.

Wellington, Arthur Wellesley, Duke of 1769–1852 British Army Commissioned into the 73rd Highlanders 1797, by 1793 he was a colonel in the 33rd Foot, saw service in the Netherlands 1794, and then went to India 1795. He became commander in chief of Mysore and fought with success against the Mahrattas 1803. He left India 1805 and fought in Denmark and Hanover before going to Portugal as a divisional commander 1808. He won the battles of ◊Rolica and ◊Vimiero but his superiors did not approve of his methods and he returned to England. He went back to Portugal in command 1809 and until 1814 conducted a brilliant campaign against the French, with a series of victories at ◊Badajoz, ◊Albuera, ◊Salamanca, ◊Vitoria, and the ◊Nive. He then crossed the Pyrenees, defeated Soult at Toulouse and advanced on Paris to overthrow Napoleon Bonaparte.

He was ambassador to Paris 1814 and was at the Congress of Vienna when word of Napoleon's escape from Elba sent him back to take command of the British Army and its allies and fight the battle of ◊Waterloo. He then commanded the army of occupation in France until 1818, when he went into politics, subsequently becoming Prime Minister.

Wellington's greatness as a soldier was due partly to his natural flair for tactics and partly to his attention to detail. He made a thorough examination of his army and had every defect attended to, was a strict disciplinarian (for which he was known as the 'Iron Duke'), and was capable of seeing and seizing upon any mistake an enemy made.

Zhukov, Marshal Georgi Konstantinovich 1896–1974 Soviet Red Army Zhukov joined the Bolsheviks and the Red Army 1918 and led a cavalry regiment in the Civil War 1918–20. His army defeated the Japanese forces in Mongolia at ◊Khalkin-Gol 1939; shortly afterward he demonstrated his strategic abilities in the High Command War Games and was made Chief of Staff. Initially overwhelmed by the German attack in 1941 he defended Moscow 1941, counterattacked at ◊Stalingrad 1942, organized the relief of ◊Leningrad 1943. He led Soviet forces in the battle in the ◊Kursk salient, planned and executed Operation ◊Bagration which resulted in the near-destruction of the German Army Group Centre 1944, and finally led his army to Berlin. He headed the Allied delegation that received the German surrender 1945, and subsequently commanded the Soviet occupation forces in Germany. After the war, he served as Soviet minister of defence 1955–57.

Chronology of Wars and Battles

This section serves as a chronological index of all the entries listed in the main body of the *Dictionary*, enabling readers to locate quickly, for example, all entries relating to the Napoleonic Wars or Seven Weeks' War in their correct historical context. It is not intended to be an exhaustive list of all wars and battles throughout history, and only those battles which are detailed in the body of the book are listed under the relevant war. For long sieges, the start and finish are indicated; in World Wars I and II, the dates given are for the commencement of battles and where these were prolonged or intermittent engagements, the finishing date is also given.

743 BC	First Messenian War (Messenia conquered by Sparta)
499–48 BC	Persian Wars (Greek states *v.* Persia)
	490 BC Marathon
	480 BC Salamis
474 BC	Etruscan-Greek War
458 BC	Second Messenian War
431–04 BC	First Peloponnesian War (Athens *v.* Sparta)
	405 BC Aegospotami
395–337 BC	Corinthian War
390 BC	First invasion of Rome by the Gauls
371–362 BC	Wars between the Greek City States
	371 BC Leuctra
343-41 BC	First Samnite War (Samnites, an Italian tribe, *v.* Romans)
338 BC	Amphyctionic War (Macedonia *v.* Athens and Confederated Greek allies)
	Chaeronea
334–23 BC	Alexander the Great's Asiatic Campaign
	333 BC Issus
328–04 BC	Second Samnite War
298–290 BC	Third Samnite War
283 BC	Etruscan War (Etruria *v.* Rome)
264–241 BC	First Punic War (Romans *v.* Carthaginians)
244 BC	Syrian Wars
218–01 BC	Second Punic War
	216 BC Cannae
	207 BC Metaurus
	202 BC Zama
215–11 BC	First Macedonian War
201 BC	War of the Hellenistic Monarchies
198–197 BC	Macedonian War (*v.* Rome)
195 BC	Roman invasion of Greece
149–146 BC	Third Punic War
113–101 BC	Cimbric War (Germanic tribes led by the Cimbri *v.* Romans)
110–86 BC	First Mithridatic War (Mithridates, King of Pontus, *v.* Rome and allied states)
83–82 BC	Second Mithridatic War
88–82 BC	Roman Civil Wars
74–65 BC	Third Mithridatic War
58–51 BC	Julius Caesar's Gallic Wars
	52 BC Alesia
60–38 BC	Parthian Wars (Parthia *v.* Romans and allied Syrians etc.)
	53 BC Carrhae
53–46 BC	Roman-Persian War
48 BC	Roman Civil War (leading to Caesar's dictatorship)
	Pharsalus
31 BC	Roman Civil War (war of the Second Triumvirate, primarily Octavian *v.* Mark Anthony)
	Actium
AD	
101–06	Dacian Wars
115–218	Parthian Wars (Parthia *v.* Rome)
315–25	War of the Two Empires
378	Gothic invasion of the Roman Empire
	Adrianople
394	Roman Civil War
412–414	Visigoths invade Gaul and Spain

Wars and battles continued

429–439	Vandals invade North Africa and conquer Carthage
451	Wars of the Western Roman Empire
455	Vandals sack Rome
533	Wars of the Byzantine Empire
665	Islamic Wars; Muslim invasion of Europe
711	Moorish invasion of Spain
1014	Norse Invasion of Ireland Clontarf
1066	Norse Invasion of Britain Stamford Bridge
1066	Norman Conquest of England Hastings
1093	Anglo-Scottish War
1095–99	First Crusade 1099 Ascalon
1106	Norman War (England v. Normandy) Tinchbrai
1119	Anglo-French War
1147–49	Second Crusade
1187	Battle of Hattin (Saracens v. Crusaders)
1189–92	Third Crusade
1203	Fourth Crusade
1214	Anglo-French War Bouvines
1216–1229	Fifth Crusade
1227	Scandinavian War
1249	Sixth Crusade
1265	English Civil War (Barons' War)
1266	Franco-Italian War
1270–1272	Seventh Crusade
1281	Chinese invasion of Japan
1260–1325	War of the Guelphs and Ghibellines (Italian civil war)
1302	First Flemish War (Flanders v. France) Courtrai
1314	Edward II's invasion of Scotland Bannockburn
1337–1453	Hundred Years' War 1346 Crécy 1356 Poitiers 1415 Agincourt April 1429 Orléans June 1429 Patay
1379	War of Chiogga (Venice v. Genoa)
1382	Second Flemish War
1385	Spanish-Portuguese War
1410	Battle of Tannenberg
1420–34	Hussite War (Bohemian civil war)
1456	Ottoman Wars Belgrade
1455–85	Wars of the Roses 1485 Bosworth
1476	Burgundian Wars Granson
1492	Spanish defeat of the Moors
1499	Swiss-Swabian War
1512	War of the Holy League
1512	Russo-Polish War
1515	Italian Wars (French v. Swiss) Marignano
1519–21	Spanish conquest of Mexico
1526–29	Ottoman War 1526 Mohács 1529 Vienna
1525–38	Hindu-Moghul Wars 1526 Panipat
1532–34	Spanish conquest of Peru
1533	Counts' War (Danish civil war)
1539	Turkish invasion of Russia
1544	Wars of Charles V
1556	Hindu Revolt Panipat
1557	Franco-Spanish War St Quentin
1562–98	French Religious Wars
1563–70	Seven Years' War of the North
1564–1648	Netherlands War of Independence 1573 Haarlem 1574 Leyden
1571	Cyprus War (Holy League v. Turks) Lepanto
1580	Spanish conquest of Portugal
1588	Anglo-Spanish War Spanish Armada
1593	Moghul invasion of India
1598	Swedish-Polish War Linköping
1618–48	Thirty Years' War May 1631 Magdeburg Sept 1631 Breitenfeld 1632 Lützen 1643 Rocroi 1645 Nördlingen
1632	French Civil War
1640	Wars of Louis XIV
1642–49	English Civil War 1645 Naseby
1643–45	Danish-Swedish War
1644	Candian War
1648–52	Wars of the Fronde (French civil war)

Wars and battles *continued*

1651–60	Polish-Swedish War
1651–67	Polish-Cossack War
1652–56	Anglo-Dutch Wars
	1653 Texel
1657–59	Danish-Swedish War
1665	War of Devolution
1677–87	Ottoman Wars
	1679 Zenta
	1683 Vienna
	1687 Mohács
1689–1700	Russo-Turkish War
1690	War of the Grand Alliance
1690	War of the English Succession (King William III *v.* the exiled James II)
	July 1690 Beachy Head
	July 1690 Boyne
1700–21	Great Northern War (Russia, Poland, and Denmark *v.* Sweden)
	Narva
1701–14	War of the Spanish Succession
	1704 Blenheim
	1706 Ramillies
	1708 Oudenarde
	1709 Malplaquet
1702	Swedish-Polish War
1706	Russo-Swedish War
1710–11	Russo-Turkish War
1713	Farukhsiyar Rebellion (Indian civil war)
	Agra
1716–18	Austro-Turkish War
	1717 Belgrade
1718	War of the Quadruple Alliance (England, Netherlands, France, German Empire *v.* Spain)
1733–38	War of the Polish Succession
1736–1739	Russo-Turkish War
1739	War of Jenkins' Ear (England *v.* Spain)
1740–48	War of the Austrian Succession
	1743 Dettingen
	1744 Toulon
	May 1745 Fontenoy
	June 1745 Hohenfriedburg
1745–46	Jacobite Rebellion
	1746 Culloden
1751	Carnatic War (England *v.* France, in India)
1756–63	Seven Years' War
	May 1757 Prague
	June 1757 Plassey

	Nov 1757 Rossbach
	Dec 1757 Leuthen
	Aug 1758 Zorndorf
	Aug 1759 Minden
	Aug 1759 Künersdorf
	Sept 1759 Quebec
	Nov 1759 Quiberon Bay
	Aug 1760 Liegnitz
	Nov 1760 Torgau
1759–61	Afghan-Mahratta Wars
	1759 Panipat
1768–74	Russo-Turkish War
1775	Spanish-Algerian War
1775–83	American War of Independence
	April 1775 Lexington
	Sept 1777 Brandywine
	Oct 1777 Saratoga
	1779–83 Siege of Gibraltar
	Aug 1780 Camden
	March 1781 Guilford Court House
	Sept 1781 Chesapeake Capes
	Oct 1781 Yorktown
	April 1882 The Saints
1782	First British-Mysore War
1788–92	Russo-Turkish (Ottoman) War
	1789 Belgrade
1778–82	First British-Mahratta War
1790–91	Second British-Mysore War
1791–93	Russo-Polish War
1792–1802	French Revolutionary Wars
	Sept 1792 Valmy
	Aug 1793 Toulon
	June 1794 Glorious First of June
	Feb 1797 St Vincent
	Oct 1797 Camperdown
	Aug 1798 The Nile
	June 1799 Zurich
	June 1800 Marengo
1794–95	Polish Rising
1798	Irish Rebellion
1803	Second British-Mahratta War
	Agra
1803–15	Napoleonic Wars
	Sept 1805 Ulm
	Oct 1805 Trafalgar
	Oct 1805 Haslach
	Dec 1805 Austerlitz
	June 1806 Maida
	Oct 1806 Jena-Auerstadt
	Feb 1807 Eylau
	June 1807 Friedland
	April 1809 Eckmühl
	May 1809 Aspern

Wars and battles *continued*

	July 1809 Wagram
	Sept 1812 Borodino
	Nov 1812 Beresina
	May 1813 Bautzen
	May 1813 Lützen
	Aug 1813 Dresden
	Oct 1813 Leipzig
	March 1814 Laon
	June 1815 Ligny
	June 1815 Waterloo
1807	Russo-Turkish War
1808–14	Peninsular War
	Aug 1808 Rolica
	Aug 1808 Vimiero
	Jan 1809 Corunna
	July 1809 Talavera
	Sept 1810 Busaco
	May 1811 Fuentes d'Onoro
	May 1811 Albuera
	March 1812 Badajoz
	July 1812 Salamanca
	June 1813 Vitoria
	Dec 1813 Nive
1809–11	Russo-Turkish War
1812–15	Anglo-American War of 1812
	May 1813 Burlington Heights
	Aug 1814 Bladensburg
	Jan 1815 New Orleans
1813	Colombian War of Independence
1814–16	British-Gurkha War
1816–18	Third British-Mahratta War
1817	Chilean War of Independence
1821–24	Peruvian War of Independence
1821	Venezuelan War of Independence
1821–70	Italian Wars of Independence
1824	Anglo-Burmese War
1820–28	Greek War of Independence
	1826 Missolonghi
	1827 Navarino
1825–28	Argentine-Brazil War
1828–29	Russo-Turkish War
1833–37	First Carlist War (Spanish civil war)
1838–42	First British-Afghan War
	1842 Jellalabad
1839–42	First Opium War
1841	Bolivian-Peruvian War
1843	Fourth British-Mahratta War
1843–48	First Maori War
1845–46	First Anglo-Sikh War
1846–47	First Kaffir War
1846–48	Mexican-American War
1848–49	Second Anglo-Sikh War

	Jan 1849 Chilianwala
	Feb 1849 Gujarat
1849	Italian Rising
1850–53	Second Kaffir War
1852–52	Second Anglo-Burmese War
1853–54	Russo-Turkish War
	Nov 1853 Sinope
	March 1854 Silistria
1854–56	Crimean War
	Sept 1854 Alma
	Sept 1854–Sept 1855 Sevastopol
	Oct 1854 Balaklava
	Nov 1854 Inkerman
	Aug 1855 Tchernaya
1855–60	Mexican Uprising
1856–60	Arrow War
1856–57	Persian War
1857–58	Indian Mutiny
	June–Sept 1857 Delhi
	Aug 1857 Agra
	July–Nov 1857 Lucknow
1859	Argentine Civil War
1860	Spanish-Moroccan War
1859–60	Italian War of Independence
	1859 Magenta
1860–61	Second Maori War
1861	Peruvian-Chilean War
1862–67	Franco-Mexican War
1861–65	American Civil War
	July 1861 Bull Run
	Jan 1862 Mill Springs
	Feb 1862 Fort Donelson
	Feb 1862 Roanoke Island
	March 1862 Hampton Roads
	April 1862 Shiloh
	June 1862 Seven Days
	Aug 1862 Bull Run
	Sept 1862 Antietam
	Oct 1862 Corinth
	Dec 1862 Fredericksburg
	Dec 1862 Murfreesboro
	May 1863 Chancellorsville
	July 1863 Vicksburg
	July 1863 Gettysburg
	Sept 1863 Chickamauga
	Nov 1863 Chattanooga
	Dec 1863 Nashville
	May 1864 Wilderness, The
	May 1864 Spotsylvania
	May 1864 New Market
	June 1864 Cold Harbor
	June 1864–April 1865 Petersburg
	Sept 1864 Opequon Creek

Wars and battles *continued*

	Oct 1864 Cedar Creek
	April 1865 Five Forks
1863—64	First Ashanti War
1863—66	Third Maori War
1864—66	Spanish-Peruvian War
1865—70	Paraguayan War (Argentina, Brazil, and Uruguay *v.* Paraguay)
1866	Austro-Prussian War (Seven Weeks' War)
	June 1866 Custozza
	June 1866 Langensalza
	July 1866 Königgratz (Sadowa)
	July 1866 Lissa
1868	Prusso-Danish War
	Duppel
1867—68	Anglo-Abyssinian War
	Magdala
1868—70	Fourth Maori War
1870—71	Franco-Prussian War
	Aug 1870 Froeschwiller
	Aug 1870 Spicheren
	Aug 1870 Gravelotte (Sainte Privat)
	Aug 1870 Vionville-Mars la Tour
	Aug–Oct 1870 Metz
	Sept 1870 Sedan
	Sept 1870–Jan 1871 Paris, Siege of
	Nov 1870 Coulmiers
	Dec 1870 Hallue River
	Dec 1870 Loigny-Poupry
	Jan 1871 St Quentin
1873—74	Second Ashanti War
1877	Satsuma Rebellion (Japanese civil war)
1877—78	Russo-Turkish War
	Plevna
1877—78	Third Kaffir War
1878—81	Second British-Afghan War
	Kandahar
1879	Zulu War
	Isandhlwana
	Rorke's Drift
1879—83	Pacific War (Chile *v.* Peru and Bolivia)
1880—81	Basuto War
1880—81	First Boer War
	Majuba
1881	Egyptian Revolt
	Tel-el-Kebir
1885—87	Third Burma War
1885	Sudan Relief Expedition (under General Gordon)

	Abu Klea
	Abu Kru
1891	Chilean Civil War
1893	Italian Sudan campaign
1893	First Matabele War
1893—94	Third Ashanti War
1894—95	Sino-Japanese War
	Yalu River
1895—96	Second Matabele War
1896	Italian-Ethiopian War
1896—98	British Northwest Frontier campaign in India
1896—98	British reconquest of Sudan
	1898 Omdurman
1897	Graeco-Turkish War
1898	Spanish-American War
1899—1902	South African (Second Boer) War
	Dec 1899 Colenso
	Nov 1899–Feb 1900 Ladysmith
	Oct 1899–May 1900 Mafeking
	Dec 1899 Magersfontein
	Feb 1900 Paardeburg
	Jan 1900 Spion Kop
1900	Boxer Rebellion
1904—05	Russo-Japanese War
	May 1904 Yalu River
	May 1904–Jan 1905 Port Arthur
	June 1904 Telissu
	Aug 1904 Liaoyang
	Feb 1905 Mukden
	May 1905 Tsushima
1911	Italian-Turkish War
1912—13	First Balkan War (Bulgaria, Serbia, Greece, and Montenegro *v.* Turkey)
1913	Second Balkan War (Bulgaria *v.* Serbia and Greece)
1914—18	World War I
	Aug 1914 Le Cateau
	Aug 1914 Charleroi
	Aug 1914 Guise
	Aug 1914 Heligoland Bight
	Aug 1914 Liège
	Aug 1914 Mons
	Aug 1914 Morhange
	Aug 1914 Namur
	Aug 1914 Meuse
	Aug 1914 Tannenberg
	Sept 1914 Drina
	Sept 1914 Aisne
	Sept 1914 Albert
	Sept 1914 Lutsk
	Sept 1914 Ivangorod
	Sept 1914 Nery

Wars and battles *continued*

Sept 1914 Marne
Sept 1914 Masurian Lakes
Sept 1914–March 1915 Przemysl
Sept 1914 Rava Russka
Sept 1914 Tsingtao
Oct 1914 Radom
Oct 1914 Ypres
Oct 1914 Yser
Oct 1914 La Basée
Oct 1914 Augustov
Oct 1914 Warsaw
Nov 1914 Coronel
Nov 1914 San
Dec 1914 Warsaw
Dec 1914 Champagne
Dec 1914 Falkland Islands
Dec 1914 Givenchy
Dec 1914 Lódz
Dec 1914 Sarikamish

1915 *World War I continued*
Jan 1915 Dogger Bank
Jan 1915 Soissons
Feb 1915 Bolimov
Feb 1915 Dardanelles
Feb 1915 Gallipoli
Feb 1915 Masurian Lakes
Feb 1915 Przasnysz
March 1915 Naroch, Lake
March 1915 Neuve Chapelle
April 1915 Courland
April 1915 Dunajetz
April 1915 Gaba Tepe
April 1915 Ypres
May 1915 Festubert
May 1915 Aubers Ridge
May 1915 San
June 1915 Dolomites
June 1915–May 1917 Battles of
   the Isonzo
June 1915 Lemberg
July 1915 Narev
Aug 1915 Brest-Litovsk
Aug 1915 Dvina
Aug 1915 Kovno
Aug 1915 Warsaw
Sept 1915 Kut-al-Imara
Sept 1915 Campagne
Sept 1915 Loos
Sept 1915 Styr
Oct 1915 Vardar
Nov 1915 Ctesiphon
Nov 1915 Kosovo

1916 *World War I continued*
Jan 1916 Dvina

Jan 1916 Dvinsk
Feb 1916 Verdun
Feb 1916 Galicia
Feb 1916 Erzerum
May 1916 Trentino
May 1916 Jutland
June 1916 Somme
June 1916 Styr
June 1916 Brusilov Offensive
Aug 1916 Gorizia
Sept 1916 Ancre
Sept 1916 Carso
Oct 1916 Carso
Oct 1916 Kronstadt
Nov 1916 Argesul

1917 *World War I continued*
March 1917 Gaza
April 1917 Arras
April 1917 Aisne
April 1917 Chemin des Dames
May 1917 Lens
May 1917 Carso
June 1917 Messines
July 1917 Tarnopol
July 1917 Ypres
Aug 1917 Maraçesti
Sept 1917 Carso
Sept 1917 Riga
Oct 1917 Caporetto
Oct 1917 Beersheba
Nov 1917 Cambrai
Nov 1917–Sept 1918 Bourlon
   Wood
Nov 1917 Piave
Nov 1917–Nov 1918 Asiago
   Plateau

1918 *World War I continued*
March 1918 Somme
April 1918 Ypres
April 1918 Zeebrugge
May 1918 Château-Thierry
May 1918 Aisne
May 1918 Ostend
June 1918 Belleau Wood
June 1918 Piave
July 1918 Marne
July 1918 Abu Tellul
July 1918 Archangel
July 1918 Hamel
July 1918 Vaux-Fossoy
Aug 1918 Bapaume
Aug 1918 Laon
Aug 1918 Scarpe
Sept 1918 Argonne

Wars and battles *continued*

	Sept 1918 Meuse-Argonne
	Sept 1918 Cambrai
	Sept 1918 Doiran-Struma
	Sept 1918 Epéhy
	Sept 1918 Flanders
	Sept 1918 St Mihiel Salient
	Sept 1918 Vardar
	Oct 1918 Le Cateau
	Oct 1918 Piave
	Oct 1918 Selle
	Oct 1918 Vittorio Veneto
	Nov 1918 Sambre
1916	American-Mexican War
1931–41	Sino-Japanese War
1932–35	Gran Chaco War
1936–39	Spanish Civil War
	July 1938 Ebro
	Nov 1936–March 1939 Madrid
1936	Abyssinian War
1939	Italian invasion of Albania
1939	Battle of Khalkin Gol
1939–45	World War II
	1939–45 Battle of the Atlantic
1939	*World War II continued*
	Dec 1939 River Plate
1940	*World War II continued*
	April 1940 Calabria
	April 1940 Narvik
	May 1940 Eben Emael
	July 1940 Britain, Battle of
	July 1940 Dakar
	Sept 1940 Blitz, The
	Nov 1940 Cape Spartivento
	Dec 1940 Sidi Barrani
1941	*World War II continued*
	Jan 1941 Agordat
	Jan 1941 Keren
	Feb 1941 Beda Fomm
	March 1941 Cape Matapan
	April 1941–Oct 1942 Tobruk
	May 1941 Amba Alagi
	May 1941 Crete
	June 1941 Barbarossa, Operation
	June 1941 Battleaxe, Operation
	June 1941 Halfaya Pass
	July 1941 Smolensk
	July 1941 Kiev
	Sept 1941–Jan 1944 Leningrad
	Nov 1941 Sidi Rezegh
	Nov 1941 Rostov
	Nov 1941 Gondar
	Nov 1941 Crusader, Operation
	Nov 1941 Moscow

	Dec 1941 Pearl Harbor
	Dec 1941 Kota Bharu
	Dec 1941 Wake Island
	Dec 1941 Hong Kong
1942	*World War II continued*
	Jan 1942 Ambon Island
	Jan 1942 Demyansk
	Jan 1942 Bataan
	Feb 1942 Java Sea
	Feb 1942 Singapore
	April 1942 Gazala
	May 1942 Sevastopol
	May 1942 Kharkov
	May 1942 Cauldron
	May 1942 Coral Sea
	May 1942 Corregidor
	June 1942 Midway
	July 1942 Alamein
	Aug 1942 Alam Halfa
	Aug 1942 Dieppe
	Aug 1942 Eastern Solomons
	Aug 1942 Guadalcanal
	Aug 1942 Milne Bay
	Aug 1942 Kokoda Trail
	Aug 1942 Savo Island
	Aug–Nov 1942 Stalingrad
	Oct 1942 Alamein
	Oct 1942 Cape Esperance
	Oct 1942 Santa Cruz
	Dec 1942 Arakan
	Dec 1942 Barents Sea
1943	*World War II continued*
	Feb 1943 Kasserine Pass
	March 1943 Komandorski Islands
	March 1943 Mareth Line
	July 1943 Guam
	July 1943 Kolombangara
	July 1943 Kursk
	Sept 1943 Salamaua
	Sept 1943 Nadzab
	Oct 1943 Hukawng Valley
	Nov 1943 Sangro River
	Nov 1943 Tarawa
	Nov 1943 Cape St George
	Nov 1943 Bougainville
	Nov 1943–March 1944 Berlin
	Nov 1943 Empress Augusta Bay
	Dec 1943 Arakan
	Dec 1943 New Britain
	Dec 1943 North Cape
1944	*World War II continued*
	Jan–May 1944 Cassino
	Jan 1944 Anzio

Wars and battles *continued*

	Jan 1944 Rapido River	**1946–49**	Chinese Civil War
	Feb 1944 Admin Box	**1946–54**	French Indo-China War
	Feb 1944 Kwajalien		1953 Dien Bien Phu
	April 1944 Imphal	**1948-55**	Burmese Civil War
	April 1944 Kohima	**1948-49**	First Arab-Israeli War
	May 1944 Biak	**1950–53**	Korean War
	June 1944 Bagration, Operation		Sept 1950 Inchon
	June 1944 D-Day		Nov 1950 Chosin Reservoir
	June 1944 Philippine Sea		April 1951 Solma-Ri
	June 1944 Great Marianas	**1950–62**	Indonesian Civil War
	Turkey Shoot	**1954–62**	Algerian War of Independence
	June 1944 Saipan	**1954–75**	Vietnam War
	June 1944 Indaw		Jan 1967 Iron Triangle
	July 1944 Tinian		Jan 1968 Khe Sanh
	July 1944 Bourgebus Ridge		Jan 1968 Tet Offensive
	Aug 1944 Mortain	**1955–72**	Sudanese Civil War
	Aug 1944 Falaise Gap	**1960–67**	Congo Civil War
	Sept 1944 Antwerp	**1961–75**	Angolan War of Independence
	Sept 1944 Arnhem	**1962–70**	Yemeni Civil War
	Oct 1944 Breskens Pocket	**1964–74**	Mozambique War of
	Oct 1944 Leyte Gulf		Independence
	Nov 1944 Bhamo	**1965**	First Indo-Pakistan War
	Nov 1944 Walcheren	**1967**	Second Arab-Israeli (Six Day) War
	Dec 1944 Bulge, Battle of the	**1971**	Second Indo-Pakistan War
	Dec 1944 Bastogne	**1973**	Third Arab-Israeli (Yom Kippur)
1945	*World War II continued*		War
	Jan 1945 Colmar Pocket	**1980–88**	Iran-Iraq War
	Feb 1945 Reichswald	**1982**	Falklands War
	Feb 1945 Iwo Jima		Goose Green
	March 1945 Balaton, Lake	**1982**	Soviet invasion of Afghanistan
	March 1945 Rhine Crossing	**1991**	Gulf War (Operation Desert
	April 1945 Argenta Gap		Storm)
	April 1945 Okinawa	**1992**	Yugloslavian civil war (Third
	May 1945 Elephant Point		Balkan War)
1944–49	Greek Civil War		